PELICAN BOOKS

A HISTORY OF MODERN FRANCE

VOLUME THREE

Alfred Cobban was born in 1901. He was educated at Latymer Upper School and Gonville and Caius College, Cambridge.

He was a lecturer in history at King's College, Newcastle upon Tyne, held a Rockefeller Fellowship for research in France and was Visiting Professor at Chicago, Harvard and other American Universities.

He was Professor of French History at University College, London, and editor of *History* on his death in 1968.

Among his publications are *Burke and the Revolt against the Eighteenth Century*; *Rousseau and the Modern State*; *Dictatorship, its History and Theory*; and *National Self-determination*. More recently he wrote *The Debate on the French Revolution*; *Ambassadors and Secret Agents: the diplomacy of the first Earl of Malmesbury at The Hague*; the history of Vichy France in Toynbee's *Hitler's Europe*; *In search of Humanity: the Role of the Enlightenment in Modern History*; and articles in the *English Historical Review*, *History*, the *Political Science Quarterly*, *International Affairs*, and many other journals.

A HISTORY
OF MODERN FRANCE

BY ALFRED COBBAN

VOLUME THREE

France of the Republics
1871–1962

PENGUIN BOOKS

PENGUIN BOOKS

Published by the Penguin Group
27 Wrights Lane, London W8 5TZ, England
Viking Penguin Inc., 40 West 23rd Street, New York, New York 10010, USA
Penguin Books Australia Ltd, Ringwood, Victoria, Australia
Penguin Books Canada Ltd, 2801 John Street, Markham, Ontario, Canada L3R 1B4
Penguin Books (NZ) Ltd, 182–190 Wairau Road, Auckland 10, New Zealand

Penguin Books Ltd, Registered Offices: Harmondsworth, Middlesex, England

First published 1965
17 19 20 18 16

Printed and bound in Great Britain by
Cox & Wyman Ltd, Reading
Set in Monotype Baskerville

CONTENTS

MAPS

INTRODUCTION

THE need to write a third volume in this history of modern France has provided a stimulus to reflection on the slow struggle of republican France to escape from its history. For a thousand years France was a monarchy; it has been a republic for less than a hundred. Monarchical traditions necessarily went deep in French society, and the establishment and consolidation of the republic was bound to be a long-drawn-out and uncertain struggle against them. When the trials of two world wars are added, it may well seem surprising that the republic, even in a series of numerical metamorphoses, should have survived. The work of those who founded and consolidated it, between 1871 and the beginning of the age of wars in 1914, must have been sounder than their critics, or perhaps even they themselves, knew. Monarchy and empire have attracted more attention and far more admiration from historians than the republic. But if the former had their moments of glory, the latter now begins to be seen as more truly an age of greatness. But it was marred by a social pattern of economic conservatism and class rigidity inherited from *ancien régime*, revolution, and empire, which produced intense political conflicts and governmental instability.

There was a time when the history of republican France seemed a tiresome story of repetitious failure, the history of a régime too weak and governments too ephemeral to master circumstances, and of would-be rebels too futile and merely negative to take their place. If this were all, there would be little justification for the production of yet another account of how one Radical Socialist replaced another Radical Socialist on the banks of the Seine and the Rhône. But in history the past gains significance from the future, and the Fourth and Fifth Republics have given a posthumous justification to the Third by the achievement of social and international aims which had seemed doomed to perpetual frustration. A merely political history of the French republics is bound to seem trivial and superficial; but envisaged in terms of the evolution of a society, the history of modern France acquires a deeper dimension. As such it has a significance which, as an account of the vagaries of day-to-day, or even year-to-year politics, it was bound

Introduction

to lack. Social history has also to be seen on a longer time-scale than political. The history of each age throws light on those that preceded and those that followed it. In writing a third volume on France of the Republics I have constantly found myself referred back by echoes of earlier régimes, and sometimes sent forward by anticipations of the latest one. The Fifth Republic seems to draw the threads of modern French history together. It has already concluded much hitherto unfinished business. But if it provides a suitable terminus for this history, it is not so much because it represents an end, as because it also represents a beginning.

I am indebted to readers, and in particular to Professor Douglas Johnson and to Lord Strang, for drawing my attention to some factual errors in the first version of this volume, which I have now corrected.

ALFRED COBBAN

University College, London
June 1966

I

THE RISE OF THE THIRD REPUBLIC

I. THE MAKING OF THE REPUBLIC

THE defeat that wrote *finis* to the rule of Napoleon III was an external event not an internal development. The Second Empire was not ended by the will of the people. The last plebiscite gave the Emperor almost as large a majority as the first. It was not destroyed by revolution: there was no revolutionary party with the power to overthrow it. The Empire had simply, in the person of a defeated, aged, and ailing Emperor, been overthrown in war, and capitulated to the invader. Its disappearance, before no predestined successor, left only a void. France was thrust into a new age, not deliberately by its own action, or in the fullness of time by the presence of new social forces, but accidentally and prematurely by the fact of military defeat. The intense conservatism of French society in 1871 was revealed by the savage reaction to the Commune of Paris, as it had been in 1848 by the repression of the revolt of the June days. The aim of the ruling classes in 1871 remained what it had been when the Empire was set up, to preserve the fabric of society unchanged; not to make a new France but to save the old one. This was the task which the National Assembly at Bordeaux, elected to get France out of the German war as quickly as possible, took upon itself.

It was an assembly of notables in more than one sense: intellectuals from all shades of the political spectrum. Louis Blanc, Edgar Quinet, Victor Hugo, Littré, Albert de Broglie, Dupanloup; old republicans like Ledru-Rollin and Delescluze, and Orleanists like Dufaure and Thiers; the as yet untried leaders of the future republic, including moderates like Waddington, Méline, Léon Say, and those who were then

9

accounted of the left – Jules Simon, Jules Favre, Grévy,
Ferry – and so far out that he resigned when the Assembly
made war on the Commune, the Mayor of Montmartre,
Clemenceau. More noticeable at the moment, since no one
knew that they already belonged to a *temps perdu* and had a
future only in the volumes of Proust, were the Noailles,
Harcourt, Haussonville, la Rochefoucauld – the old *noblesse
de cour* come back to Versailles to haunt the galleries and
corridors of its former greatness for the last time. They might,
if they had possessed sufficient perception, have perceived
an omen in the fact that despite its predominantly monarchical complexion, the Assembly chose the republican Jules
Grévy – admittedly known as the enemy both of the Empire
and of Gambetta – as its first President. More significant was
the fact that Thiers had been elected in twenty-six departments and thus practically chosen by a national vote to form
the new government. He appointed three republicans,
Favre, Picard, and Simon, to the key posts of Foreign
Affairs, Interior, and Education respectively.

The first task was to make peace. Thiers settled with the
Germans even before he settled with Paris. The southern
part of Lorraine, all Alsace except Belfort, the payment of
what seemed at the time a huge indemnity of two milliard
of francs, German occupation of the eastern departments of
France until the indemnity had been paid, and of Paris until
the treaty was ratified – such was the cost of defeat in war.
The Assembly, desiring peace and a return to normal conditions before everything else, accepted the terms as soon as
they were presented, and so reduced the German military
occupation of Paris to a parade of a single day. By the peace
France lost a population of nearly a million and a half,
though there was a considerable migration to France from
the surrendered territories. She lost the mines and industries
of Lorraine, the textile mills of Alsace, and the great provincial capital of Strasbourg, a French city since the time, two
hundred years earlier, when Louis XIV had marched his
armies to the Rhine. The sums necessary to pay off the in-

demnity were raised, by means of loans, far more rapidly than had been expected. The first half milliard was paid in July 1871 and brought the evacuation of five out of twenty-one occupied departments. In March 1873 Thiers was able to pay another half milliard, and the remainder in four monthly instalments from June to September. The last German soldier left France in September 1873. In spite of the burden of the indemnity, the French budget, with the aid of favourable world economic conditions, was balanced by 1875.

Elected to liquidate the war, Thiers and the National Assembly had succeeded in their task by the simple process of paying the price demanded by the victors. The Assembly found the other task, for which it had not been elected but which it took upon itself, that of framing a new constitution for France, a more difficult one. The only solution which at first seemed definitely excluded was the Bonapartist one. In 1871 the political and administrative personnel of the Second Empire had followed its predecessors into the increasingly overcrowded Valhalla of defunct régimes, whose memories filled the history books and whose ghosts haunted the French political scene. It was not quite the end of Bonapartism. A nostalgia for the high days of the Empire survived among army commanders, high ecclesiastics, dispossessed officials, and Corsicans; and the death of Napoleon III in 1873 was to leave the young Prince Imperial as a more appealing representative of the dynasty. Subsequently the selfish policies of monarchists and conservative republicans revived Bonapartist sentiments among those suffering from economic distress; and yet later it was to be seen that plebiscitary dictatorship had not exhausted its attraction for the people. But for the time being, at least, Bonapartism was excluded from the political agenda.

If the elections of February 1871 had adequately represented the political wishes of France, a restoration of the monarchy should have been a foregone conclusion. Even if they did not, the predominance of monarchists in the

Assembly would have brought the same result if the fatal division of monarchist forces had not stood in the way. The legitimist claimant was the comte de Chambord, *l'enfant du miracle*, posthumous son of the duc de Berry, who had passed his life with a little court of exiles in a castle in Austria. Devout to the point of mysticism, trained as he said himself to expect everything from God and nothing from man, free from worldly ambition or knowledge, lame, isolated, living in and for the past, perhaps the noblest of his line, he was beyond doubt now the last for he had no children. In this fact seemed to lie the possibility of a deal with the rival house of Orleans, by which the comte de Chambord might occupy the throne while he lived, and on his death be followed on the throne in due line of succession by his Orleanist heir.

This seemed a very reasonable plan to the Orleanist comte de Paris, a very different kind of person, who knew the world and might seem almost to have modelled himself on the career of Louis Napoleon in preparing his own candidature to the throne. He had studied trade unionism in England, travelled widely and written books to describe his travels, fought in the American Civil War and written a history of it. Unfortunately for the hopes of the Orleanists it was quite out of the comte de Chambord's character to do a deal with anybody, or offer any concession to obtain his legitimate rights. He made this plain in a manifesto issued as early as July 1871, when he declared that he would never abandon the white flag and fleur de lis of his ancestors: 'I will not let the standard of Henry IV, of Francis I, of Jeanne d'Arc be torn from my hands.' Decentralization, provincial liberties – the old demands of the aristocratic revolt of 1787, universal suffrage 'honestly applied' – whatever that meant, parliamentary government – these he could and did promise. He was willing to give up the substance so long as he kept the shadow, the symbols of legitimate monarchy, which had a mystical value in his eyes. This was his first and his last word and it was fatal to the prospect of a restoration, for these were the symbols that France had twice rejected.

For some years the French monarchists continued to hope for a compromise and to pursue their vain negotiations with Chambord. Indeed in the autumn of 1873 their envoy returned with the glad news that he had accepted the national flag. Preparations were at once set on foot for the *joyeuse entrée* of the last of the Bourbons into his capital, which shows how crucial was the question of the flag. Alas, it was all a misunderstanding. Chambord issued a repudiation of the report. Notwithstanding this, with ineffable faith and that contempt for the facts which was the hall-mark of the French royalists, he still continued to believe, apparently, that all he had to do was to appear in France for his right divine to be recognized. When he did come, in 1874, it was to arrive in secret and return in silence.

The one thing that Chambord and his supporters could do was to block the path to a restoration of the hated house of Orleans. That under neither dynasty would it have been an easy or peaceful restoration was shown by the first elections to be held under normal conditions. These were the supplementary elections of July 1871, in which 99 republicans, as against 9 Orleanists, 3 legitimists, and 3 Bonapartists, were elected. Subsequent by-elections continued the same trend: between 1871 and 1874, 126 republicans were elected and only 23 monarchists and 10 Bonapartists. There was thus a great change in the composition of the Assembly, which explains in part how an initially monarchist assembly came to agree to a republican constitution. At the same time the significance of the election results must not be exaggerated.

In 1873, however, the monarchist majority still surviving in the Assembly was becoming increasingly restive under the yoke of the republican ministers it had felt obliged to accept in 1871. If the monarchists could not set up their own régime, at least, they felt, they did not have to endure the rule of their enemies. Grévy was forced out of the presidency of the Assembly in favour of an intransigent clerical. Thiers, who had made up his mind that the Republic was going to win and had cautiously been throwing his influence on that side, had not been quite cautious enough for the taste of the monarchists of the majority. When it became evident that he was no longer a safe bulwark against the advance of the left they repudiated him. This was after a Paris by-election in which the conservative candidate, Thiers's own Foreign Minister, was well beaten by the republican candidate Barodet, a former mayor of Lyon who had been dismissed by the government for his advanced views. After this the Assembly decided to rid itself of Thiers. By a vote of 24 May 1873 the monarchists repudiated the old man, who now seemed to them only an embarrassment, and he resigned.

In his place as head of the state they chose Marshal MacMahon, whose reputation had somehow survived defeat. Perhaps defeat itself was not so loathsome if it bore the precious jewel of a restoration in its head. MacMahon, although a former bonapartist Marshal, was reckoned sympathetic to the cause of monarchs. He was rather stupid and did not understand politics. The headship of the government was now separated from that of the state and was taken over by the Orleanist duc de Broglie. The abnormal situation in which practically supreme authority had been concentrated in the hands of a single man was thus brought to an end and replaced by a parliamentary government. Ironically, the monarchists in 1873, as after 1815, were temporarily and for their own ends the restorers of parliamentary government. It was restored under very aristocratic auspices. Along with Broglie the government included Decazes and d'Audiffret-Pasquier, only three it is true, but enough to let historians dub the new régime the republic of the dukes. The witticism may have some point if it is true that the aim was as much to preserve the rule of a now rather adulterated *noblesse* as to restore that of an over-pure monarch.

Until legitimists and Orleanists had reached an agreement, and the legitimist claimant had given way on the question of the flag, the restoration of the monarchy was not practical politics. MacMahon himself, when Chambord made his secret journey into France in the autumn of 1874, had sufficient common sense to see what patent folly an attempt at restoration would be and Chambord returned to his castle as he had come, incognito. Broglie, seeing that the monarchy could not be restored in the person of Chambord, and unwilling to accept the Republic, fell back on the device of prolonging the provisional. Chambord and his flag, an Orleanist may have thought, would not stand in the way of a restoration for ever. The solution was the *septennat* of November 1873, by which MacMahon was to be head of the state for seven years. This settled nothing but it enabled Broglie to remain in office pursuing a resolutely conservative policy.

The failure of the restoration should not lead us to underestimate the strength of monarchist feeling in the country, just as the strength of the republicans had been underestimated a few years earlier. In the Assembly, and the country, right and left were – as they were to be throughout the history of the Third Republic – fairly evenly balanced. The future government of France was to depend on which could win the support of the body of opinion in the centre which held the balance.

The weakness of the monarchists lay, where their strength also lay, in their religious affiliations. The religious revival that had begun early in the century was still strong. Religious sentiments played their part in the masochistic tendencies manifested by the French right after 1871, as they had after 1815 and were to again in 1940. The nation was called to repentance by the Church for the sins that had brought disaster on it. There was also a general fear of social revolution, and religion was, perhaps more than ever before, seen as a social sanction. The identification of the Church with the protection of the interests of birth, wealth, and social status became almost total with the Third Republic. The *noblesse* were now practising Catholics almost to a man and even more woman, and the bourgeoisie, at least since 1848, had come to feel that religion was necessary both to protect

the virtue of their daughters and to keep the socially dangerous classes at bay.

The strength of the religious bulwark of society had greatly
increased under the Second Empire. The numbers in the
male religious orders had multiplied by ten to some 30,000,
and in women's orders by four to about 120,000. Much of
boys' and practically all of girls' education was under their
control, as was assistance to the poor, aged, and infirm.
Influence over the voters was, however, more easily won by
an appeal to their sentiments than to their intellect or even
their interests. The propaganda motive, as well as the
dominance in the Church of a wealthy class with peculiarly
little aesthetic sense, may have been responsible for the
remarkable vulgarity of most of the religious art of the
period. The attempt to win back the people to religion was
above all the work of the new order of the Assumptionists,
founded in 1845, who promoted a raging, tearing propaganda, one feature of which was the development on a vast
scale of the cult of the Sacred Heart. The foundation stone
of a great new church, dedicated to the Sacré Cœur, was
laid in 1873 on the heights of Montmartre, where Loyola
and his first group of followers had met and the Counter-
Reformation had in a sense begun. Its building was conceived as an act of national penitence. Individual penitence
took the form of great mass pilgrimages to Lourdes and
other shrines, organized with the aid of special railway ex-
cursions. The methods of the popular press were brought
into play in the cause of religion by the Assumptionist paper
La Croix, which attained a circulation of half a million.

Religious agitation was, as usual, not unconnected with
political aims. Linked with the cult of the Sacred Heart and
the sorrows of France were those of a Church whose head
was now the prisoner of the Vatican. In July 1871 the
French bishops petitioned the Assembly to take action to
restore the temporal power of the Pope. In the Churches
Roman Catholics prayed '*Sauvez Rome et la France au nom du
Sacré Cœur*'. The restoration of the monarchy to France and

of the Pope to his temporal domains became the joint aims of French Catholicism, but such militancy was only to the taste of a minority. To those who were less ardent the prospect of war with Italy for the sake of the temporal possessions of the Papacy, and a parallel agitation against the religious policy of Bismarck which threatened further hostilities with Germany, were alarming. The result of the close link between legitimacy and the Church was to saddle the monarchists with the joint encumbrance of clericalism and war-mongering. Meanwhile they were falling out among themselves. To serve permanently under an Orleanist was more than some legitimists could manage, and the two legitimists in Broglie's government retired in November 1873. In May 1874 the extremer legitimists, who were known from the name of the street where they had their head-quarters as the *chevau-légers*, voted to the number of fifty with the republican opposition to overthrow Broglie. He had to resign and MacMahon set up a caretaker government in his place.

At the same time the republicans, including Gambetta who had returned to active politics in 1872, had been behaving with conspicuous moderation which was gradually conciliating centre opinion. Both republican and moderate monarchists were now becoming alarmed at signs of a recrudescence of Bonapartism. In the National Assembly there were some twenty-five to thirty admitted Bonapartists, led by the Second Empire survivor Rouher. This was not many, but enough, given the narrow margin of votes separating republicans and monarchists, for them to inaugurate the wrecking policy which was to be the hall-mark of Bonapartism without a Bonaparte, as it was later to be of monarchism without a monarch, under the Third Republic. The Bonapartists played their part in bringing down Thiers in 1873 and Broglie in 1874, and so long as France remained without a constitution, even of the most provisional kind, the door seemed open to a Bonapartist revival.

In January 1875 a motion defining the government of the

Republic was defeated only by 359 votes to 336. It was followed, on 25 February, by the famous *amendement Wallon*,
which laid down the method of electing the successors to
MacMahon at the head of the state. The effect of this was
to turn the presidency of the Republic from a temporary
expedient into a permanent institution. 'My conclusion,'
Wallon ended his speech, 'is that it is necessary to leave the
provisional. If the monarchy is possible, show that it will be
accepted, propose it. If on the contrary it is not possible, I
do not say to you: decide for the Republic, but I say: recognize the government now established, which is the government of the Republic. I do not ask you to proclaim it as
definitive – what is definitive? But all the same do not call it
provisional.' The amendment was passed by 353 votes to
352, so that it could be said that the Republic was established by a majority of one vote.

The Third Republic never had a constitution. In its place
there was passed a series of constitutional laws, determined
more by practical than theoretical considerations. The
monarchists, knowing that they would lose heavily in a
general election, were prepared to compromise to avoid a
dissolution of the Assembly. So it came about that a republic
was set up by an Assembly which still had a monarchist
majority. Naturally the constitutional laws included as many
potentially conservative elements as the Assembly could
manage to introduce into them. The President, chosen for
seven years and re-eligible, with extensive and broadly
defined political powers, including, with the agreement of
the Senate, the dissolution of the Chamber of Deputies, to
which he was not personally responsible, was the next best
thing to a king; and the door for an easy transition from
republic to monarchy was kept open by establishing a simple
procedure for constitutional revision. While republican institutions lasted, the conservative interests in society were to
be entrenched in an upper chamber, or Senate, with powers
in theory practically equal to those of the Chamber of
Deputies. One third of the members of the Senate were to be

chosen for life by the existing monarchical Assembly, while the remainder were to be elected indirectly by electoral colleges drawn from local government bodies, with a strong weightage in favour of the small, rural communes. The elected Senators, moreover, were to hold office for nine years, one third retiring every three years.

What happened was, of course, very different from what had been expected. Only in the later years of the Third Republic did the Senate come to assume the conservative role planned for it, while the strong executive intended for the presidency was never to materialize. However, the natural play of social forces ensured that the Chamber of Deputies should itself be for long immunized against social experiment.

Having given birth if not to a constitution at least to a small litter of constitutional laws, the National Assembly had no longer any reason for existence. It was dissolved in December 1875. The elections of 1876 produced a Chamber with over 340 republicans against under 200 on the right, including, most significantly, a Bonapartist group of about 75. When the new Chamber chose the life members of the Senate, the legitimists of the committee of the rue des Chevau-légers vented their hatred on the Orleanists by joining with the republicans in an electoral manoeuvre which produced 57 republican life Senators out of 75.

After the elections MacMahon found himself in the position of a President elected by a defunct Assembly which had been repudiated by the country, and faced with a republican Chamber which could claim to represent the voice of the people. If the monarchists accepted this situation they abandoned any hope of achieving their aim in the foreseeable future. Rather than do this they played the only card in their hand: MacMahon dissolved the Chamber on 16 May 1877. This became known as the *coup d'état* of *seize mai*, though in fact he was acting strictly within his constitutional rights. He called Broglie to lead a government which was to make – literally it was hoped – the new elections. The ground was prepared by a wholesale administrative purge. Over 70 prefects and 226 sub-prefects and secretaries-general were replaced, 1,743 municipal councils dissolved and their mayors dismissed. To conduct the new elections Broglie had to call in the only men with experience in the job of electoral management, those who had run the former Bonapartist political machine. All the traditional methods of influence were revived. Pressure was brought to bear on government officials or employees; opposition journals were prosecuted, opposition cafés were closed, and licences to sell pamphlets were revoked. MacMahon was sent to tour the provinces, making speeches in the larger towns, and with the whole-hearted backing of the Church and the *bien-pensant* gentry whose authority customarily dominated the small towns and villages of France, he and Broglie might reasonably have felt confident of success.

The left replied with a policy of republican concentration under Gambetta and Thiers. When, in the middle of the campaign, Thiers died, Paris forgot that he had made war on it and turned his funeral into a great republican demonstration. His place at the head of the republican coalition was taken by Jules Grévy, a provincial lawyer from Franche-Comté with a reputation for moderate republicanism, a safe man on all matters affecting property and particularly interested, the chansonniers alleged, in its acquisition, which was to involve him in difficulties later.

The election of 1877 can be regarded as the real foundation of the Third Republic. It was not only a political turning-point, it was a more decisive social revolution than anything that had occurred in 1830, 1848, or 1871. It was the point at which rural France repudiated the authority of the notables, those men of landed estate, composed of an amalgam of *noblesse* from a series of régimes with *haute bourgeoisie*, conservative and clerical, whose influence had kept the great rural masses of France steadily on the side of social conservatism whatever political changes might come about. The attempt to make the elections was a total failure:

the republicans won 326 seats and the right 207. After this
there was nothing for MacMahon to do but resign. Broglie
naturally disappeared and was followed into the wilderness
by his prefects. Also, to bear witness that this was a major
defeat for the executive, the Vice-President of the Conseil
d'État and nine Conseillers were dismissed, the first and last
such purge until 1945. Grévy moved into the vacant presidential chair.

2. THE TRIUMPH OF THE REPUBLIC

THE crisis of 1877 had done more than register the failure
of the monarchists. In his first message the new President
declared, 'Subject to the great law of the parliamentary
régime, I will never enter into opposition against the national
will expressed by its constitutional organs.' The balance
of the constitution had been decisively shifted in favour of
the Chamber and against the Senate and the President. The
Senate was for long after this to be a mere 'theatre of the
left bank', not a stage on which the greater dramas of
national life were enacted. Its influence gradually increased,
but it was only in the last years of the Third Republic that
it became practically the headquarters of the general staff
of republican politics. The presidency, on the other hand,
never recovered from the failure of MacMahon's attempt to
make himself an effective head of state. It became practically a constitutional convention of the Third Republic that
no strong statesman should be elected President; Poincaré in
1913 was an exception attributable to the threatening international situation. The President's duties were henceforth
mainly honorific: he has been described as an elderly gentleman whose function it was to wear evening dress in day-time.
Yet he alone was in a position to provide continuity in
policy – very necessary in a régime of rapidly changing
governments – and his right to nominate the new head of the
ministry made him the key figure when a government fell.

His skill in manoeuvring could often determine whether a political crisis should be of short duration, or long and severe. But at best the President could do no more than grease the wheels of politics. After 1877 power resided in the parliament and chiefly in the Chamber of Deputies.

The years 1877 to 1881 witnessed the establishment of the republican régime. It was fortunate in that it came to birth at a time when economic affairs were prospering and the budget was balanced. It was also fortunate, considering the strongly conservative nature of French society, in coming to power with a conservative policy and bias. The attempted *coup* of the *seize mai* had saddled the right with a tradition of unconstitutional action which alarmed moderate opinion. The republicans had previously been committed to radical demands based on Gambetta's Belleville programme of 1869, including separation of Church and State, liberty of press and meeting, free and compulsory public education, removal of the laws against trade unions. The *seize mai* was a not altogether unwelcome diversion, which enabled them to escape from these advanced proposals, and when they came to power it was with more modest commitments. The abandonment of the 1876 programme was also responsible for the description of Opportunists, given them by the satirical journalist Rochefort.

The ruling personnel, as well as the policy of the new republic, was to be conservative. Grévy was determined that a popular tribune with dangerous reforming ideas, such as Gambetta, should be kept out of power. When it was necessary to choose, in December 1879, he therefore called to office not Gambetta but his former *aide* in the Prussian war, Freycinet – small, dapper, aloof, subtle, insinuating, who was for a whole generation to run up and down the corridors of the Third Republic like a little white mouse, which was what the political world called him, not a great figure but a useful, worthy, likeable one – eminently a serviceable man.

The defeat of the right in the legislative elections of 1877 was followed by a corresponding republican victory in the local elections of 1878, which was bound in due course to influence the composition of the Senate. After further elections in 1881, the republicans had control of some 20,000 communes out of 36,000, and a majority in 66 departmental Councils out of 87. This has been called the *révolution des mairies*. The notables, having been defeated in their struggle for the central government, had also lost control of the provinces.

A series of political changes marked the increasing republicanism of the régime. *La Marseillaise* became the national anthem and 14 July a national holiday. In 1879 the Chamber of Deputies and the Senate returned to Paris from Versailles. This was a less dangerous move than it might have been a generation earlier, for Paris was ceasing to be the left-wing and proletarian city of the past hundred years.

The major political problem for the left was presented by the exiled Communards of 1871. The agitation on their behalf was led by small groups of Socialists, for whom it provided a focus of unity which in other respects they lacked. The tiny group of French Marxists, which was just beginning to appear, seized on the Commune as a ready-made historical legend for themselves and began the propaganda which was to root the cult of the Commune deeply in French working-class consciousness. A partial amnesty, granted in spring 1879, reduced the number of Communard prisoners or exiles to about one thousand. Those who were released were the best plea for an amnesty to the remainder. Ill, wasted, and in rags, they staggered off the ships that had brought them back across half the world, and the appeal of humanity was stronger than the fears of property and respectability. With new elections due in 1881, the republicans were anxious to remove from the political agenda a question which divided them, though the Socialists were now less keen for an amnesty which would rob them of one of their strongest grounds for agitation against the régime. Freycinet introduced the proposal for a full amnesty in June 1880, but it was the authority of Gambetta which carried the measure.

Among other progressive measures of the same year were a law freeing public meetings from the requirements of official authorization; and a press law abolishing 'crimes of opinion', leaving only direct provocation to crime or to disturbance of the peace, insults against the President, defamation, and the like as press offences. The latitude allowed to the press to slander and incite to violence with almost total impunity was not yet seen as the danger to democratic institutions that it was to become later.

The legislative election of 1881 continued the swing to the left, giving the republicans a large majority in the Chamber. The Republican Union of Gambetta emerged as the strongest group with over 200 members; but perhaps the most significant feature was the continued growth of the Bonapartists, who included half the strength of the conservative forces in the Chamber. Clearly the right was changing, and with hindsight we might say that it was ominously evident in what direction.

With the constitutional crisis settled, the chief area of strategic conflict between left and right now shifted to the field of education, in which political and social divisions were exacerbated by their identification with religious ones. In 1879 a determined opponent of clerical control, Jules Ferry, had become Minister of Education. He belonged to a distinguished family of the Vosges and had been a strong critic of the Second Empire and a member of the Government of National Defence. Though able and determined, he was too rigid and uncompromising to win popularity. Conservative in social matters, he was a convinced republican and fiercely secularist in educational policy. There was a general feeling, in republican circles, that French education did not meet the requirements of the time. The disaster of 1870 was regarded as a victory for the German teacher. Whereas German schools provided instruction in the sciences and modern languages, French education, it was alleged, was still following the methods and aims of the seventeenth century. An attempt at modernization in 1872, by Jules

Simon, had been frustrated by the influence of the Church, particularly of the great cleric, Dupanloup, and it seemed unlikely that reform would be possible so long as education remained in clerical hands. As the clergy were in the main monarchist in their political sympathies this was another reason for fearing their influence on the educational system.

Ferry launched his attack with characteristic single-mindedness and vigour. He began by secularizing the Conseil Supérieur de l'Instruction Publique, expelling the bishops and other high ecclesiastics from it. He confined the granting of degrees and other educational qualifications to the State. Education in the public primary schools was made free and by a subsequent law compulsory. For the training of women teachers, *écoles normales* for girls, which hardly existed as yet, were to be founded in every department. Religious instruction was excluded from the State schools: it was the coming of the '*école sans Dieu*', declared de Broglie.

The bitterest opposition to Ferry's educational laws was provoked by the notorious article 7: 'No one is allowed to take part in state or independent education or to control an educational establishment of any kind if he belongs to an unauthorized congregation.' Among the unauthorized congregations were Jesuits, Marists, Dominicans, and indeed all but five of the orders for men. The Senate rejected the article but the government retaliated by taking advantage of the distinction drawn by Napoleonic legislation between religious bodies that were legally authorized and those that were merely tolerated. It decreed the dissolution of the Society of Jesus and ordered that the other orders should apply for official recognition. Ferry himself was prepared to let the parish priests give religious education in secular schools, but the extremists on both sides rejected this compromise and Catholics and anti-clericals united to vote it down. The Premier, Freycinet, a Protestant, was willing to agree to a compromise in respect of all orders except the Jesuits, and the Pope, Leo XIII, was prepared to accept an agreement by which the government would abandon its demand for official authorization and in return the orders would renounce their political opposition to the Republic, though without affording it formal recognition. This was too much, on one side for the superiors of the orders and the French hierarchy, monarchist almost to a man, and on the other for the extreme anti-clericals. As soon as information about the proposed compromise leaked out, Freycinet, attacked from both right and left, was driven out of office.

The clerical party did not gain by this, for Ferry took his place and began a piecemeal expulsion of the unauthorized orders. The decrees presented a real *crise de conscience* to many good men. Two hundred magistrates, who had scruples about applying them, resigned their positions. Members of the orders often barricaded their houses, though they generally did not wait in them to be arrested when the police, or sometimes the army, occupied the empty premises. This was only a preliminary skirmish, not the major battle. After the passions aroused by the struggle had died down, the orders filtered back, with even less love for the Republic than before, while the decrees were allowed to fall quietly into disuse. It was the beginning of a conflict which was to embitter the politics of the Third Republic almost to the end.

In spite of the success of the republicans, their real leader, Gambetta, had remained excluded from office. Grévy reflected conservative hostility against the man whom Thiers had damned as the '*fou furieux*'. It was the first of many occasions during the Third Republic when the reasonable, sensible, moderate, intriguing, little men, of whom Grévy was no unworthy representative, joined to exclude a man whose greater stature made him seem dangerous. Not until 1881 did Gambetta form a ministry and then it proved a sad anti-climax. Whether as a result of Grévy's continual hostility against him, or of the suspicions of other politicians, or of Gambetta's own dictatorial temperament, his great ministry proved to be a cabinet of lesser lights, including none of the brighter luminaries of the republican galaxy. Perhaps, also, Gambetta was too much a man of panaceas.

He attributed the weakness that was already affecting republican politics to the influence of the electoral system of single-member constituencies – *mares stagnantes* as they were later to be called – and began his legislative programme by introducing a law to replace *scrutin d'arrondissement* (single-member constituencies) by *scrutin de liste* (voting on a departmental basis). When the Chamber rejected the proposal he resigned, in January 1882, less than three months after taking office. The same year he died prematurely, at the age of forty-four, taking many hopes and fears for the new Republic with him.

After a short hiatus Ferry, the biggest figure among the republicans after Gambetta, came again to office. The membership of Ferry's two ministries of 1880 and 1883 reads like a roll-call of future premiers and presidents. In his second ministry, beginning in February 1883, Ferry continued the task of republican consolidation with the notable law on municipalities of 1884, which established the free election of *maires* by the local councils everywhere except in Paris. The full importance of this step can only be appreciated if we realize the extent of the powers of the *maire* – the agent of the State for proclaiming and carrying out the laws and regulations of the central government; registrar of births, marriages, and deaths; a judicial officer entitled to denounce breaches of the law, and in default of the police commissioner prosecute them in the courts; the executive agent of the commune, the president of the meetings of the local council, who prepares its agenda and draws up its budget. In the light of all this it is not difficult to see why the Republic has been described as the régime of the elected *maire*.

Other laws passed at this time included a prohibition of any revision of the republican form of government, and of the election of any member of a family which formerly reigned in France to the presidency; the abolition of life Senators as and when the existing ones died; the recognition of trade unions; and the introduction of a law of divorce.

These were the work of Ferry and those moderate republicans whom their critics condemned as Opportunists. Ferry's achievement has seemed greater to historians than it did to his contemporaries, dominated by a personal hatred of the man. Hardly any other politician of the time aroused such bitter hostility; but it was not his domestic policy but his contribution to building a new colonial empire that brought about his downfall.

It is ironic that the Third Republic should have been the régime which built up France's great colonial empire, for at least in the earlier stages this was against the will of most of its political groups. The left was opposed to colonial conquests on principle, as well as to anything that might increase the influence of the army, while the right regarded overseas acquisitions as a diversion from the task of revenge on Germany. The creation of the colonial empire under the Third Republic has been explained in terms of the personal policy of Ferry, but this is to attribute too much to the influence of one man, as well as to read back into Ferry's actions at the time a colonial policy that may never have been in his mind, or only been thought of later, when he had undeservedly suffered for what was supposed to be his policy. Coming from an industrialized area of the Vosges and from a family of manufacturers and financiers, it is easy to suppose that he might have envisaged colonies as providing markets for surplus manufactures and a source of supply of raw materials. But this is to read an economic motivation into the colonial policies of the Third Republic for which there was at the time little evidence. A more important factor than the economic may well have been the religious one, for France was the great missionary power of the Roman Catholic world in the nineteenth century. By the time of the Third Republic among some 4,500 missionary priests outside Europe three quarters were French. If trade followed the flag, the flag sometimes followed the cassock. More influential than either economics or religion was perhaps mere prestige. When France occupied Tunis, in 1881, Gambetta wrote to Ferry that she was resuming her rank as a great power.

In spite of such motives, the reluctance of politicians to launch France on extensive colonial enterprises was clearly exhibited when a debt-collecting Anglo-French fleet sailed to Alexandria to overthrow Colonel Arabi in 1882. The Chamber of Deputies reacted against the possibility of being entangled in a war in Egypt and left the liquidation of the affair to the British. A little earlier, in 1881, a decision had been taken by Ferry to establish a protectorate over Tunisia, but this was for strategic reasons and under pressure from the Army and the Foreign Office. The whole of the decaying Turkish empire of North Africa had fallen into a state of chaos in which the only stable point was the French military hold on Algeria. It was evident that either France or Italy would move into the vacuum in Tunis, and Bismarck's diplomacy encouraged the French to do so, both to divert French interests from Europe and to alienate Italy from France. It was not even necessary to organize a *casus belli*: in those days retaliation by the stronger against aggression by the weaker was not invariably regarded as a form of international immorality. Forays into Algeria by Tunisian tribes provided the Army with an excuse to take action, and after minor military operations the Treaty of Bardo, in 1881, established a French protectorate over Tunisia in the name of a puppet Bey.

Ferry's next major colonial commitment was also hardly the result of deliberate choice. The Second Empire had established a foothold in Indo-China. Trouble with pirates and the loss of a small French force there turned a minor expedition for police purposes into a substantial war with China for the possession of Tonkin. The credits required for the expedition were resented and there was a heavy loss of life from disease. As the colonial war dragged on it became more and more unpopular in a country that was not interested in colonial expeditions and had unhappy memories of the Mexican adventure, which had followed rather a similar

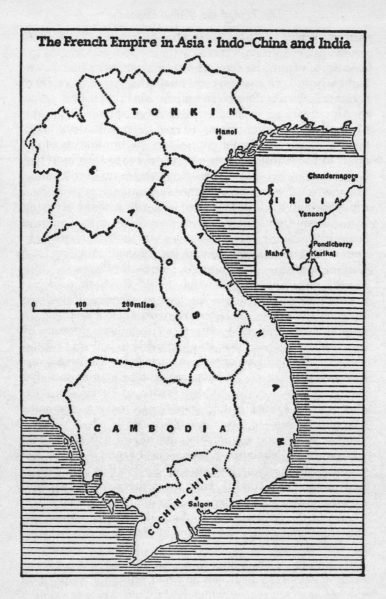

The French Empire in Asia : Indo-China and India

TONKIN

Hanoi

Chandernagore

INDIA

Yanaon

Pondicherry
Mahé   Karikal

0   100   200 miles

CAMBODIA

COCHIN-CHINA

Saigon

pattern. When, in 1885, the report arrived of a French reverse, the enemies of Ferry saw their opportunity. Led by Clemenceau from the extreme left, they shouted him down with cries of 'Tonkin-Ferry' and hurled him from office. The Tonkin affair was soon afterwards concluded successfully, but Ferry's name had been linked with colonial aggression and disaster and his reputation never recovered from the attack.

He fell at a time when political and economic developments were leading up to the first great crisis of the Third Republic. Economic conditions, which had given the Republic a good start in the seventies, became much less favourable in the eighties. The world slump, which had begun in 1875, was now affecting France, always slower than most other countries to experience the effect of external economic regression. In addition, competition from America was bringing down agricultural prices and land values were falling with them. The disease of phylloxera, which had begun to affect the vineyards in 1865, continued to spread until 1885, when the vines were reconstituted by grafting on immune American stock. Finally, a financial crisis developed in 1882, when one of the leading banks, the Union Générale, established under Catholic influence to challenge the financial dominance of Protestants and Jews, suspended payment. Speculation in central Europe had brought the bank into a conflict with the more powerful Rothschilds from which it emerged the loser. The failure of this Catholic financial venture, a panic on the Bourse, and a number of bankruptcies, were perhaps not unconnected with a growing agitation against Jewish financiers. Also, for the first time under the Third Republic, there was a deficit on the budget in 1882, which continued until 1887. A general industrial slump, in which prices and wages fell and unemployment rose, followed the financial crisis. The conclusion was drawn that economic depression was the result of the weak and unstable policies of republican governments, whereas in fact it would have been more reasonable to suppose that it was their cause.

The republican parties therefore entered the elections of 1885 in unfavourable conditions. They were disunited because of the growth of a left wing, now beginning to be called Intransigents or Radicals, who were hostile to the social conservatism as well as to the colonial policy of the dominant Opportunists. The right, on the other hand, as a result of the deaths of the Prince Imperial in 1879 and of the comte de Chambord in 1883, were left with only one candidate for the throne, the Orleanist comte de Paris. It is true that the more rigid legitimists never reconciled themselves to his claim, and that the Bonapartist tradition was to develop in a different direction, but for the moment the monarchists were less divided than usual. Throughout the history of the Third Republic the strength of the right in the country was greater than their generally inferior position in the Chamber of Deputies would lead one to suppose, but this permanent parliamentary inferiority was partly responsible for their tendency to flirt with revolution. In the elections of 1885, which were conducted under the system of *scrutin de liste*, they had 3,500,000 votes against the republican 4,100,000. The obvious danger forced an electoral coalition on the republican parties in the second ballot, which gave them 383 seats against 201 to their opponents.

In the new Chamber the Opportunists secured the re-election of Grévy as President, but they were only able to form a government with the aid of the more radical republicans, and to this extent were at their mercy. The left wing – and particularly its leading figure, Clemenceau – was now responsible for a miscalculation which endangered the Republic. The later development of his political career had already been foreshadowed in the transfer of Clemenceau from his working-class constituency of Paris to the representation of the old Jacobin stronghold of Draguignan in the Var. A new left was appearing which he could not but repudiate. He would not follow it, he declared, into the barracks and convents of socialism. He was more attracted, as indeed were many on the left, by a reforming general, whose martial air and panache had aroused the enthusiasm of the crowd. Boulanger was appointed Minister of War, largely by the influence of Clemenceau, in January 1886. When, by a law passed soon after, the heads of families which had formerly ruled in France were excluded from the territory of the nation, Boulanger manifested his republicanism by going a step further. Despite earlier indebtedness to Aumale, he rather meanly stripped the Orleanist princes of their military rank. This doubtless won him some support from the left. The attention that Boulanger in his new office paid to the welfare of the troops also increased his popularity, which was not diminished by German attacks on him for verbal fireworks directed against Germany. The Opportunists becoming alarmed, in May 1887 he was dropped from the ministry; but he was now a national figure, round whom opposition, from left and right, began to rally. Popular discontent, arising from economic difficulties as much as anything, found a cause to concentrate on in November 1887, when it was revealed that the President's son-in-law, Daniel Wilson, had been turning the Élysée Palace into a market for the sale of decorations and other favours in the presidential gift. Grévy, though discredited by these revelations, clung to office until he was forced out. The obvious successor was Ferry, but the popular hatred that had been built up against him was such that his nomination might well have provoked a revolution. Instead, therefore, Sadi Carnot, a worthy moderate republican and the bearer of a great republican name, was elected.

The situation was still dangerous, for the right had now taken up Boulanger. They saw in his popularity a lever with which they might overturn the Republic. The episode that followed is a watershed in the history of French politics. It marks the end of the old-fashioned monarchist tradition, whether of Legitimists or Orleanists, and the beginning of a new nationalist, plebiscitary, anti-parliamentary one, based on an appeal to left and right against the centre and relying on the cult of a man rather than on a policy. Summed up, it was Bonapartism without a Bonaparte. The government gave Boulanger and his supporters their opportunity by forcing him into retirement from the army in March 1888. He had now lost the backing of most of the radical leaders but not necessarily of their voters. On the extreme left Blanquists were attracted to a potential dictator. Many Socialists, in their enmity to the conservative Republic, favoured Boulanger, and unemployment brought the workers on to his side. Rochefort, once editor of *La Lanterne*, who had returned to France with the amnesty of 1880 and as editor of *L'Intransigeant* conducted a guerrilla war against the Republic, contributed to his clientele. Boulanger was backed by a committee of monarchists and Bonapartists, his campaign was financed by the legitimist duchesse d'Uzès, and he had much support in the Army and the Church. In a series of by-elections he won overwhelming majorities culminating in a victory by 244,149 to 162,410 in the Paris election of January 1889.

When the Paris result was announced huge excited mobs surrounded Boulanger crying '*À l'Élysée*'. The Ligue des Patriotes, founded in 1882 by Paul Déroulède with the intention of reviving French national spirit by a mass appeal, was ready to give the lead, which many would have followed, for a *coup d'état*. It is difficult to see what but his own faint-heartedness – unless the persuasion of his ailing mistress – stopped Boulanger from attempting to seize power. He has been charged with losing his head in this crisis and with an unmilitary preference for parliamentary methods, but this is to forget that, apart from Louis Napoleon, who had the First Empire and the Napoleonic tradition behind him, there was as yet no modern precedent, outside Latin America, for this kind of dictatorial seizure of power. Possibly Boulanger may have realized – what was certainly true – that his supporters were so diverse that they could never have agreed on a coherent policy. If they had obtained power they would not have known what to do with it. It is more difficult to explain why he gave up the game altogether. When a comparatively weak government began legal proceedings against Boulanger and he believed himself in danger of arrest he fled the country, to commit suicide on the grave of his mistress a few years later. With his flight the whole movement collapsed. In the elections of September 1889 conservatives and Boulangists could win no more than 210 seats; the republicans gained 366. Among them the Opportunists with some 216 were the dominant element, for the Radicals suffered because of their flirtation with Boulanger.

3. THE CONSERVATIVE REPUBLIC

THE next ten years was a period of confused and changing policies. Superficially it could be described in terms of personal rivalries and the political intrigues of parties and factions, but to do so would be to miss the real significance of the decade. A summary of political developments is perhaps necessary in the first place.

The new Chamber of September 1889 continued to support the cabinet of republican concentration which had weathered the Boulangist storms. It was 'replastered', to use the French term, twice, under different leaders, but achieved nothing in particular until November 1892, when, under a nondescript republican premier, Loubet, it had to face a new crisis, caused by the collapse of the Panama Canal Company. After his triumph with the Suez Canal, Ferdinand de Lesseps had launched a plan to drive a canal through the isthmus of Panama. This proved a much more difficult undertaking than had been expected and called for far more capital than had originally been envisaged. To raise the new money the Panama Company issued shares repayable at an enhanced price and by lot, which required parliamentary authorization. In spite of the new money, the difficulties of the canal project proved too much for the resources of de Lesseps and the Company went bankrupt to the tune of some sixty million pounds, all sunk without hope in the hills and mosquito-ridden swamps of Panama.

Two survivors of the Boulangist movement, the author Maurice Barrès, who had been elected by Nancy to the Chamber in 1889, and Édouard Drumont, editor of the anti-semitic *La Libre Parole*, saw in the affairs of the Panama Company an opportunity to discredit the parliamentary régime. Drumont opened the attack with *Les Dessous de Panama*, an exposure of the bribery of politicians that had accompanied the promotion of the company and the raising of funds for it. He based himself on information supplied by a baron Jacques de Reinach. This was curious, since Reinach had himself been the agent responsible for the bribery. Possibly he was trying to confuse the issue and so conceal his own activities; but when he died, suddenly and possibly by suicide in November 1892, it appeared that he himself had not been a free agent. For years he had been blackmailed by an international adventurer named Cornelius Herz, who, as was the way of international adventurers, was well placed in the social world of Paris and had influential political connexions. With Reinach's death the scandal burst out into the open. The names of deputies and journalists charged with receiving bribes were published. Violent scenes occurred in the Chamber. Ministers resigned, the government fell. A judicial inquiry was instituted. Among those implicated in the affair were the Minister of Finance, Rouvier, the President of the Chamber, Floquet, and the *franc-tireur* of the left, Clemenceau.

It was on the head of Clemenceau, whose ruthless attacks had earned him so many enemies, that the most violent storm fell. Though he came from Catholic and royalist Vendée, Clemenceau's ancestors, small proprietors and doctors, were anti-clerical and Jacobin. La Réveillière-Lépeaux, regicide and Director, had been a cousin. Clemenceau's father narrowly escaped deportation under the Second Empire. He himself was *maire* of Montmartre during the siege of Paris, and one of the *maires* who attempted to mediate

between the Commune and Versailles. In the Chamber of
Deputies he became the most feared of the guerrillas of the
left, notorious for his violent speeches, vitriolic articles, and
duels. Now he was to fall a victim to the kind of onslaught he
himself knew so well how to launch. Suspicion that he had
been the power behind Cornelius Herz was crystallized in a
speech by Paul Déroulède. Everyone knew who was the
guilty man, Déroulède proclaimed, but they dared not say
it for they feared three things – his tongue, his pistol, and
his pen. 'I defy all three and name him: it is M. Clemenceau.' A duel naturally followed, which was bloodless, but
the fatal blow had been struck. Clemenceau was hounded
out of public life with cries of 'Aoh yes!', for to the charge of
Panama corruption was added, to sink him beyond hope of
rescue, that of being an English agent.

The republicans, having shed their more compromised
members, got over the Panama affair as well as they could.
The elections of August 1893, in which there were many
abstentions, returned a majority of about 310 moderate
republicans, some 150 radical republicans, and a small
group of independents or socialists on the extreme left –
these last the electoral witness of rising social unrest. The
republican cabinets of the next few years had to govern amid
a wave of violence which culminated, in June 1894, in the
assassination of Sadi Carnot. Casimir-Périer, who replaced
him as President, only held office for six months, after which,
frustrated at the powerlessness of the presidency, he resigned.
In his place was chosen the amiable man-of-the-world,
Félix Faure. The new government of June 1894 was more
notable for its members than for its head. With Delcassé,
aged 43, Hanotaux 42, Poincaré 33, and Barthou 31, it was
evident that a new generation, and a notable one, was entering republican politics. In November 1895, under Léon
Bourgeois, for the first time a radical cabinet took office. It
was undermined by its attempt to introduce financial
reforms, including an income tax, and in April 1896 was
replaced by a cabinet of moderates under Méline, who had

no such dangerous ideas. General elections in May 1898 once again proved that despite all the faults of the republican parties the country remained republican. But now a new crisis had unexpectedly arisen. In January 1898 Zola published in the journal which Clemenceau used as his political forum after his parliamentary débâcle an open letter, *J'accuse*, and the Dreyfus affair broke.

Before this, however, and behind the petty political manoeuvring of the nineties, major developments had taken place, which fundamentally changed the meaning of right and left. First, the old right, the monarchists, whether legitimist or Orleanist, ceased to be an effective political force. The Boulangist movement showed the pattern of the future right, in which neither Church nor King, nor the inherited traditions of the old monarchist parties, were to have much real part to play.

There had been, after the failure of Boulangism, an attempt to refashion the right on different lines, which must first be mentioned. This was the Ralliement. So long as Pius IX remained on the papal throne there had been no possibility of any relation between the Church and the Republic other than a state of open or barely concealed war. The accession of Leo XIII in 1878 brought the opportunity of a *détente*, especially after the death of the comte de Chambord in 1883 had made an Orleanist prince the claimant to the throne. In 1884 a papal encyclical enjoined the French bishops not to exhibit hostility to the established authorities of the state. Papal awareness of the strength of anti-republican sentiments among French Catholics was shown by the long interval that elapsed before a further step was taken towards a *rapprochement* with the Republic.

This came in 1890 and its chosen agent was the tall, bearded, authoritarian, irascible primate of Africa, Cardinal Lavigerie. A Bonapartist prelate, though converted after 1870 to legitimacy, and the embodiment of French missionary zeal, he was an odd choice for the role. The occasion of the announcement of the new policy was equally unexpected. It was a banquet at Algiers to the officers of the Mediterranean fleet, monarchist and reactionary to a man. Though Lavigerie had acted under instructions, that he had accurately represented papal policy was not made clear before 1892, when Leo XIII issued the encyclical *Au Milieu des Sollicitudes*, which advised French Catholics to rally to the Republic and defend the interests of the Church by taking part in political life.

The policy of Ralliement was not the only evidence of a new wind blowing from the Vatican. Leo XIII also saw that the increasing alienation of the Church from the poorer sections of society, which resulted from the identification of its interests with those of the wealthier classes, had already gone a long way towards duplicating the social cleavage in urban society with a religious one. The encyclical *Rerum Novarum*, of 1891, called on Catholics to adopt a positive attitude towards the problem of wages and hours and the social welfare of the workers. The French hierarchy, confined to the society of the *haute bourgeoisie* and *noblesse*, took but a languid interest in the new ideas enunciated by Rome; but lower down appeared a sprinkling of what came to be called – not necessarily in praise – democratic priests, who engaged in missionary activity among the poor and even went so far as to suggest that they might have rights as well as duties. The hierarchy and the *bien-pensant* upper classes could hardly be expected to tolerate this. Like the followers of Lamennais and the Catholic democrats of 1848 earlier, or the worker-priests much later, the democratic priests of the nineties went further than respectable society was willing to accept or than Rome was ready to follow them. The implicit repudiation, in 1901, of these steps towards social *rapprochement* by the Vatican was a severe blow to the Ralliement, because it drew its main strength from the areas that were both Catholic and industrial, especially the departments of the Nord and the Pas-de-Calais.

Heirs of the Social Catholics of half a century earlier, the *ralliés* drew their leaders largely from old legitimist families.

Albert de Mun, an orator of the extreme right but also a social reformer, was their most notable figure, but perhaps the most influential convert in the long run was a young cavalry officer named Lyautey. Under the influence of the new school of Catholic thought, he put forward, in an article in the *Revue des Deux Mondes* in 1891, a new role for the army, now composed mostly of conscripts spending their time in peaceable manoeuvres or kicking their heels in barracks. The army, said Lyautey, should be a school of citizenship and the officer an educator. All that an attempt to put his ideas into practice with his own squadron gained for the young officer was a severe reprimand and the advice to transfer himself and his unsuitable ideas to the colonies. Curiously, the first steps towards putting his ideas into practice in France were taken after 1901 by the anti-clerical War Minister, André.

Between the radical anti-clericals and the dervishes of the Catholic revival, there was never much room for a party of liberal Catholicism. Even Dupanloup, whose liberalism was very diluted, had never been made a cardinal. As an effort to reconcile the Catholic Church and the Republic, the Ralliement proved almost a complete failure. Faced with the choice between the advice of a Pope (which another Pope might reverse) and their deeply ingrained hatred of republican ideas, most of the monarchists and Catholics remained irreconcilable. Even the bishops closed their ears to the appeal from Rome. There is this to be said for them, that it was not a mere matter of accepting republican institutions, but also republican symbols and dogmas, which were profoundly secularist and anti-clerical. On the republican side, while the moderates were prepared to accept the support of Catholics, the radicals feared them even when they brought gifts.

The failure of the Ralliement meant that the conservative and monarchist right ceased to be a real force, or to have more than a nuisance value, in French politics. Even though the monarchy was still a flag that was waved, a different party now fought under the same banner and directed its efforts towards a different objective. The logic of the situation made it a revolutionary party, and being this it had to adopt a revolutionary pattern of behaviour. It still found its allies naturally in the two great professional bodies which had not been reconciled to the Republic – the army and the church. Hence militarism and clericalism became the hallmarks of the new right. From Bonapartism it inherited a contempt for parliamentary government and from Panama had learnt the cry of '*À bas les voleurs*'. It took over from the Opportunists a belief in the colonial mission of France, which it added to the hope of revenge on Germany and the recovery of Alsace-Lorraine. Therefore it stood for war, as well as, and perhaps partly as a means towards, the overthrow of the régime. It drew its support largely from the urban middle classes. Never more than a revolutionary minority, with only a small representation in parliament, it could provoke a permanent feeling of insecurity by continual agitation. Henceforth the Republic had always to live on the brink of a threatened *coup d'état*, and the conservative elements that should have provided ballast for the state were weakened by the existence of a revolutionary party on their right, which might capsize the ship by a sudden lurch at any moment.

The conservatives, properly so called, were to be found among the right-wing republicans, and the minority Catholics of the Ralliement naturally gravitated towards them. This alliance was, however, not without its harmful effect on the original social ideals of the Ralliement; for the conservative republicans, who were now changing the title of Opportunists for that of Progressivists, had taken over from the Orleanist and Second Empire notables the defence of property. The bitter class struggles of 1848 and 1871 were now a historical memory, labour was beginning to organize itself, and Socialist parties were effecting a breach in republican politics. But the wealthy propertied classes were still prepared to resist all concessions and to do no more to improve the conditions of the lower classes than they were compelled to. As has already been mentioned, when, in 1896, Léon Bourgeois proposed a reform of the inequitable system of taxation by the introduction of a modest income tax, the Chamber of Deputies reacted violently and turned to Méline to save them from what they saw as a monstrous attack on the rights of property, involving an inquisition into the jealously guarded secrets of individual wealth.

Financial reform had little chance in a nation in which social influence and administrative position were still largely in the hands of the wealthy, and political power rested with the votes of peasant proprietors and independent shopkeepers and artisans. The influence of organized labour was too weak to do much to redress the balance. This situation accounts for the backwardness of social legislation in France. Even the reforms that were passed into law often remained ineffective for lack of the machinery to put them into practice. One can hardly count the abolition of the worker's *livret* in 1890 as such; in fact it had fallen into disuse much earlier, for it involved obligations on employers as well as on their workers. A law of 1892 establishing labour conciliation remained unapplied. Such modest reforms as passed, usually only did so after a prolonged struggle and much delay.

Freedom of individual enterprise, however, did not involve any dogmatic adherence to ideas of free trade. Gradually an alliance of agriculturalists and manufacturers, aided by the slump of the late seventies, secured the abandonment of the liberal commercial policy of the Second Empire. In 1881 a tariff law imposed duties of between ten per cent and thirty per cent on imported manufactures. Agriculture, which had been suffering from bad harvests and the competition of overseas products, demanded protection in its turn. Its cause was championed by the Minister of Agriculture, Méline. A senator from the Vosges, he particularly represented agricultural interests, and was the spokesman of the economic Bourbons of the Third Republic, for whom economic progress equalled social danger. He combined a policy of energetic state aid and protection for agriculture with strenuous opposition to any interference with the free play of economic forces in industry. Méline's campaign reached a successful conclusion in 1892 with the introduction of a tariff covering practically the whole of agricultural and industrial production. The system of high protection provided a platform on which small and big men, peasant proprietors and large farmers, craftsmen and capitalists, could stand together, the rich uniting to defend the poor against the threat of cheap food and cheap manufactures. France was one of the greatest wheat-producers of the world, but the price of wheat inside France remained far above the world level.

The interests of the propertied classes were even more closely touched by the question of taxation. In 1895 and 1896, as we have seen, proposals were tabled for a progressive income tax, with a compulsory declaration of income to be officially checked. Some such way of making French tax methods more modern, more elastic, and more equitable was badly needed, and it had been part of the programme of the radical wing of the republicans. The moderates and the right reacted almost unanimously against the proposal. Here, again, the small businessman and the peasant provided the rank and file of the army that fought in defence of the social irresponsibility of wealth. Méline, who had already been the agent of class interests in his protectionist campaign, became Premier with the task of defending the interests of property against the new tax proposals. This was practically the only policy of his cabinet, but it was enough to guarantee it a solid majority for over two years, from 1896 to the elections of 1898.

France evidently remained under the Republic what it had been under the Monarchy and the Empire, socially an intensely conservative country. Political and social changes had indeed increased the strength of conservative forces. The peasantry had been a revolutionary element in 1789; 1848 demonstrated that they were on the side of law and the

established order; and the fact that this was now a republican order did not materially change its social implications.
Paris also had ceased to be a stronghold of the left, as
Boulangism showed. This was the point at which the political
kaleidoscope was given the decisive twist which settled
French politics in their new pattern. Although the Boulangist movement was followed by Radical victories in the
capital, changes in the social composition of Paris proper,
consequent on Haussmann's rebuilding, finally found political expression in the municipal elections of 1900 and 1902,
when the right gained control of the municipal council. It
was the end of the *bras nus* and the barricades. Only a few
Blanquists and their successors among Marxist or Leninist
historians continued to hanker after the legend of the revolutionary *journées*. The excitement of the descent *dans la rue*, of
swirling mobs surging through the streets, beleaguering the
Hôtel de Ville, breaking into the Assembly, now passed
from left to right. The threat of revolution was henceforth
to come from the other end of the political spectrum.

In the industrial regions there was a growing, but in
relation to the whole population still small, wage-earning
proletariat of factory and mine, disciplined by its conditions
of life, lacking the initiative or the political instincts of the
master craftsmen and the middle class, more capable of the
dumb, passive resistance of the strike than the active effort
to overthrow governments and seize power by *journée* or *coup
d'état*, lacking also the middle-class leadership that can
usually be traced in the revolutionary mobs of the past.
What the industrial proletariat was capable of, what indeed
it was conditioned to accept, was organization in trade union
or political party. The nineties saw the real development of
the trade unions, or *syndicats*, and of the Socialist party or
rather parties, though the previous decade had been one of
preparation for them.

After the Commune, left-wing leadership had temporarily
been eliminated from France; the older socialist ideologies
were moribund, and the new influence of Marx had as yet

hardly penetrated to France. The first positive step towards
the organization of a socialist political party was taken by a
Congress at Marseille in 1879, which formed a Fédération
des Travailleurs Socialistes, with a very moderate programme of nationalization. The return of the exiled Communards after the amnesty of 1880 gave an impetus to the
left-wing movement but also introduced strong elements of
dissension. The Blanquists formed a Central Revolutionary
Committee under Vaillant. Their opponents joined the
Federation, but it split in 1883, when Jules Guesde, the
earliest of the Marxist leaders in France, repudiated the
policy of social reform and founded a new Parti Ouvrier,
drawing its chief support from the areas of mining and heavy
industry in the North-east and the Centre.

The passing of the law of 1884 authorizing the formation
of trade unions, or *syndicats*, was evidence that the Opportunists recognized the existence of a new force in French
society, though the unions were bitterly opposed by employers, and state employees, including railway workers,
were prohibited from joining them. The new unions were
profoundly suspicious of politics and politicians; they believed in direct action to improve the workers' conditions,
and distrusted the Socialist leaders as mere bourgeois
ideologists. In fact, all except one of these, Allemane, were
middle-class. However, under the Marxist influence of
Guesde, a Fédération Nationale des Syndicats was formed
for political action in 1886. In opposition to this, Bourses de
Travail, founded in 1887 as popularly controlled centres of
mutual aid, workers' education, and employment exchanges,
formed a national federation in 1892. The period from 1889
to 1892 was one of economic progress, when the membership
of the *syndicats*, 140,000 in 1890, multiplied by three; then,
in a period of economic recession, it rose very slowly and was
still only 580,000 in 1899 – this in a country with a total
population of some thirty-nine millions. Even this modest
progress of the *syndicats* was marked by strikes, violence on
both sides, and repression. In 1890, 1 May was recognized

45

as the annual Labour Day. Its first celebration, in 1891, served to demonstrate the reality of class fears and hatred in French industrial society. A demonstration in the Nord for an eight-hour day got out of hand. Troops were called in and opened fire on the crowds, killing nine demonstrators, including four young girls, and wounding over one hundred.

The situation darkened when 1893 brought an industrial slump, and about this time also the infection of anarchism, hitherto not much more than a literary freak, broke out in France. The anarchists upheld a doctrine of propaganda by action, in which bombs were the chief form of conversion, though a knife was used to kill President Carnot in June 1894. The disease worked itself out after a year or two, but provided a justification for the cabinet of Casimir-Périer to pass what the left called the '*lois scélérates*', imposing severe penalties on press offences and on the instigation or organization of attacks on persons or property.

However, the left was now in a better position to defend itself politically. Socialist and syndicalist agitation had created an effective workers' vote, which in some constituencies could materially influence or even decide the elections. The result was the arrival in the Chamber of Radical Socialists (strictly 'socialist radicals') and even Socialists. The four Socialist parties, with the aid of the votes of former Boulangists and of radicals upset by the Panama scandal, won eighteen seats. In addition there were some thirty independent Socialists, including Alexandre Millerand and Jean Jaurès, who had moved over from the Radicals or Opportunists. They were too few in number to provide more than a small weight in the political balance, but they offered a reminder that, though politically the Republic had survived longer than any other régime France had known since 1789, the social problem still remained. A hard struggle was evidently ahead between the intensely conservative propertied classes and the growing class of employees. The agricultural population, which had been suffering from a prolonged depression, had not yet awoken to the use of its potential political power to secure better conditions, but even this was to come. These issues, however, could be fought out by ballot box and in the debating chamber: they did not threaten the stability of the régime. Though the ideology of the Socialists was revolutionary, they were already beginning to show their capacity for being absorbed by the parliamentary system. The real danger arose from the fact that there were other elements, which were unreconciled to the Republic and fundamentally opposed to its ideology.

The Ralliement, by its very failure, had underlined the hostility of the Catholics to a political régime which was on principle secular and seemed to be the deadly enemy of religion. Though the political personnel was now overwhelmingly republican, the higher ranks of the administration continued to be recruited from families of the *haute bourgeoisie* which, whatever their origins, now had, or were rapidly acquiring, Catholic connexions. Literature in France has always tended to lean towards the opposition, and the opposition was now on the right. Most important of all, a new political trend was appearing which may loosely be called nationalism and which appealed to a new generation of angry young men in revolt against the boredom of a régime that had lasted for a quarter of a century. In their enmity to the parliamentary régime the nationalists were the heirs of Bonapartism, with which Boulangism was the link, while their anti-intellectualism harked back to the theocrats. The most characteristic, and indeed the common feature of all sections of nationalism was a peculiarly vicious strain of anti-semitism. The new right drew, geographically, on the traditional centres of right-wing support. Despite the changes in name, and even in ideology, the electoral geography of France remained remarkably stable, except that, as well as Paris, Lorraine moved, after 1871 when many Alsatians settled there, to the right. In 1898 the nationalists elected fifteen deputies, to whom might be added four anti-semites from Algeria. In 1902 their strength had risen to fifty-nine. Their support in the nation was limited. The danger they presented to the Republic lay not so much in their political power as in their ideological hold over Church and Army. Though the nationalists of the early years of the twentieth century often used bellicose language and were xenophobic, their aggression was directed more against their compatriots than against foreigners.

4. THE DREYFUS AFFAIR

ONE of the most important developments in the Third Republic was the change in the composition of the officer class in the Army. The older legitimist families had abandoned the Army, as well as all other forms of government service, after 1830, while the sons of the wealthy bourgeoisie avoided a career that brought neither gain nor social prestige. However, this situation did not last. Gradually, during the Second Empire, the status of the Army officer rose and recruitment from aristocratic families revived. This tendency was intensified, rather unexpectedly, in the early years of the Third Republic, perhaps because the agricultural depression made a profession more necessary for the sons of the old landed class. The result was that by the end of the century, when in other fields the republicanization of the state was becoming effective, the higher ranks of the Army were an almost solid conservative, monarchist, and Catholic monopoly. There were the ingredients here of a dangerously explosive situation, though no one could have guessed in advance what was to be the spark that would set it off.

This came in 1894, though the train that led to a nationwide conflagration was a long and slow-burning one. In September 1894 a list of French military documents, apparently handed to the Germans, was rescued by a minor French agent, in the normal process of collecting information, from a wastepaper basket in the German Embassy.

This was the famous *bordereau* or memorandum. It was examined by the counter-espionage branch of the French Army, which operated under the title of the Statistical Section and was practically a law to itself, being answerable only to the Chief of Staff. It followed its own ways – rather eccentric and devious ones, be it said – in blithe freedom from all outside control. The dominant influence in the little office – its staff only numbered some seven altogether – was a career officer who had risen by his own ability from the ranks, one Major Henry, a heavy and powerful peasant type, brave, ruthless, and, as it turned out, with peasant cunning and an extraordinary gift of invention that accorded ill with his blunt, bull-like appearance. It was evident from the *bordereau* that there was a spy at work in the French officer corps, and, looking for a culprit, the Statistical Section hit on the name of Captain Alfred Dreyfus. Member of a wealthy textile-manufacturing family of Alsatian Jews which had chosen French nationality in 1871, Dreyfus entered the Army as an artillery officer, and had recently been seconded to the War Office in Paris. The evidence against him was not merely negligible, it was entirely non-existent. Even the writing on the *bordereau*, the one material fact, did not resemble Dreyfus's hand. In the whole story, while we meet, naturally, with some ingenious rogues, what strikes one most is the monumental stupidity that was exhibited, not least in the Intelligence branch, by the Army.

What settled the fate of Dreyfus was the fact that he was a Jew and as such a rare – possibly unique – phenomenon on the General Staff. Anti-semitism, formerly, in so far as it existed in France, a prejudice of the left and the people, under the Third Republic had moved over to the right and become a mark of those who were, and therefore of those who wished to be regarded as, socially superior. Before about 1890 there had been some 80,000 Jews in France, mostly well assimilated except in Alsace. By the end of the century immigration from eastern Europe had more than doubled their numbers and this great influx of a new and obviously alien element into French society provided an opportunity and stimulus for the spread of anti-semitism on a much wider scale than before. Its chief propagandist was the journalist Edmond Drumont, who founded in 1892 a paper called *La Libre Parole* to inculcate his ideas. One of the earliest features was a series called '*Les Juifs dans l'armée*'. In 1886 he had given the anti-semites a text-book in *La France juive*, and in 1889 he founded the Anti-semitic League.

The one part of France in which anti-semitism was indigenous – it had appeared in 1789 and again in the Revolution of 1848 – was Alsace. Now, not only was Dreyfus an Alsatian Jew, but the head of the Statistical Section was also Alsatian: this may have helped him to settle on Dreyfus as the guilty man. He reported his discovery to the War Office. The Minister, General Mercier, who was to play a sinister role from beginning to end of the affair, ordered a court-martial. It might have been thought that the absence of evidence would prove a difficulty at this stage. By now, however, the press was on the scent. With its usual determination that justice shall be done, or at least seem to be done, and a victim be found, it proclaimed that a rich Jewish traitor was about to buy himself immunity for his crimes. The War Office being anxious not to provide any opening for such a suspicion, the conviction of Dreyfus became a political necessity. Major Henry, who was a practised hand at producing forged papers to be planted on foreign agents, supplied the necessary evidence. Though the result was rather crude, it was good enough for a secret court-martial which had, to use French legal terminology, an intimate conviction of the guilt of the accused. Dreyfus was unanimously found guilty and sentenced to be cashiered and deported for life. There was a good deal of public indignation that he was to escape being shot. Clemenceau, admitting that in the past he had supported the abolition of the death penalty, urged that here if anywhere was a case for its infliction. The socialist leader, Jaurès, expressed his alarm at the evidence of sinister forces at work: a rich Jew, who was a proved spy and traitor, was going to escape his rightful punishment.

The War Ministry did not really deserve this criticism. Enraged that Dreyfus had refused to commit suicide as a gentleman should when found out, or even to confess, although promised better treatment if he would do so, General Mercier ordered him to be sent to the severest possible solitary confinement on Devil's Island. The order was faithfully carried out for the next four years.

The case was now closed, but there was still a desire to get to the bottom of the crime. What was the motive of Dreyfus? What was he after? It could hardly be money for he was a wealthy man. Efforts were made to uncover a woman. A secret love nest was in fact ferreted out, but it proved to be only a mare's nest, belonging to quite a different Dreyfus. Moreover staff papers continued to disappear and the invaluable wastepaper basket of the German Embassy produced another document, this time an express letter – a *petit-bleu* – addressed by name to a French officer named Esterhazy. There was now a new head at the Statistical Section, Major Picquart, yet another Alsatian, who had represented the War Office in the trial of Dreyfus. Put on the track of Esterhazy by the *petit-bleu*, Picquart obtained specimens of his writing and discovered to his astonishment its similarity to the writing on the *bordereau*. One might have thought that this would be the end of the case: it was only the beginning. Major Henry rapidly appreciated the danger of the situation and proceeded to manufacture some better evidence against Dreyfus for Mercier to use. The War Office also became alarmed, and before he could cause trouble by any more inconvenient discoveries Picquart was removed from his position, sent to Tunisia, and subsequently ordered to the fighting area where there was at least a chance that his inconsiderate activities might be brought to an end.

Major Henry's mind was still not at ease, and his alarm was shared by two highly placed members of the War

Office, General Gonse and the Marquis du Paty de Clam, who had taken part in the original investigation of Dreyfus. Gonse was a good office man, and as it turned out prepared to lie through thick and thin to cover up for the Office. Du Paty de Clam had been a dashing young officer and still fancied himself as something out of a romantic novel. Henry, who was obviously the brains of the triumvirate, now had the fantastic idea of using Esterhazy to consolidate the case against Dreyfus, with a promise of protection, though he was a notorious debauchee, permanently in debt, and known to the foreign attachés, if not to the Intelligence branch, as prepared to do anything for money. But he was also the son of a French general, had himself formerly been a member of the Statistical Section, and had an imposing aristocratic air. Because of the discovery of the *petit-bleu* it was not possible to avoid a court-martial, which took only three minutes to acquit him. Esterhazy's sardonic imagination was now added to the cruder cunning of Henry, and more and more officers were entangled in a web of forgery and false evidence so complicated that even its inventors began to lose the threads.

The family of Dreyfus had all this while been struggling unavailingly to reopen the case. They had obtained only a little outside support and that chiefly from other Jews; but Picquart, who had already sacrificed his career to his sense of justice, was trying from a distance to prevent his suspicions from dying with him. He therefore sent a statement to a friend in Paris, who, armed with this, approached the eminent Alsatian senator, Scheurer-Kestner, who was convinced by it of the need for a retrial. Scheurer-Kestner interpellated the government in December 1897 but received no satisfaction. Indeed, Méline prematurely announced, '*Il n'y a pas d'affaire Dreyfus.*' This made it an affair on the political level. Public interest was aroused: evidently something mysterious was going on. It burst on the general public in January 1898, when the novelist Zola, who had already written one or two articles expressing his concern, published in Clemenceau's *L'Aurore* an open letter to the President of the Republic – the famous *J'accuse* – in which he indicted the War Office of a judicial crime. The Office and the government fought back – they could do nothing else – even though it meant bringing out some of the secret evidence against Dreyfus. Zola was tried, found guilty, and eventually took refuge in flight to England. Picquart was charged with indiscipline and dismissed the service. Surely the case was now closed.

The case may have been closed, the Affair had just begun. Press and public opinion were aroused and a campaign for revision of the sentence on Dreyfus was started. For some, justice and the fate of an innocent man were at stake; for others it was a heaven-sent opportunity for a campaign against the enemies of the Republic. A petition calling for revision of the judgement on Dreyfus was signed by leading writers and artists – Lanson, Seignobos, Brunot, Viollet, Blum, Langevin, Anatole France, Proust, Halévy, Briand, Herr, Péguy, and many others. The League for the Defence of the Rights of Man was founded. Naturally, the majority of those who took an active part in the campaign for revision were anti-clericals, freemasons, Protestants, and Jews. The Army, monarchists, Catholics, nationalists found themselves attacked by all those they hated most. The veil that had been cast over old grievances was rudely torn aside and recent attempts at reconciliation went for nothing. The *anti-dreyfusards* had most of the press behind them and the campaign against the revisionists was waged without mercy. The small party of Catholic reformers was committed by Albert de Mun to the defence of the Army, and though there were Catholic *dreyfusards* neither side was willing to draw attention to their existence. One who could not be ignored was Péguy, for whom the stake in the Affair was not the physical safety of France, which the Army and the politicians imagined themselves to be defending, but its spiritual salvation.

The Archbishop of Paris had a different idea of what was

needed spiritually; he became the patron of the Laborum League of anti-semitic army officers. In its journal *La Croix* the Assumptionist Order carried the Church into the struggle with a raging, tearing campaign which did much to stir up anti-clerical feeling on the other side. The question, wrote one commentator, is not whether a wretched individual is guilty or innocent, it is whether the Jews and the Protestants are, or are not, the masters of this country. The factions of the right had the incitement to fight back against enemies whose political control of France had seemed unshakeable, and in anti-semitism they had a symbol, a flag, a common cause to bind them together. Anti-Jewish riots broke out in many towns; in Algiers there was widespread looting of Jewish property.

The line between *dreyfusards* and *anti-dreyfusards* did not invariably coincide with other divisions; old associations were broken and families split. The political parties of the left at first tried to keep themselves uncommitted. The Radicals were anti-revisionist, the Socialist groups unwilling to be outbid in patriotism by the Radicals and themselves not uninfluenced by anti-semitic feeling. The Foreign Minister, Hanotaux, believed that a retrial would weaken the French image abroad. A manifesto drawn up by Guesde and Jaurès called on the proletariat not to enlist in either of the clans of a bourgeois civil war. Jaurès, however, found his sense of justice stronger than his socialist ideology and became one of the leading advocates of revision. Politically, the fate of Dreyfus had come to be bound up with the survival of the Third Republic. The attempt to pretend that this was not the issue collapsed with the resignation of Méline in June 1898. The War Office had so far played its cards with complete success – this was not so difficult since Major Henry was always there to provide it with extra aces whenever they were needed. General Mercier, in particular, fought each move in the direction of revision with every weapon he had. The fanatic obstinacy of the War Office has led some historians to the supposition that there was somebody much more powerful than Esterhazy involved in espionage, who was determined to use the supposed guilt of Dreyfus to cover himself. Indeed it does seem possible that a second spy had been at work, though beyond this we cannot go. Whatever the reason, in its anxiety to beat down all criticism the War Office committed the tactical blunder of prosecuting Picquart, which involved a re-examination of the documentation used against Dreyfus. The new War Minister, though *anti-dreyfusard*, was an honest man who could not pretend that a forgery if it convicted Dreyfus was not one. He subsequently resigned. Colonel Henry, whose capacity for covering up one forgery with another had at last come to an end, was put under fortress arrest. He was a brave man who had done his best for the Office without thought of personal reward. Realizing he could do no more, he cut his throat that night. Esterhazy, realizing that *his* game was up, fled to England.

In fact the game was not yet up. To admit the innocence of Dreyfus would be to incriminate the War Office, the aristocracy, and the Church. A Ligue de la Patrie Française rallied intellectuals, artists, poets – Charles Maurras, Émile Faguet, Mistral, François Coppée, Heredia, Lemaître, Rimbaud, Jules Verne, Léon Daudet, Forain, and many others – in their defence. The most powerful writer among the *anti-dreyfusards*, Maurice Barrès, converted what had become a defensive struggle against the revisionists into a mystical offensive on behalf of the nation. The country seemed on the verge of civil war.

What saved it was perhaps that spirit of *fonctionnairisme* with which the Army, like the other great organizations which emerged from the Consulate and Empire, was imbued. Its officers in the last resort were servants of the state, bound by an oath to whoever held the legal authority of the government. Hence, of all the revolutions or *coups d'état* between 1815 and 1958, none was made and none was prevented by the Army. The revolutionary move had to come from civilians. The poet-politician Paul Déroulède, who had founded his Ligue des Patriotes for such a purpose, saw an opportunity to exploit the feverish state of public opinion early in 1899, when the President, Félix Faure, collapsed in the Élysée and the arms of a terrified lady friend. His funeral was used by the Ligue des Patriotes to stage an attempt at a *coup*; it was a farcical failure.

The tide was now running fast the other way. There is no need to recount the delaying tactics by which one barrier to revision after another was set up. In September 1898 the case of Dreyfus was referred to the appeal court; in June 1899 it decided for a new trial, and Dreyfus, in total ignorance of everything that had happened since his trial, was brought back from Devil's Island, white-haired and broken. He was to be tried again, before a new court-martial, at Rennes. It was no better conducted than the former trial: the generals and colonels lied like troopers in defence of the honour of the Army. By five to two the court reached the ridiculous verdict that Dreyfus was guilty of treachery with extenuating circumstances and sentenced him to ten years' detention. It was clear that no military court would admit to an error of justice. A presidential pardon was therefore issued. A retrial before the Appeal Court in 1906 quashed the Rennes verdict, but the case was really over in 1899.

In the summer of 1899 it had seemed that the republican régime was breaking down. A trivial incident in June proved the turning-point. In the course of a visit to the races at Auteuil by the new President, Loubet, a royalist baron knocked his hat off with a stick. This was going too far. It was only a straw but it came at the end of a history that had aroused intense passion. At last the republicans, moderates as well as the extremer factions, had had enough. The compromising, appeasing cabinets that had held office so far during the Affair came to an end. In June 1899 a cabinet of republican defence was formed under Waldeck-Rousseau, a conservative republican and a former colleague of Gambetta and Ferry. The new premier was a distinguished lawyer with a clear mind, a cool temperament, and a cold manner. He was a moderate in his political views, but added a sense of justice to his sense of order, and he was capable of giving the country what it needed most, a government that would govern. Perhaps only Ferry, among the politicians of the Third Republic, had an equal sense of authority, and Ferry aroused too many enmities. Waldeck-Rousseau drew his ministers from the whole gamut of republican politics. Their names are worth remembering for it was a cabinet of strong men, not afraid of taking decisions, chosen for what they were rather than for the number of parliamentary votes they could bring with them. General de Gallifet at the Ministry of War, hated by the left as the 'executioner' of 1871, was balanced against the socialist Millerand, even if the latter's acceptance of a ministerial post aroused resentment among other Socialists; Delcassé was at the Quai d'Orsay, Caillaux at the Ministry of Finances; Lépine, strongest and most popular of Prefects of Police, brought Paris back to order.

The Waldeck-Rousseau cabinet obtained a majority of only twenty-five, but the new Premier was not deterred from taking energetic measures. The appointment of the new Minister of War, though it aroused bitter opposition from the left, was in one respect a stroke of genius. Gallifet was a professional in the best sense of the word, not a political general like Mercier, and free from any inclination to play at politics. His reputation with the Army put him beyond attack on that side and enabled him to quell all symptoms of unrest in it. To subject the Church to republican discipline was to be a longer and most costly process. But the critical decade had passed. The Affair, though at a heavy price both at the time and in drafts on the future, had ended in the triumph of the Republic. It was to survive for another forty years, and then only to be overthrown by a foreign enemy.

5. PROLOGUE TO REFORM

THE struggle for justice in the Dreyfus affair had united, as perhaps nothing else could have done, the republican forces in France. Under a premier like Waldeck-Rousseau this meant justice not only for Dreyfus but also – of a retributive kind – for the enemies of the Republic. One of the first steps of the new government was to order the arrest and trial of those who had attempted to exploit the affair in the interests of revolution. Something also had to be done about the Assumptionist Fathers, who in their papers had been conducting a Holy War against the Republic and the Jews. They had been rather unwise in thus putting themselves in the forefront of the political battle, for as an unauthorized congregation they were in a weak position if the government chose to take action against them. Not without provocation – one of the last efforts of the Order had been to subsidize opposition candidates in the election – it did take action and the Order was dissolved.

Waldeck-Rousseau was not anxious to extend the attack to those religious bodies which had not flung themselves into the political struggle. He put forward, in November 1899, a scheme compelling religious congregations to apply for legal recognition. It also included certain steps for assimilating clerical and lay schools, so that, as he said, there should no longer be *deux jeunesses* in France. It is doubtful if the Church would have accepted such proposals in any case, but the plan was diverted from its original intention. One of the basic weaknesses of the parliamentary system of the Third Republic was that no government had control of its own legislation. Its proposals were seldom voted on in the form in which they were presented; they automatically went into the machine of the Commissions of the Chambers, from which they might emerge in an almost unrecognizable shape. Thus Waldeck-Rousseau's proposals, when they became law on 1 July 1901, had been vastly changed. By the new law each congregation had to apply for legal authorization or be dissolved, and no member of an unauthorized congregation was to be allowed to teach. However, the law was applied with moderation and did not seem likely to provoke serious opposition.

The country registered its approval, after a close electoral struggle, in May 1902. The government won some 370 seats against 220 held by the opposition, though once again the division was a much more even one than these figures might suggest, for in actual votes there was only some 200,000 difference between the two blocs. But they were now divided by the whole gulf of the Dreyfus affair. The bitterness of the feelings that had been aroused by the series of attempts to overthrow the Republic, and the moral revulsion against appeals to violence and anti-semitism, were now added to the traditional anti-clericalism; and a strong element of class hostility reinforced the attack on a Church which was identified with the ruling class. The aristocracy was pretty solidly Catholic, the wealthier middle classes and higher officials had largely abandoned their former scepticism or indifference to religion and now supported the Church. On the other hand the lower middle classes and lesser officials retained all their fervid anti-clericalism, and the breach between many of the workers and Roman Catholicism was becoming total. The attitude of the peasantry varied greatly. In the South there was widespread anti-clericalism; elsewhere – for instance in Brittany, the Vendée, Normandy, and Lorraine – the Church was still deeply rooted.

The particular form which anti-clericalism took among the middle and lower middle classes was Freemasonry, which was also closely linked with radicalism in politics. In 1896 there were 364 lodges and about 24,000 freemasons. By 1926 the numbers had risen to 583 and 52,000, though possibly at the price of some dilution of quality. Indeed, by this time the masonic movement could be described, not altogether unfairly, as very largely an employment agency for lower civil servants. Being a secret society, its actual activities and membership can only be guessed at, but it undoubtedly exercised considerable political influence.

The extremer anti-clericals regarded the elections of 1902 as their particular victory. Waldeck-Rousseau was left behind by the violence of the passions that had been aroused in the course of the electoral struggle. Unwilling to give the new majority what it wanted, he resigned in June 1902 and in 1903 strongly attacked the policy of his successor, though without any effect. He died a year later. His place was taken by a second-rate, elderly senator named Combes, indicated for such high office only by the fact that as an ardent anti-clerical himself he might be expected to hold an anti-clerical majority together. No one has a good word to say for this product of a seminary education, who would have made a typical narrow-minded and vindictive bishop in a backward diocese, for Combes was originally intended for the priesthood. He added to the *odium theologicum* the petty malignancies of small-town politics and carried both into national life. The corrupting influence of clericalism and anti-clericalism on French public life can be seen fully displayed, the first in the Dreyfus affair and the second in the ministry of Combes.

With Combes in office everything was subordinated to the anti-clerical campaign. To reassure the interests of property, the Ministry of Finances was given to Rouvier, who – as had been shown in the Panama affair – had close, if in the past a little shady, connexions with the financial world. To keep his parliamentary majority in line Combes set up a Délégation des Gauches as a sort of occult government in the Chamber. It arranged parliamentary strategy, disciplined individuals who were tempted to act on their own, and checked any tendency on the part of moderate elements in the left to compromise with the right. The Socialists were divided in their attitude to the new government. For Guesde and the more orthodox Marxists the radical onslaught on the Church was a distraction from the class struggle; on the other hand, Jaurès played a leading part in the work of the Délégation des Gauches. Along with the majority of the parliamentary Socialists he believed that the weakening of clerical influence was a necessary preliminary to the introduction of socialism. Like the philosopher of the liberal republic, Renouvier, he saw the French Church as a fortress for the defence of the privileges of the wealthy bourgeoisie.

In the country Combes brought the whole administrative machinery into play in support of his anti-clerical campaign. A circular of June 1902 instructed the prefects to reserve 'the favours which the Republic disposes of' for supporters of the government. In communes where the *maire* belonged to the opposition an 'administrative delegate' was appointed instead, to advise the government on the distribution of these favours. The law against congregations was applied ruthlessly. Those that asked for legal recognition under the new law found, with few exceptions, their requests rejected: eighty-one congregations of women were dissolved and fifty-four of men, the latter containing some 20,000 members in 1,500 houses. By October 1903 more than 10,000 schools conducted by unauthorized orders had been closed, though some 6,000 were to be reopened later, still under religious control. A law of July 1904 prohibited members of religious orders from teaching. Priests were excluded from the state examination for the *agrégation*; responsibility for burials was attributed to the secular authorities and crucifixes were removed from law courts. The property of the banned orders was put up for sale and conscientious anti-clericals felt it their duty to support the government by purchasing it, often at prices well below its real value.

It is surprising that such measures, though they produced demonstrations of protest, did not lead to more violent resistance, especially in the large areas of France where Catholicism was dominant. These formed a kind of ring, beginning in the mountains of Savoy and Franche-Comté, and passing through Lorraine, Flanders, and Artois, Normandy, Brittany, and the Vendée, down through the Bordelais to the Basque country and Béarn in the extreme South-west; in the Massif Central also there were strong Catholic enclaves. Yet only in Brittany did disturbances worthy of the name occur.

Combes found an enemy of his own metal in Rome. There Leo XIII had died in 1903. The representative of the Emperor of Austria in the Sacred College vetoed the election of a francophile candidate who seemed to be leading the field, and the choice fell on Pius X, a simple priest with little knowledge of the world but a great sense of the authority of his office, who appointed as his Secretary of State the young and uncompromising Spanish Cardinal, Merry del Val. The conflict with Rome which the policy of the French government had prepared was precipitated by an official visit of President Loubet to the King of Italy. A papal protest against the visit leaked out and the French government recalled its ambassador to the Vatican. The action of the Papacy was widely resented in France, and the French cabinet's retaliation was endorsed by a vote of 427 to 95 in the Chamber. The conflict was exacerbated by differences between Rome and Paris over the appointment and dismissal of bishops. Finally, in November 1904, Combes, not very reluctantly, tabled a law for the separation of Church and State.

Though his majority was weakening, it still held together, and it was in fact not his anti-clerical legislation that brought down the government of the '*petit père*' Combes but the indiscretions of his Minister of War, General André. One of Gallifet's reforms had been the reorganization of the Army Council and the attribution to the Minister of War of all promotions and appointments in the Army. This was obviously a desirable measure, on condition that it was put into effect with discretion, which was the quality André lacked. He had been chosen as the only general with strong republican sympathies, and had suffered throughout his career for his views. It was therefore with enthusiasm that he set about breaking down the Catholic and monarchist monopoly of the higher command. Its fantastic behaviour in the course of the Dreyfus affair did indeed suggest that drastic changes were needed, and Gallifet had taken the first steps towards them. André turned the tables with a vengeance. Promotion now went only to those who could demonstrate their sound republican and anti-clerical sentiments. This was not altogether unreasonable in a republic, though it was not guaranteed to improve the morale or quality of the army command. To obtain the necessary information, André organized, with the aid of informers, especially Freemasons and often from the lower commissioned or non-commissioned ranks, a great collection of *fiches* on the religious affiliations of the members of the officer corps. In October 1904 his system was revealed by an employee of the Masonic Grand Orient, and public indignation was such that the Minister had to resign. Combes followed him in January 1905.

The problem of separatism had still to be tackled. In a new ministry it was taken over by a young lawyer and journalist from Nantes, Aristide Briand, who had begun his political career as a socialist but was too little a doctrinaire and too much a politician to stay in any of the Socialist groups. Supple, conciliating, and infinitely persuasive, Briand was to move in and out of the highest posts of government for the space of nearly thirty years with equal nonchalance. His gift for political manoeuvre secured the passage, in December 1905, of a law of Separation which, he hoped, would offend the religious susceptibilities of the Catholics as little as possible. In principle it went back behind the Napoleonic Concordat to the year III, recognizing absolute liberty of religion but denying that any Church had special claims to the patronage of the state. Religious bodies were to be allowed to keep their property, including religious edifices, on condition of forming recognized associations to manage it. Thus the state would not have to contaminate itself by having any dealings with the Catholic Church as such, which would satisfy the anti-clericals, while the Churches would continue to function legally and preserve their corporate identity under a different name.

The French bishops, mostly appointed during the comparatively liberal régime of Leo XIII, were prepared to make the best of the situation by accepting Briand's conciliatory proposals and working the proposed religious associations, but for Rome separation meant the creation of a godless state and Pius X was in no mood for compromise. Besides, whatever the original intention of the Napoleonic Concordat, in practice it had proved too favourable to the interests of the Church for the Vatican to be willing to abandon it without a struggle. The papal encyclical *Vehementer* therefore barred the road to compromise and prevented the French Church from forming the religious associations provided for by the new law.

In practice, of course, there had to be some kind of compromise. An unofficial *modus vivendi*, worked out by the Conseil d'État, allowed the use of church premises for religious ceremonies and permitted religious processions. The opposition of Rome merely underlined the fact that the anti-clericals had won a great victory. 'We have torn human consciences from the clutches of credulity,' proclaimed Viviani; 'we have demonstrated that behind the clouds there are nothing but chimeras. With a magnificent gesture we have put out the lights of heaven and they will never be lighted again.'

One unanticipated result of the law of Separation was greatly to increase papal control over the Church in France. The Papacy could now appoint bishops without, as it normally had done in the past, taking into account the preferences of the French government. Moreover the poverty which fell upon the lower clergy, which made their recruitment more difficult, at the same time helped to ensure that only those with a real religious vocation entered the priesthood. The *curés* and *vicaires*, who in the nineteenth century had represented a privileged class in the villages, perhaps gained more respect now that economically they were no better off than their parishioners; whereas the *instituteur*, the teacher, who had been one of themselves to the village people when he was a downtrodden usher eking out a meagre living by acting as bell-ringer, clerk, and general drudge to the *curé*, now that he was a better-paid official of the state seemed to represent a superior and alien element. Paradoxically, the Concordat, framed, at least in the mind of the Vatican, to protect the interests of the Roman Church in France, had in the long run done it much harm; the separation, which was so bitterly resisted, was to prepare the way for the recovery of some of its lost spiritual authority.

On the whole separation, while it temporarily exacerbated relations, in the end tended to reduce the tension between Church and State. The majority of the Catholics were not yet reconciled to the Republic, but with the decline of clerical interference in politics the violence of anti-clerical sentiment inevitably declined. The discredit resulting from the methods and narrowness of Combes was to some extent wiped out by the moderation of Briand. On the other hand, the policy of the Vatican remained rigid and uncompromising. Its victims were inside as well as outside the Church. Those who were suspected of having been infected by the abbé Loisy with the taint of modernism came under severe disciplinary measures.

Another French movement which incurred papal censure was Le Sillon. This was the creation of Marc Sangnier, who in 1898 gave up an army career to devote himself to proselytizing the laity. He was a spell-binder, capable of winning total devotion, though even at its height Le Sillon never had more than some 25,000 adherents and never formulated any clearly defined programme of action. This did not matter, for Marc Sangnier envisaged its task as the formation of an élite, and its essential coherence in loyalty to his own person. He drew his followers largely from students and the lower middle classes. To protect his meetings he organized a 'young guard', which was treated as a sort of modern order of knighthood with ritual observances and a uniform. Opposition to the authority of the leader was not tolerated. All this might sound as though Le Sillon was a sort of religious Fascism; though its bias was towards the left rather than the right. Politically the aim of Le Sillon was to reconcile the Church with the Republic. Socially it upheld the idea of cooperation. Because he acted in independence of the hierarchy, Sangnier was viewed with suspicion by the Church. His movement was particularly opposed by the Action Française, which directed its propaganda at a similar clientele and also hoped to spread its view by the indoctrination of an élite. To the influence of the Action Française has been attributed the papal condemnation, in 1910, of Le Sillon as a movement 'placing authority in the hands of the people and tending towards the levelling of classes', which was perhaps to give it too much credit.

Thrust back upon themselves by their defeat in the struggle with the state, the leaders of the Church identified the spirit of conciliation with weakness or covert disloyalty. The attempt to come to terms with the Republic, which had begun when Cardinal Lavigerie made his speech at Algiers in 1890, had failed, and on the whole it may be said that the Republic had emerged strengthened from the prolonged crisis. The hold of the republicans on the state, even though still based on a narrow electoral margin, was unshaken. It was reaffirmed by the elections of May 1906. And now it seemed possible that the social and political reforms, held up while the dog-fight between the Church and State had been going on, might at last have a chance of enactment. In October 1906 Clemenceau, *bête noire* of the right, for the first time formed a government, towards what might have seemed the end of such a long and chequered career. After his disastrous involvement in the Panama affair of 1893 even the staunch Jacobins of the Var had rejected him and he had turned back to journalism. His daily article in *La Justice* kept him still a force in the country. Back in parliament, he resumed the role of hunter-out of scandals – he liked to call

himself '*le premier flic de France*' – and destroyer of governments, that suited a republican with no faith in the people.
At last in office, he chose a cabinet inclining to the left and
announced an impressive programme of reforms, few of
which were to be carried into effect even though his government was to last for the astonishingly long period of three
years.

One of the first steps of the new parliament was to increase
the pay of its members from nine to fifteen thousand francs a
month – a gift not only to themselves but to the agitators of
the right, who now had a new anti-parliamentarian cry in
denunciation of the *quinze mille*. The Clemenceau ministry
also passed a law nationalizing the Chemin de fer de l'Ouest,
which had for long been surviving only with the aid of a
subsidy from the state. After this its reforming ardour lapsed.
The trouble was that the social reforms that were urgently
needed could not be carried through without injury to the
interests of the great mass of property-owners which constituted its electoral clientele. A pensions law was passed by
the Chamber of Deputies, but as usual opposition in the
Senate could be relied on to safeguard the Chamber from the
effects of its own generosity and the law was held up until
1914.

The issue which aroused the strongest feeling was the
proposal for an income tax. First discussed by the Chamber
in 1888, this took a whole generation to be passed into law
and come into effect. The government of Léon Bourgeois
had brought it forward again in 1896, only to be defeated by
the Senate. Caillaux introduced an income-tax bill in 1907,
and after two years succeeded in getting it through the
Chamber. Naturally, the Senate vetoed the bill. Only on the
eve of war, in 1914, did the Senate relax its opposition as
part of a political deal over military service, and a very
modest income-tax law came into effect, finally, in 1917.

The party which should have represented the cause of
social reform, the Socialist, was weakened, as throughout
its history, by internal divisions. It achieved little in the pre-

war years, despite the leadership of the man who must count
as one of the greatest of French politicians of the time. Jean
Jaurès was an orator who could sway the masses, an inspiring personality who won the loyalty of individuals, a distinguished historian whose work on the French Revolution
is still a major historical contribution, a powerful journalist,
editor of the socialist daily paper *L'Humanité*, a Socialist who
had learnt Marxism at the École Normale, and at the same
time a liberal idealist. His genius bestrode the French
political stage but could not overcome the opposition of the
great body of small property-owners, whose votes kept the
Radicals in power and the Socialists out. Even among the
Socialists the power of Jaurès was limited by the rivalry of
the sterner Marxist, Guesde, the pope of French socialism
and certainly papal in his anathemas and excommunica-
tions.

On the surface the two main tendencies into which the
French Socialists were split had been brought together by the
mediation of the Second International in 1905. The Socialists
were united as the Section Française de l'International
Ouvrière – S.F.I.O. The development of a specifically
Socialist, as distinct from a republican, French revolu-
tionary mystique, was symbolized by the abandonment of
La Carmagnole and the substitution for it of *L'Internationale* as
the party song. Born at Lille in 1888, sung at the Congress of
Troyes in 1895, it had become the official anthem by 1899.

In the policy of the new party the more doctrinaire views
of Guesde prevailed over the belief of Jaurès in the possibility of collaboration with bourgeois parties and progress
by constitutional methods. Both sides could appeal to the
experience of Millerand's entry into the Waldeck-Rousseau
cabinet. Millerand was not merely a traitor, he had introduced an element of reformism into a non-Socialist government. He created a labour section inside his Ministry of
Commerce to deal with the problem of social insurance,
established arbitration tribunals and inspectors of labour,
brought representatives of the workers into the Conseil

supérieur de travail, prescribed minimum wages and maximum hours of labour for all work undertaken by public authorities, and established an eight-hour day for postal workers. The maximum working-day of eleven hours instituted in 1900 was reduced to ten hours in 1904. These were not negligible achievements but they did not win Millerand any favour from his former socialist colleagues, who believed that half a loaf was much worse than no bread.

The Socialist movement was further split by the cleavage between its political and industrial sides. The trade union organization, the Confédération Générale du Travail, under the influence of former Blanquists and anarchists, and more recently of Georges Sorel's *Réflexions sur la violence* (1908), was profoundly suspicious of the political movement. It advocated revolutionary syndicalism and believed in the myth of the General Strike, which had been accepted as the basis of trade-union action at a congress in 1892 by a large majority, under the influence of an eloquent speech by a young socialist named Briand. In 1906 a congress at Amiens laid down the programme known as the Amiens Charter and reaffirmed the General Strike as the means of achieving it.

At this time the membership of the C.G.T. was rising, from some 715,000 in 1904 to nearly a million in 1909, and militancy was increasing. Strikes were often accompanied by violence, which was not confined to industrial workers. In 1907 the vineyard owners of the South reacted to over-production and a fall in the price of wine by a series of outbursts, in one of which the *préfecture* at Perpignan was looted and burnt. The government retaliated against strikers by sending in troops and arresting and imprisoning their leaders. Clemenceau, though relying on a majority of the left, repressed such movements ruthlessly, but it remained for his successor, Briand, to invent and put into use the decisive weapon. In 1910 a strike on the Chemin de fer du Nord, for an increase in wages and a weekly day off work, developed into a general railway strike. Briand smashed it by the simple process of mobilizing the strikers and sending them back to work as soldiers.

While industrial action by the trade unions was becoming more vigorous, politically the years from 1906 to 1914 were a period of evolution towards the right. The Radicals, losing votes on the left to the Socialists, who in the election of 1910 garnered over a million votes and by 1914 had 100 deputies in the Chamber, turned for support to the right in a sort of anticipation of the later Bloc National tactic. The history of the Third Republic bore out the saying that France was politically to the left and socially to the right. Governments of the left could only achieve and keep power on condition of not using it to introduce social reforms.

Whatever the political trend, the social structure of France was a guarantee of conservatism. Nearly half the labour of France was still engaged in agriculture. Of some forty million population, seventeen to eighteen million, or nearly half, lived in communes of under 2,000. Nearly forty per cent of the 5,700,000 farms in France were less than $2\frac{1}{2}$ acres in size; and only 33,000 over 250 acres. The electoral system still overweighted the rural vote. The small peasants, who were politically dominant in the Third Republic, were not disposed to favour social reforms in the interest of the workers of the towns. Apart from occasional depressions, such as that which produced the outbreak of 1907 in the South, they had reason for satisfaction with the Third Republic, under which they were at last beginning to escape from the depressed conditions of life that had been their lot from time immemorial. In their farmhouses floorboards were replacing beaten earth and tiles the more picturesque thatch; oil lamps and coal stoves were coming in; the blue blouse and sabot were disappearing. The Méline tariff kept the price of agricultural produce high; and because of the railways its transport to the towns was now easier. The opening years of the twentieth century were a period of agricultural prosperity. Although agricultural methods were still very backward, France was second only to the United States and

Russia in the production of grain, and produced more wine than any country except Italy.

Industry was also mainly on a small scale. Out of 1,100,000 workshops, 1,000,000 had fewer than 5 employees, and only 600 employed over 500. At the same time, the process of industrialization begun under the Second Empire was continuing under the Third Republic, particularly between 1890 and 1914. The use of steam power in industry (excluding transport) multiplied ten times between 1870 and 1914. Between 1880 and 1914 the production of coal doubled, from twenty to forty million tons, that of cast iron went up nearly four times, and that of steel was multiplied by twelve.

What French production still lacked in quantity it made up in quality. France was what Louis XIV and Colbert had made it, the world's chief producer of luxury goods – fine fabrics, *haute couture*, perfumes, and cosmetics, *objets d'art* in general. The race of craftsmen still survived and there is no irrelevance in adding that Paris under the Third Republic was more than ever the artistic capital of the world. The picture of French social conservatism and economic backwardness in this period must therefore not be exaggerated. There were, of course, reasons why the economic development of France was lagging behind that of other Western countries. The structure of a society dominated at the top by the official and professional classes and *rentiers*, and at a lower level by peasants and small employers, was not favourable to economic progress. The family was dominant not only in social life but also in business, and the preservation of the family business took precedence over expansion or even efficiency. This helped to preserve a host of small family firms from the pressures of competition, while the larger ones were protected by cartellization. Firmly prevented from interference in the interests of the workers by the electoral influence of the mass of small employers and proprietors, the state was biased by the same influences in their own favour, particularly through the protective system of tariffs. While private enterprise would not take the risk of starting new undertakings, it could prevent the state from supplementing its deficiency; as was shown in 1879, when Freycinet, a real technocrat, put forward plans for the development of roads, canals, and feeder railways, only to be defeated by the opposition of the great banks.

One must not forget, of course, that France was not well endowed in the natural resources of the industrial revolution. French production of coal in 1913 was one-seventh of British or German production. In iron and steel she produced less than a third as much as Germany. The slow growth of population was also a handicap. France, so long predominant in Europe, had been overtaken. In 1871 the population of France, at 36 millions, had been above that of Great Britain and only slightly lower than that of all Germany. By 1914 France had grown only to 39½ millions, Great Britain had 45 millions, and the German Empire 67 millions. Various explanations have been given for the stagnation of the French population, such as the influence of the rule of the division of inheritance among all children, generalized by the Napoleonic Code, or the persistence of a high rate of infant mortality, itself not unconnected with the absence of social reforms.

While French economy suffered from lack of capital, the savings of the French flowed out to fertilize the rest of the world, nearly one-quarter of the foreign investments being – for reasons not unconnected with high politics – placed in Russia. By 1914 French investments abroad, at about fifty milliards of francs, represented one-sixth of the national wealth, but only four milliards of this was invested in France's own colonies. The large commissions which went to the credit houses which handled the loans were, of course, not a negligible factor in determining their direction and ensuring their success.

When all this has been said, it must be added that in the first decade of the twentieth century France was clearly beginning to move out of the phase of social rigidity which had marked its history in the nineteenth century. The political conflicts on which attention had been concentrated were beginning to give place to social problems in the public mind, and the balance was beginning to be weighted on the side of reform.

6. AN AGE OF GREATNESS

IF survival was a test of political success, the Third Republic had passed it. By 1914 it had long outlasted all previous régimes since 1789. Its economic progress had been slow, but only in comparison with that of the more advanced industrial countries. The status and economic conditions of the peasantry, who constituted the largest section of the French nation, had risen to the point at which it would not have been very exaggerated to describe France as a peasants' republic. What, more than anything else, made this one of the great ages of French history was its achievement in arts, letters, and sciences. Its periodization in this respect reflects unusually closely the political calendar. As in the political history of the Third Republic, 1914 is something like an end, though 1871 is in no sense a beginning. The fall of the Second Empire was not a date in artistic, literary, or scientific history. French art and literature had already revolted against the philistinism of the Second Empire before 1870. It is significant of an age of individualism that the public arts of architecture and town-planning, which had reached a high degree of excellence under the *ancien régime*, continued to decline. The only advantage that the official architecture of the Third Republic has over that of the Second Empire is that there is possibly less of it, though ecclesiastical building, unfortunately, flourished. Sculpture did not develop beyond the romantic tradition, but it reached a level of mastery that won immediate appreciation with the popular and powerful work of Rodin (1840–1917). A less dramatic but persisting appeal is to be seen in the lovely nudes of Maillol (1861–

1944). Not all was of this quality. The sculpture of the Third Republic, like its architecture, was largely dependent on the commissions of nineteenth-century officials and bourgeois, who, unlike their predecessors of the previous century, were notably lacking in taste.

Painting would equally have suffered from the philistinism of society if it had not been a comparatively cheap art, which the artist could pursue for his own pleasure and that of a few friends. France, of course, had an Academy art, like Great Britain, of painters whose works, having gratified a generation of town councillors, civil servants, and politicians, now clutter up provincial museums, and whose names are forgotten. The mid century had not been a period of great distinction in painting. A pastoral spirit, like that of the Berrichon romances of George Sand, illumined the poetic landscapes of Corot (1796–1874) and the Barbizon school. The growth of a social conscience had appeared in the paintings and cartoons of Daumier (1808–79), in the harsh realism of the Socialist and Communard Gustave Courbet (1819–77), and the unsentimentalized and affecting peasants of Millet (1814–75). A combination of realism with a purer interest in pictorial values appears in such paintings as the *Déjeuner sur l'herbe* (1863) of Manet, whose naked girl at the picnic seemed so much more shocking than all the romantic odalisques who had preceded her, or in his *Bar aux Folies Bergères* (1882).

Manet forms the link with the great school of the Third Republic, the Impressionists, who inaugurated an artistic renaissance which casts a glow over the society that in their own day rejected them. Paris of the Third Republic, damned by the Hôtel de Ville and Sacré Coeur, is saved by the painters it despised or ignored. A roll of honour of artists decorates its days – Monet, Pissarro, Sisley, Degas, Gauguin, Seurat, Toulouse-Lautrec, the Douanier Rousseau, and the great names of Cézanne, Renoir, Matisse; nor should it be forgotten that Picasso and Braque, both born in 1881, belong to the Third Republic. To see in this galaxy of artists an element of greatness is obviously justifiable. To go beyond this is perhaps not justifiable, but it is tempting to see also the reflection of an intensely vital society, full of colour and character, in which the individual vision mattered most, a fundamentally stable society in which experiments were possible because they were firmly rooted in tradition, and which through them rose to the achievement of a great classical art.

The Third Republic came to its greater musicians more slowly. Offenbach had delighted Second Empire society, but after him the world of music was bestridden by Wagner. *Carmen* was first performed in 1875 and *Manon* in 1884, but Bizet, César Franck, Massenet, Saint-Saëns could hardly challenge Wagner's genius. A new note was heard in 1902 with the production of *Pelléas et Mélisande* by Debussy. Soon after, Ravel joined him, and with composers such as Gabriel Fauré, Paul Dukas, Erik Satie, the Third Republic had a school of music of its own, not unworthy to be mentioned along with its great painters.

In letters the great names of the first half of the century had been succeeded by somewhat of a hiatus during the Second Empire. Romanticism, when the gloss had been worn off, was felt to be meretricious and false. A period of 'realism' in literature followed; its greatest figure, Flaubert, produced an exposure of romantic love in *Madame Bovary* (1857) which was also a detailed anatomy of life in a provincial town; and a picture of Paris from the Orleanist monarchy to the Second Empire in *L'Éducation sentimentale* (1869). None of the other realists of this time has left work that counts besides Flaubert's masterpieces. Notable writers appeared later in the century under the label of Naturalism, which was merely Realism pushed to a more brutal extreme and given a scientific theory by Taine. Vice and virtue, he proclaimed, are but products like vitriol or sugar; the three factors of race, environment, and conjuncture (which he called moment) determine absolutely the character of men and nations. The novelist therefore is really a kind of social scientist registering and recording the facts of social life which added together explain the men and women of his day. The Goncourt brothers applied this theory to writing the social and artistic history of the eighteenth century; they recorded the literary history of their own time; and they produced under the Second Empire a series of novels describing on the basis of a careful documentation the more sordid aspects of French life. They were followed on a monumental scale by Zola, whose *Les Rougon-Macquart* is the natural and social history of a family under the Second Empire. It appeared in twenty novels between 1871 and 1893 and its characters – all drawn from the same family circle and revealing in combination after combination the same hereditary traits – range from scheming Senators or financiers and the dissolute high society of the Empire to the degraded and wretched victims of social injustice and their own vices and follies at the bottom of the social scale. Sheer power carries Zola's sordid concerns and pseudo-scientific theories into the rank of literary art. The other naturalists are lighter in weight. Guy de Maupassant, a disciple of Flaubert and Zola, still remains the greatest master of the *conte*. Another important contributor to *Les Soirées de Médan* (1880), a naturalistic symposium in which Maupassant published *Boule-de-suif*, was J.-K. Huysmans, but he was to move on to the higher realms of decadence and religious mysticism.

Naturalism in literature may be regarded as in some sense the reflection of the positivist movement in philosophy. This was itself the secular reflection of the religious revival of the nineteenth century, it was *la foi des sans foi*, envisaged by its prophet, Comte, as a sort of religion of science based on the laws of social progress. Freemasonry also, in some aspects, was a kind of secular faith. This semi-religious element in French freemasonry explains why it met with such bitter opposition from rival faiths like Roman Catholicism and later Communism.

That the fundamental influence of positivist social thought was conservative was shown by the historical writings of

Taine. His hatred of democracy and fear of the people ante-
dates the shock of the Commune of Paris, to which it is
sometimes attributed, and is inherent in his positivist social
philosophy. It is arguable that Taine played a larger part
than any other writer in the development of an anti-
democratic trend of thought among the intellectuals of the
Third Republic. A whole generation of French students
learned from him to condemn the Revolution which had
founded French republicanism, and to see Jacobinism as the
source of all social evil. The '*petits faits bien choisis*' of his
history, presented in a coruscating style, were convincing,
and if Taine's gems are now seen to be paste, they still have
the power to dazzle. Even the greatest of the republican
historians who came after Taine, Georges Lefebvre, could
not but pay a somewhat reluctant tribute to his power of
social analysis, which should remind us that in spite of all
other differences they both shared the tradition of positivism. Another great influence among the positivists was Émile
Littré (1801–81), who began life as a student of medicine,
became a disciple of Comte, and won his fame as the com-
piler of the masterly *Dictionnaire de la langue française* (1863–
73). He combined a rigidly materialist determinism with
an idealistic conception of human progress.

From the positivists also grew a school of sociology, in
which the greatest name was that of Émile Durkheim.
Theories of group or mass psychology were developed, which
exposed the irrational content of democratic action and
taught the enemies of democracy how to exploit its weaknesses against it.

Positivism exercised a surprising influence over the academic world during the Third Republic, but both its
austerities and its dogmatism stood in the way of a wider
influence. A more inspiring form of scientific idealism was
derived from the writings of Ernest Renan (1823–92). A
Breton, educated in a seminary, he became a distinguished
Hebrew scholar. When he published the first volume of his
Vie de Jésus in 1863, its literary charm could not make up for

its unduly rational and historical attitude to the founder of Christianity and Renan was expelled from his chair as Professor of Hebrew at the Collège de France. In many later works he developed the views on religion as a historical phenomenon which he had sketched out in *L'Avenir de la science*, written as early as 1848 though only published in 1890. Religious dogmatism was in much more danger from such moderate, historical criticism than from its more violent enemies. Even a religious historian and archaeologist like Duchesne (1843–1922), Professor of Ecclesiastical History at the Catholic Institute in Paris and achieving the rank of Monseigneur, contributed to the undermining of nineteenth-century orthodoxy by applying the methods of historical criticism to many a cherished legend of the Church.

Reference has already been made to the modernist controversy in the Roman Catholic Church, stirred up by the writings of the abbé Loisy (1857–1940). A professor at the Catholic Institute, he also applied historical criticism to the Scriptures, showing how religious ideas had changed and developed in the course of their long history. In this Loisy, however, went much further than Duchesne, and further than the Church could follow him. He was removed from the Institute and sent to be chaplain at a girls' boarding school in a fashionable suburb of Paris, where it was presumably hoped that his dangerous historical inquiries would do no harm. Unfortunately he continued to write and to acquire followers by his writings. He was excommunicated but this did not prevent him from being appointed Professor of the History of Religion at the Collège de France.

Not only a heretic like Loisy, but many other French ecclesiastics and laity, whose orthodoxy was hardly suspect, were to suffer in the early years of the twentieth century from a witch-hunt run from Rome, under the patronage of Pius X, by those who called themselves 'integral Catholics'. The lead in this anti-modernist campaign was taken by the journal *Correspondance de Rome* along with a secret international federation of Catholic groups associated with a neo-Thomist revival. The bitterness of the attacks, and the strength of the modernist defence, were at least evidence of the vitality of religious interests.

On the other side, philosophy was moving back towards a neo-Kantian idealism with Charles Renouvier (1815–1903), whose optimistic belief was in progress towards rationality, marking the moral advance of the human race – for reason was still, at the end of the nineteenth century, in the ascendant and along with it science and history. The need to cultivate science seemed to be one of the lessons taught by defeat in the Franco-Prussian War. The Third Republic continued the great tradition of French science with names such as those of Henri Poincaré, the mathematician, the Curies, famous for their work on radium, the chemist Berthelot, and Pasteur, genius of the famous Institute founded in 1888 and named after him. On a lower level, yet not without significance for the future, was the technological development shown when, in 1894, the Lumière brothers made the first short films in France and in 1896 Méliès built the first film studio.

The same empirical spirit produced a school of critical historians, centred on the Sorbonne and the École des Chartes, with Fustel de Coulanges, Lavisse, Seignobos, Halphen, Lot, among many others. Even the Académie Française included an Albert Sorel among its members – though the historians in its ranks were mostly on a much lower level. There was a deep gulf between the historical scholarship of the University and the smart-society historical journalism of the Academy. Of course, the scientific and historical achievements of French genius were confined to a small *élite*. It is remarkable that they were possible at all, for tradition was still so strong in French education that the predominantly literary culture of the schools was as yet hardly affected by the newer disciplines.

Even in literature, however, new trends were appearing towards the end of the century. In poetry, as in the other arts, there had been a sort of pause after the ebb of the flood-tide of romanticism. It was occupied by the Parnassians, whose aim was to write a more classical verse, free from the passionate individual and social concerns of romanticism. They had learnt the doctrine of 'art for art's sake' from Théophile Gautier. Among them were Leconte de Lisle, Sully-Prudhomme, and José-Maria de Heredia, whose sonnets, *Les Trophées*, published in 1893, are still the most read poems of the school.

A profounder and more permanent influence than that of Gautier flowed from Baudelaire, whose *Les Fleurs du mal* had appeared, only to be burnt as indecent, as early as 1857, and who died in 1867. His poems, and even more his literary criticisms, were only appreciated at their real value by a subsequent generation. Baudelaire is the real founder of Symbolism, which began to put forth its fruits when Verlaine met the boy Arthur Rimbaud and the latter wrote *Le Bateau ivre* in 1871. Verlaine's own *Romances sans paroles* followed in 1874 and Mallarmé's *L'Après-midi d'un faune* in 1876. The influence of Symbolism was to be continued into the heart of the twentieth century in the rare poems of Paul Valéry.

The last decade of the nineteenth century saw the passing of a great generation in literature. Rimbaud, Verlaine, Mallarmé ceased to write then. Renan died in 1892, Taine in 1893, Edmond de Goncourt, author with his brother (who died much earlier) of the *Journal* which is the literary history of their time, in 1896. Maupassant died in 1893 and his master Zola in 1902; among the Parnassians Leconte de Lisle in 1894.

The new age in literature opened on a lower level, with the decadence and mysticism of *fin de siècle*. The critic and novelist Rémy de Gourmont continued the Symbolist movement, but his novels, combining mysticism with physiological naturalism, illustrate its weaknesses rather than its strength. The half-Dutch Joris-Karl Huysmans moved from a naturalism in which he tried to outdo Zola to a literary cult of Satanism, with the usual appurtenances of black magic, orgies, sacrilege, and religiosity. Like the hero of his own novel, *Là-bas* (1891), he then moved over to religion, becoming for a time an oblate in a Benedictine abbey. By way of decadence and mysticism the road back to religion in literature was opening up. Barbey d'Aurevilly (1808–89), flamboyant critic and novelist, anticipates the militant royalist and Catholic writers of the next generation such as Léon Bloy (1846–1917), whose apocalyptic writings preached death and destruction on existing society.

With religious and secular inspiration, from both left and right a politically committed literature was appearing. The growing pressure of politics can be traced in the life and writings of Anatole France (1844–1924), for whom, as for many, the Dreyfus affair was the catalyst which brought literature and political life together in a more active, and in some cases even an explosive, reaction. Anatole France's erudition, his scepticism, irony, moderation, the patina of the past with which he misted over nearly everything he wrote, the sense of being too consciously a literary man, have robbed him of much of the adulation that he received in his lifetime. His fine novel of the French Revolution, *Les Dieux ont soif* (1912), could be disliked equally by those who favoured the revolution and the counter-revolution. *L'Île des pingouins* (1908), a satiric history of the Third Republic, and the four volumes of *L'Histoire contemporaine* (1896–1901), were too understanding to political enemies, too lukewarm to friends, and altogether too humane, to appeal to the generation that followed him. It is a curious comment on changing ideas that France, who to his predecessors seemed to have sacrificed literature to his commitment to social and political causes, was seen by the next generation as a mere man of letters, too lacking in serious interests to be taken seriously.

Another writer, primarily a music critic, also brought into political consciousness by the Dreyfus case, was Romain Rolland (1868–1944), in whom the commitment was above all to the problem of international relations and peace. His ten-volume *roman fleuve*, *Jean-Christophe*, published between 1906 and 1912, reflects the shift in the main concentration of French interests from domestic to foreign problems. Its hero, a German musician who makes his home in France, is the embodiment of Rolland's belief in the need for Franco-German friendship. This was also to be expressed in 1915, during the First World War, by his pamphlet *Au-dessus de la mêlée*, an appeal for international understanding, which was not to be listened to until another generation had been sacrificed in another world war.

In Anatole France and Romain Rolland reason was still in the ascendant. The influence of the second-rate mysticism of the nineties had so far done little to weaken it. But times were changing. Perhaps the strongest single influence over French thought in the opening years of the twentieth century was the philosophy of Henri-Louis Bergson (1859–1941). *L'Évolution créatrice*, published in 1907, which elevated Bergson to the rank of one of the society stars of the Collège de France, postulated the existence of an *élan vital* inspiring all life. Reality, he proclaimed, is discovered not by the intelligence but by intuition. The problems that he propounded were perhaps more important than his solutions, and both Bergson and his brilliant literary style have long been out of favour. But philosophy has its fashions and these are as much a reflection of the spirit of an age as is its fiction. The philosophy of *élan vital* belongs to a period when rationalism was passing under a cloud.

The anti-intellectualism, which had risen to the surface in the last years of the old century and which marks the decline of a great age in French literature, was becoming dominant in the years before the First World War. A straw, which showed the way the wind was blowing, was thrown up in 1909 by the Italian poet Marinetti. His Manifesto of Futurism, an appeal to and glorification of war, chaos, and destruction, was more prophetic of the future than its adherents guessed or could have hoped. It anticipated both the Dadaism of the war years by its apotheosis of meaninglessness, and the surrealism of post-war years by its suggestions of sinister hidden meanings.

The inculcation of violence as a legitimate method in domestic politics was a more immediately significant development, and one in which literature and politics came closest together. One of the peculiarities of the Third Republic was that revolution, hitherto a force of the left, was now transferred to the right. It was essentially an inheritance from Bonapartism, and the transition from Bonapartism to the new right came in the Boulangist movement. Among the supporters of Boulanger was a young writer from Lorraine, Maurice Barrès. The German annexation of what he felt to be part of the French nation and French soil was the first conditioning factor in his life. A second was the dislike of a provincial for the centralizing influence of Paris. In *Les Déracinés* (1897) Barrès portrays the disillusionment of a group of young Lorrainers robbed of their traditions by the indoctrination of a Kantian schoolmaster, and of their roots in their native soil by transplantation to Paris. Barrès was the chief literary exponent of nationalism in France, but his literary interests, though dominated by a national ideology, were never completely subjected by it. The same cannot be said of his friend Charles Maurras, with whom we leave the category of literature and enter that of political journalism.

Literature and politics met and influenced one another in the cafés of the Left Bank, but the spirit of the greater literature, as of the painting and music of the Third Republic, transcended its passing political interests. By its writers and painters and musicians, even if the society of their time failed to recognize their full stature, the Third Republic becomes one of the great ages of French history. They represent the flowering of a free and vital society. Time has only magnified their achievement. In the poetry of the Symbolists, the painting of Impressionism, and the music of Debussy, Fauré, or Ravel, can be detected a common artistic vision, which transcends physical reality but never abandons the world of the senses, which intensifies the significance of sensations by seizing them in the immediacy of the single moment with a piercing clarity. What they lacked, and it was perhaps an artistic loss, was self-confidence. There is in them all a last, fading glow of romantic melancholy, a feeling of impermanence, of the transient as the all, as though something were coming to an end, which becomes the dominant note in the last and greatest of the writers of the age before the world wars.

Marcel Proust, born with the Third Republic in 1871, produced the first volume of *À la recherche du temps perdu* only in 1913. When he completed the work and his genius was recognized, shortly after the First World War, it was becoming clear that something had indeed come to an end. Yet the fundamental optimism, the belief in their world that is radiant in the Impressionists, persists in spite of everything in the Combray of Proust, and by it he belongs to a Republic in which, after so many uncertain and changing régimes, France seemed at last to have found the security of firm achievement and faith in the future.

II

THE DECLINE OF THE REPUBLIC

1. RUMOURS OF WAR

By 1910 it might have seemed that the major political problems of the Third Republic had all been solved or were well on their way to solution. Political divisions could still arouse intense feeling but there was no real danger of the Republic collapsing by its own weakness or being overthrown by the strength of its enemies. Social problems still remained to be tackled, but however powerful the forces of opposition, social reform was at least on the agenda.

There were signs in the general election of 1910, however, that France might be taking a new turn and one that was less encouraging. In that year over 200 new deputies were elected, and the new Chamber represented a marked swing to the right. On the other hand, the left-wing elections of 1914 were to show that this was not necessarily a permanent trend. More significant were new developments appearing in the realm of ideas. A mystical Catholicism and conservatism was manifest in the works of Paul Claudel, who, although he was born in 1868, only became recognized with his poetic drama *L'Annonce faite à Marie* in 1912; but his real influence belongs to the post-war years. A rather different figure is Charles Péguy, Catholic and Dreyfusard, Socialist and patriot, killed on the Marne in 1914, who left behind him a legend to which some of the finer elements of both left and right could look back. Even Péguy, however, represented a reaction against republican politics in the name of some undefined superior authority. His saying '*tout commence en mystique et tout finit en politique*' became classic, but in fact it was the other way round. The real trouble lay in the tendency to introduce religious mystique into politics.

This was the work above all of the movement known as the Action Française.

Its founder, Charles Maurras, has some claim to be considered the evil genius of the Third Republic. Born and bred in the little provincial town of Aix-en-Provence, son of a minor official who died when Maurras was six, thin, dark, solitary, from the age of fourteen deaf, he came to Paris when he was seventeen to make his way in the literary world. Though he became, and was to remain, a permanent feature of the Paris literary scene for the rest of his long life, he soon took up and never shed the perhaps more genuine pose of that other provincial, Barrès, against the cosmopolitan capital that was his adopted home, and was so different from what he believed to be the real France. It was the kind of romantic nostalgia for the scenes of boyhood and youth that Rousseau had once felt for *Les Charmettes* and Annecy, and that Proust was to express in his memories of Combray, given a less peaceful and a more feverish form in the politics of the anti-republican, right-wing Paris journalism, and the left-bank cafés.

Maurras's first aim was literary success. He endeavoured to chisel his early works like a classical statue, with a cold rejection of emotion; but in the course of the Dreyfus affair he adopted a passionate political commitment, the keystone of which was anti-semitism. The argument ran – Dreyfus was a Jew, therefore he was a traitor. Since he was a traitor, any method of bringing him to justice was rightful: hence Henry's forgery was justified, or rather, since its purpose was to establish the truth it could not be a forgery at all. From beginning to end anti-semitism was the essence of the teaching of Maurras. It provided the motive for the foundation in 1898, by a little group of young writers, of the Comité de l'Action Française, which struggled on in obscurity, but only began to make an impression on the public in 1908, when its journal, the *Action Française*, with the aid of unexpected financial support, became a daily paper. Its editor, Léon Daudet, was one of the most brilliant and un-

scrupulous political journalists of the day. A fanatic nationalist and lion of cosmopolitan society, a practising Catholic
and the author of pornographic novels, with the physical
appearance of a *bonhomme* and the qualities of a *faux bonhomme*, a dangerous man by his gifts and his lack of scruple,
Daudet was a master of invective who could give literary
shape and expression to a mass of disorganized hatred and
resentments. Another frequent contributor to the *Action
Française*, Jacques Bainville, made a successful career out of
writing popular histories with a royalist bias.

We have now moved away from literature and into the
field of politics. If the *Action Française* was to be a successful
organ of propaganda it had not only to be distributed to
members of the league of the Action Française but to be
sold to the general public on the streets. For this purpose a
volunteer corps of *Camelots du roi* was recruited. This turned
out to be a brilliant innovation: the Camelots were the first
of the organized, later shirted and booted, street-fighters and
agitators of the political leagues. Their title is a reminder
that the Action Française was a royalist organization. This
was curious, for the movement and its leaders were descended
in no way from the old royalist parties, which indeed had
largely sunk into apathy and faded out of political life. The
business and financial interests which had formerly provided
the royalists with their funds had now largely transferred
their support to the conservative republicans. The Action
Française as a monarchist organization was the creation of
Maurras. He claimed to be a monarchist because the monarchy stood for order and the classic discipline in literature,
because it was the antithesis of a hated parliamentarism,
because as the living embodiment of French history a king
stood for the permanent interests of the nation against the
transitory selfishness of the individual. Yet, on a closer in-
spection, one cannot help asking whether the royalism of the
Action Française was ever more than a stalking-horse for
different and more sinister designs. It is remarkable what a
little part the monarchy seems to play in the actual political

proposals of Maurras, so far as he had any. They were never given coherent and systematic expression, but certain leading themes can be picked out. Thus he takes up the agitation of the nineteenth-century regionalists for a revival of the old provincial divisions of France. He would limit the duties of the central government to the control of foreign policy, military and naval affairs, national finance, and justice. All other functions should be left in the hands of local or corporate bodies. In order to provide a new ruling class great landed estates and industrial corporations should be created, or re-created, and, to prevent them from being split up, the rule of equal inheritance abolished. This is essentially an aristocratic creed, calculated for the promotion of an independent, governing *élite*, in no way in the tradition of Bourbon absolutism. It looks back not to the monarchy but to the ultra-royalists of the Restoration and beyond to the Counter-revolution and the *révolte nobiliaire* of the seventeen-eighties which set its mark on all subsequent right-wing movements in France.

So long as the men of wealth and position remained in effective control of France, as they did up to 1870, there was little scope for such a creed. With the Third Republic it found a real target. Maurras supplied all those who resented the arrival of even a limited measure of political democracy and social egalitarianism with an outlet for their resentment and a rationale for views based primarily on self-interest. For a generation after 1871 the right had been on the defensive, continually out-manoeuvred and defeated and driven back from the positions it took up. Politically it continued to be beaten, but at least it was now on the offensive. This is why Maurras and the Action Française won the sympathy of many who were not willing to go all the way with them. Maurras provided the conservative classes with a stimulus for their morale which they so badly needed, but they did not reflect on the illogicality of basing a conservative creed on the advocacy of revolution. The supposed classic rationality of Maurras is an illusion, only possible because he put forward his ideas fragmentarily, through the medium of daily journalism. The king was the least essential element in his political scheme. If it ever came to the point he would have been as expendable as Louis XVI and Marie Antoinette had been for the counter-revolutionaries. The deafness which afflicted Maurras may have assisted him to isolate himself from political reality and create an illusion of doctrinaire consistency, which he inculcated with remorseless fanaticism for the space of over half a century.

The Action Française recruited its support because it offered a specific for social as well as for political discontents. Its local leadership was often in the hands of members of noble families disgruntled at their elimination from political life, though rarely of the higher aristocracy. Some half of its adherents were professional men, often lawyers, and there was a fair proportion from the lower middle class – shopkeepers, commercial travellers, and so on, either attracted by its snob value or finding an outlet for their natural resentment against a society which did not give them the rewards they felt their due.

The student element in the Action Française, at least before the First World War, seems to have been less numerous than the vociferous rowdiness of those who did belong suggested. It was numerous enough, however, to stage impressive student riots in Paris, such as those of the academic year 1908–9, when one M. Thalamas proposed to deliver a course of lectures on what might have been thought the not very provocative subject of pedagogical method. However, several years earlier the same M. Thalamas had distinguished himself by making rude remarks about Jeanne d'Arc, who had been adopted as a sort of nationalist patron saint by the Action Française, and this made him a suitable object for a rather artificial outburst. The Vatican seemed to give its blessing to the proceedings by announcing, in April 1909, the beatification of Jeanne d'Arc.

In spite of the atheism of Maurras and the libertine novels of Daudet, the Action Française won the sympathy of many

French Catholics and was treated as an ally by Pius X. The French hierarchy was less certain of the value of its support and a number of French bishops laid an information in Rome against the writings of Maurras. The congregation of the Index could hardly avoid prohibiting them in 1914, but the Pope ordered that the decree should be kept secret and the Action Française continued to retain the allegiance of good Catholics. Moreover the complexion of the hierarchy was gradually being changed under Pius X by the appointment of bishops who were favourable to the movement. On the other hand, the methods by which the Action Française was endeavouring to promote the causes of the monarchy were a little too crude for old-fashioned royalists and in 1910 the Pretender disavowed it. Conservative society was not yet accustomed to the use of irresponsible youth to create rowdy demonstrations, chanting slogans and smashing up private and public property.

In the columns of the *Action Française* an unremitting war was conducted, with all the weapons of slander, denunciation, and incitement to violence, against the Third Republic. The French Marianne, converted by the Bonapartist journalist, Paul de Cassagnac, with the anti-patriotism characteristic of the French right, into *la gueuse* – the slut – was the daily target of venomous darts in Maurras's journal. The corruption of its politicians was a constant theme, usually in combination with an appeal to the anti-semitism of nationalists and Catholics. Yet in spite of the brilliance of its propaganda the Action Française never became a real political party or more than a merely destructive force. After the First World War, when there were evident signs of the onset of social disintegration, the vultures might gather with better hope, but it would be a mistake to regard the Action Française in the years before 1914 as other than a noisy nuisance and a symbol of dangers to come.

Nationalism in France before the First World War, whether in the form of the Action Française or any other form, was directed primarily against domestic enemies. It became more significant when in place of imaginary foes at home it found real ones abroad, but this situation was slow to develop. The one major external threat to the peaceful progress of the Third Republic was the prospect of war with Germany, and for some time this, despite the nationalist cult of *la revanche*, seemed to be receding. After 1871 France had recovered its position among the Great Powers with remarkable speed. A system of alliances had been built up which enabled her to enter the conference room on equal terms with Germany; and despite the agitation on the right, and a genuine if fading regret for the lost provinces, there was no serious thought of aggressive war to recover them. The international situation, of course, was far too complex to be summed up briefly. All we can do here is to attempt to trace in outline the evolution of French foreign policy under the Third Republic.

In the first years after 1871 clerical agitation kept both Germany and Italy concerned with the possibility of a French attempt at intervention in either country in support of the Roman Catholic Church against the state. Despite the agitation of the bishops this was never a very serious danger, and the republican victory in the elections of 1877 eliminated it as a source of international tension. The condition of almost total isolation that the Republic had inherited from the Second Empire came to an end when French representatives took their seats at the Congress of Berlin.

It was understood, in the course of conversations at the Congress, that the other Powers in Europe would not regard colonial expansion by France as a threat to their security. Indeed, it was felt that the diversion of French interests outside Europe might take the French mind off Alsace-Lorraine and help to stabilize the international situation. Whether or not it actually had this result, the colonial activity of France during the Third Republic was remarkable both for its scope and its success. Yet if the French colonial empire was not acquired in a fit of absence of mind, it can hardly be described as a conscious creation of French government. There was not the machinery for a deliberate and coherent colonial policy. Colonial affairs had been the direct responsibility of the Ministry of the Marine until 1881 when Ferry put them under a sub-department. Only in 1894 did they have a separate ministry of their own, and even then Tunis and Madagascar, as protectorates, as well as the Indo-Chinese colonies, were under the Foreign Office.

A beginning had been made on the re-creation of a colonial empire earlier in the nineteenth century, but only in Algeria had the process been an extensive and continuous one, though punctuated by savagely fought Algerian revolts. After 1871 the European population was increased by the immigration of a considerable number of Alsatians, followed later by Italians, Spaniards, and others. By the end of the century there were some 665,000 Europeans in Algeria, though less than half of these were French in origin. They came to Algeria with different languages and different traditions, and if there were to be a policy of assimilation in the colony it needed to be applied to the European immigrants in the first place. At the same time assimilation seemed possible, since there were only some two and a half million native Algerians.

The policy of assimilation was therefore not an unreasonable one. Algeria was divided into three departments and given representation in the parliament at Paris. A major step was taken in 1881, when most of the Algerian public services were put directly under the ministries at Paris. In 1896, however, there was a move in the opposite direction, towards decentralization, which greatly increased the powers of the Governor-General at Algiers. The fatal weakness in the policy of assimilation was one that might not have been anticipated in the colonial policy of a state that was secular in principle and often anti-clerical in practice. The essential condition laid down for the extension of political rights to native Algerians was acceptance of the Napoleonic Code. One cannot help wondering how far this was a conscious device for excluding the native population from political rights. It certainly did this, for no follower of Islam could fulfil the prescribed condition. On the other hand the Jews of Algeria, numbering some 30,000, had been enfranchised by a decree of October 1870 by Crémieux, which helped to precipitate an Algerian revolt at the time. The new republican government repressed it ruthlessly, but the privileged position of the Jews of Algeria was one of the causes of the anti-semitism which was particularly marked there. Possession of the franchise was not a mere symbol of status. It brought with it more specific advantages in law, and with the aid of these, when the French land laws were introduced, a large part of the more fertile area was taken over by European settlers. With the coming of phylloxera to France, Algerian vineyards developed on a large scale. The benefit was almost wholly to the Europeans. The native Algerian population remained a rural proletariat working the great European *latifundia*.

The establishment of a protectorate in Tunis in the early eighties has already been mentioned. The fall of Ferry did not mean the abandonment of colonial ambitions in Indo-China. Cochin-China, Annam, Cambodia, and Tonkin were united under French rule in 1887, Laos being added in 1899. In 1885 a loose protectorate was established in Madagascar, and in 1895 once again a badly prepared and unsuccessful military expedition – in which some 6,000 out of 15,000 young French soldiers died, mostly from fever – proved the prologue to annexation. Farther north, in East Africa, France found a foothold in Djibouti, though trade or discovery did not draw her beyond the coastline there.

In the west it was a very different story. From trading centres in Guinea, the Ivory Coast, Dahomey, and above all from Faidherbe's colony of Senegal, French traders, explorers, missionaries, expeditionary forces – not necessarily in that order – extended French rule deep into the interior. After the usual setback to a premature and inadequate force in 1893, Timbuktu was successfully occupied by a column under a young officer named Joffre.

Although North Africa was a natural area for French expansion, there were other powers in the same field. In 1890 a Franco-British convention fixed a line of demarcation between the respective spheres of interest of the two countries in Africa from the Niger to Lake Chad, in spite of which a point of collision was reached in 1898. A French plan to stake out a claim to the southern Sudan by expeditions from east and west coasts was only belatedly and inadequately implemented. The leader of the latter expedition landed in July 1896 and struck out from the basin of the Congo in April 1897. Colonel Marchand's foray across the heart of desert Africa, with a handful of French and about 150 Senegalese, was a brilliant exploit. By July 1898 his small expedition had reached Fashoda, a strong point of the Sudan, only to be met in September by Kitchener with a British force ten times as large coming down from the north, where he had destroyed a Sudanese army at Omdurman. To send reinforcements to Marchand was practically impossible, and the French Foreign Minister, Delcassé, was not prepared to go to war for the sake of a large area of what Lord Salisbury called light agricultural territory. He was already looking to Great Britain as a potential ally against Germany. Therefore, in spite of popular fury in France, Marchand was given the order to withdraw and French and British zones of influence in the Sudan were delimited.

By now the room for expansion in the extra-European world was much more restricted. In Africa only Morocco remained. French intervention here was to produce a series of international crises. But before this the attention of French governments had been drawn back to Europe. The inherent contradictions in the Bismarckian system made it increasingly difficult for Germany to keep in step with Russia and Austria at the same time. The discontent of Russia with the results of the German alliance provided an opportunity for French diplomacy, as the monetary needs of the Tsarist government did for French finance. In 1888 the Russian government borrowed 500 million francs on the French market. Other loans followed, promoted with the aid of an extensive Russian-subsidized campaign in the French press. Franco-Russian friendship was further stimulated when, in 1891, the French fleet paid a formal visit to the Russian naval base at Cronstadt, returned by the Russian fleet in the following year. Finally, in January 1894, a Franco-Russian defensive alliance was announced. The *rapprochement* with Russia was immensely popular in France which no longer felt itself isolated. Though it was a natural and inevitable reply to the Bismarckian system of anti-French alliances, it is not quite so obvious now as it seemed at the time that the Russian alliance was ultimately in the interests of France. Even then some feared that – like Austria in the eighteenth century – Russia might turn the alliance to her own exclusive interests without any consideration for her ally; and that if she made a serious mistake she might drag France into an unnecessary war with her. Such doubts hardly existed in 1896 and 1897, when the Tsar and the French President exchanged highly successful visits.

After this, France was swallowed up in the Dreyfus affair and its sequel, and too preoccupied with the domestic problem to pay much attention to foreign affairs. They remained for seven years, under five successive premiers, in charge of the same Foreign Minister. This was Delcassé, small, dark, short, a provincial from the remote Pyrenees, apparently insignificant, bureaucratic, but immensely hard-working, pertinacious, and secretive, and, above all, a passionate enemy of Germany, determined to build up a counter to the now decaying Bismarckian system. His aim was, without damaging the Russian connexion, to bring Great Britain into the French alliance, to restore friendship with Italy, and to consolidate the French position in the Mediterranean by securing control of Morocco. Only Delcassé's unreasonable optimism could have conceived the possibility of achieving such incompatible ends. If he did achieve them it was partly owing to the maladroitness of German diplomacy, and partly owing to the skill with which his chief agents executed his policy in the capitals of Europe.

The Third Republic had a brilliant corps of diplomats, notably the two Cambon brothers – Paul at London from 1898 to 1920, Jules at Berlin from 1907 until his ambassadorial career there was brought to an abrupt end in 1914. Launched into the Foreign Service by Ferry, they bore a name that evoked memories of the Convention, the First French Republic, and the struggles of the year I. Another great ambassador, who had been given his start by Gambetta, was Camille Barère, at Rome from 1897 to 1922. A further element in Delcassé's success was that he had the work of his predecessor at the Quai d'Orsay, Gabriel Hanotaux, to build on. Hanotaux's achievements have hardly received adequate recognition, but it was Hanotaux who took the essential steps towards the alliance with Russia and the first step to the *rapprochement* with Italy. In 1898, when Delcassé became Foreign Minister, France had already taken the first moves towards what was to be a major diplomatic revolution.

The success with Russia was followed up, in 1900, by a secret understanding with Italy. France agreed that Italy should have a free hand in Tripoli, in return for Italian recognition of French interests in Morocco. In 1902, when Italy renewed the Triple Alliance with the Central Powers, a further secret declaration promised that she would not join in any aggressive action against France. Thus by 1902 Russia was an ally, and Italy was in effect neutralized in any future Franco-German conflict.

Relations with Great Britain presented a more difficult problem. The key to the situation was Morocco, artificially preserved in its native state of anarchy by British concern that no other Great Power should hold the southern shore of the Straits of Gibraltar. French intervention there could only take place by agreement with Great Britain, but the British government, uneasily conscious of its isolation at the time of the Boer War, was looking towards Germany, while French opinion was violently anglophobe. Fashoda was not quickly forgotten. The right-wing press alternated anti-British and anti-semitic cartoons, repulsive enough to have satisfied the most exacting demands of the Nazis, who did indeed make use of them in their propaganda forty years later. Delcassé's approaches to the British government had therefore to be made cautiously and under cover, by way of the French ambassador in London, Paul Cambon. An exchange of visits by Edward VII and the French President Loubet in 1903 did something to replace the mutual hostility of their two countries by a more cordial atmosphere. In 1904, behind the innocuous terms of a diplomatic expression of friendship, the Entente Cordiale, were negotiated secret clauses by which France and Great Britain recognized each other's freedom of action respectively in Egypt and Morocco. Even more significant for the future were the accompanying military and naval conversations, though it is doubtful if the British government realized at the time, or even much later, how far they committed it.

The change in the international atmosphere, and the restoration of France to an effective weight in the diplomatic balance, was revealed in the successive crises, provoked mainly by Germany, over the Moroccan situation. To the German government it seemed that the time had come to put a limit to the rapid improvement in France's international position. The defeat of France's ally Russia in the Far East, and the unrest produced in the French Army by the policy of the Combes government, apparently provided a favourable moment for intervention. The Emperor Wilhelm II was therefore sent to Tangier, where he insisted, in a speech that was calculated to resound through Europe, on the independence of the Sultan and the maintenance of German interests in Morocco. This was in effect a demand that France should repudiate the policy of Delcassé, who was prepared to accept the challenge by a formal rejection of the German *démarche*. The Chamber was less bellicose and did not support his demand for an uncompromising reply. Moreover his influence in parliament, which he had almost totally abandoned for work in his bureau, had greatly diminished. The German government therefore had the satisfaction of having forced his resignation. It was a Pyrrhic victory, for an international conference, held at Algeçiras in 1906, recognized, as well as the general international interest in Morocco, the primary role of France there.

This was a rebuff to Germany, which had gained nothing by her bellicose gesture, and the progressive military occupation of Morocco by French troops continued. In 1908 an affair of German deserters from the French Foreign Legion produced another international incident, without any serious consequences this time. In 1911, a further French military advance brought the sending of the German gunboat, the *Panther*, to Agadir, to reinforce a German demand for territorial compensation in the French Congo. The international situation, which up to this point had never been more than a minor sub-plot in the history of the Third Republic, now takes the centre of the stage. Three times, in 1905, 1908, and 1911, Germany had rattled the sabre – not, it is true, without some cause on each occasion, but the effect was cumulative. In 1911 the French and German Foreign Offices were prepared to work up a nice little war between them, but the French Premier Caillaux and the German Foreign Minister Kiderlen-Wächter chose to compromise: Germany recognized a French protectorate in Morocco, and France ceded part of the Cameroons to Germany, to the fury of the nationalists on both sides.

Nationalist agitation in France was now directed against external as well as internal enemies. The international crisis of 1911 marks a real turning-point in French politics. Already in February 1911, with the defeat of Briand's ministry, the dominance of the great republican bloc, which Waldeck-Rousseau had gathered behind him when he formed his cabinet in 1899, had come to an end. The influence of the Union Républicaine Démocratique, founded in 1903, and led by Louis Marin, was increasing. Representing Catholic and conservative France, and backed by much of the landed and industrial wealth of the country, it provided a responsible rallying-point for the more sober elements of the right. But even these were undergoing the influence of Action Française propaganda, which had an effect well beyond the circles that accepted the political creed of Maurras and Daudet. Through its influence in the world of letters it was changing the spirit of *tout Paris*, as Roger Martin du Gard shows in his novel *Jean Barois*.

The vociferous nationalist minority which seemed to dominate Paris society and journalism was, of course, far from representative of France. On the left there was a strong vein of pacifism and internationalism, which had been one of the reasons why the Socialists abandoned the left-wing alliance in 1905. French intervention in Morocco did not go unopposed in France; the Russo-Japanese war suggested that the Russian ally might be a liability; the suppression of the revolution of 1905 alienated the Socialists, and the money the Tsarist government was known to spend on the French press did not conciliate them. The leading spokesman of Socialist pacifism, Gustave Hervé, was a former teacher, who had set out on a demagogic career which was to bring him in the end to near-fascist journalism and the authorship of *C'est Pétain qu'il nous faut*. This was a long way ahead. Before the First World War, he was editor of *La Guerre Sociale*. '*Notre patrie*,' he wrote, '*c'est notre classe*,' and called for revolution if mobilization were proclaimed. This was only an exaggerated statement of a common illusion of the left. Jaurès, who did not go so far, himself believed that the international action of socialism could prevent the outbreak of war.

The moderate and the right-wing parties are hardly to be blamed if they did not share these optimistic illusions. It did not require any very great foresight to be alarmed about the international situation by 1912. A left-wing cabinet under Caillaux found a compromise solution to the international crisis of 1911, but Caillaux was not the man to cope adequately with any major crisis, domestic or foreign. Son of a cabinet minister, recruited into the bureaucratic *élite* of the Inspectors of Finances, at an early age Minister of Finances in the great Waldeck-Rousseau government, in Caillaux technical ability and a powerful intelligence were combined with fatal conceit, ambition, intolerance, and a weakness – surprising in one who was by birth a member of the republican *élite* – for hob-nobbing with shady characters in journalism and politics. He had no love for his fellow politicians and they had little for him. For his loss of office in January 1912, however, he was hardly to blame: the reasonable compromise he had found for the international crisis drove the nationalists to fury.

Foreign policy was now increasingly pushing domestic issues into the background, and the Chamber turned to a very different type of politician to lead a government of national union. Raymond Poincaré, lawyer cousin of the mathematician Henri, belonged to a University and Polytechnic family. Deputy in 1887 and Senator in 1903, he was profoundly conservative but counted as a man of the left since he was also an anti-clerical. He had the nationalist sentiments of a Lorrainer. Aloof, cold, and unsympathetic – Curzon, worsted in a diplomatic encounter after the First World War, was to call him 'that horrid little man' – Poincaré was one of the great technocrats of the Republic. He had intellectual powers at least equal to those of Caillaux, and combined them with a rarer personal integrity and an inexorable pursuit of the policy he thought right for his country. His reputation, and his combination of nationalism with anti-clericalism, and republicanism with conservative social views, made him the essential man for the situation. His premiership in January 1912 was only a step to the presidency, to which he was elected with the support of the right by a majority of 483 to 296 in January 1913.

The international sky continued to darken. Before the threat of growing German military power it seemed necessary to increase the period of conscription in France to three years. This had been reduced to two years in 1905, though – since the previous term of three years had been riddled with exceptions for those who possessed educational qualifications, which in effect had meant those from the better-off sections of society – this had not involved as great a reduction in manpower as might have been supposed. The bitter conservative resentment at the reduction to two years, along with a removal of the exemptions, was therefore not entirely on patriotic grounds. In spite of the energetic opposition by Jaurès and Caillaux, a law was passed in August 1913 prescribing three years' service, with seven years in the territorial army and a further seven years in the reserve.

The question that now arose was how the necessary re-armament was to be paid for. This produced an even bitterer controversy. The French bourgeoisie remained, like its predecessors of the *noblesse*, willing to sacrifice everything rather than accept a more equitable system of taxation. Caillaux's attempt to revive the income-tax proposals of 1909 added to the intense hatred which he gained from the right by opposing the three years law. A fanfare of wrath, probably orchestrated by Poincaré from the Élysée, blew round his head. His own capacity for equivocation and making enemies did not help him. Ruin came when Mme Caillaux assassinated the editor of *Le Figaro*, who had played a leading part in a very dirty campaign against her husband including the publication of early love-letters.

Judging by the press and Paris, France was on the point of being carried away on a wave of nationalist and bellicose ardour. The legislative elections that came in 1914 revealed the true sentiments of the country. Joint opposition to the three years law on the part of Radicals and Socialists brought them together again in a revived left-wing bloc. The noisy nationalists of *tout Paris* kept the support of the traditional conservative and Catholic crescent stretching round from the Vendée, through Brittany and Normandy, with a gap in the industrial regions of the North-east, but strengthening again in the border departments of the East. For once there was a clear-cut issue between left and right, and the line of cleavage was not confused, as was more usual, by an active clerical and anti-clerical issue. The right set up Caillaux as a bogey-man, with his *grand fonctionnaire* personality and association with high finance, which went so ill with his presidency of the Radical Socialist party. Opposition to the three years law was denounced as unpatriotic. On the other hand the left was at least excusable in believing the seriousness of the international situation to be exaggerated when it found the right unwilling to pay an extra sou for the defence of the country. The election proved that even in the existing state of international tension French opinion was profoundly pacific and non-aggressive. Memories of 1870 were fading, colonial conquests only really interested a minority, the political consolidation of the Republic seemed completed and the task of social reform ready to begin. To the left, the threat of war was obviously a fifth ace smuggled into the hand of the right and smacked triumphantly on the table to take the electoral trick; the idealistic Radicals and Socialists refused to believe it could be true. The country was so little warlike that it agreed with them. The result of the elections was a victory for the left, with 104 United Socialists, 24 Republican Socialists, and 172 Radicals and Radical Socialists. On the right were 37 members of the Republican Federation, 23 Liberal Action, 15 Right and 44 Independents, 119 in all. The centre and the centre left included 66 Radical Left, 23 Republican Radical Socialist Union, 7 'Dissidents', 53 Republicans of the left, and 32 Democratic left, making a floating vote of 181. This catalogue well illustrates the leading features of the French political system: the dominance of the group system; the bias to the left, so strong that the real left only began where parties ceased to label themselves as such; the inability of the members of the extreme right to present a coherent programme and their disposition to disguise themselves as independents; and the disproportionate influence that could be exercised by small groups in the – perhaps literally – dead centre of French politics, which were in a position, by throwing their votes on one side or the other, to bargain for office and set up and destroy governments at will.

The intense political struggle going on inside France was dramatically demonstrated now by the appearance and disappearance, in a single day, of the shortest of all the short-lived governments of the Third Republic. When the conservative Ribot presented his cabinet to the Chamber, on 12 June 1914, it was immediately shouted out of office by the parties of the left.

An unusual element in the political situation at this time was the presence of a President who was not content with the normal restricted role of his office. Despite the verdict of the electorate Poincaré was determined to maintain the three years law. After failing to obtain a Premier from the right, he accepted Viviani, now a member of a small group mid-way between the Radicals and the Socialists, who agreed not to press for the immediate reversal of the law on condition of the Senate's lifting its *non possumus* on the income tax. The tax was in fact voted in principle, though the details were not to be worked out until 1917, by which time France had accumulated a colossal burden of war debt. With the three years law respited, President and Premier, on 16 July, took ship for a state visit to the Tsar arranged earlier in the year.

Nobody knew that the event that was to lead to the First World War had already occurred. On 28 June 1914, a Yugoslav criminal, or nationalist, brutally murdered the Austrian Archduke Francis Ferdinand and his wife at Serajevo. The situation evolved at first slowly, while the peaceful populations of Europe went about their work and their pleasures in the warm summer weather. It seemed that this crisis would be got over, as had so many others in the recent past, peacefully; but there were those, in Vienna and Berlin, who thought otherwise. When Poincaré and Viviani left Russia, on 23 July, their visit concluded, they did not

yet know of the Austrian ultimatum, on the same day, to
Servia.

It is not necessary to summarize here the fatal events of
July 1914, through most of which France could only stand
by and watch passively the moves on the international
board that were pushing her helplessly and inexorably into
war. That the most pacific Chamber the country had ever
known should have led France into a world war was ironic.
One might be tempted to transfer the blame back earlier on
to that policy of the Russian alliance which tied France to
the support of her Russian ally; but in fact the struggle of the
great military despotisms of Germany and Austria-Hungary
against Russia was written on the tablets of fate – or only
avoidable on the supposition of quite different governments
in the three countries. In such a struggle Russia was bound
to be defeated, and to assume that after this victory the
Reich would abandon the path of conquest, and that the
German eagle would settle peacefully on its perch, side by
side with the rather clamorous but essentially domesticated
Gallic cock, would have been to expect the impossible.
Whether France would stick to her alliance with Russia, and
equally what the entente with England would amount to in
practice, did not really concern the directors of German
strategic policy. They viewed British military potential with
contempt, and the French, even if they got as far as honour-
ing their commitments to Russia, as a decadent race of
immoral artists and corrupt politicians incapable of standing
up to the *furor Teutonicus*. It was to be a short war. The great
German General Staff had its Schlieffen plan, according to
which the German army, by disregarding an old and therefore obsolete treaty of neutrality and marching through Belgium – obviously a justifiable measure because Belgium could
offer little serious opposition – would be able to turn the flank
of the French army and crush resistance within a few weeks.

On 28 July Austria-Hungary declared war on Servia. The
next day Poincaré and Viviani landed at Dunkirk. On 31
July Germany, having issued an ultimatum to Russia, called

on France to declare what she would do in the event of war between Germany and Russia. This seemed a clever move: if France replied with a declaration that she would stand in shining armour beside Russia (as Wilhelm II had in relation to Austria-Hungary a few years earlier) this could be presented as a threat of aggression; if, on the other hand, the French offered to remain neutral, then Germany intended to demand the occupation of Toul and Verdun as a guarantee. Viviani escaped the trap by replying evasively that France would consult her interests. Public opinion was now becoming excited in all countries. In France, mounting nationalist fervour, fed by years of irresponsible agitation, led to the assassination of Jaurès by a fanatic, but there was no widespread agitation for war. Small chauvinist demonstrations were easily suppressed by the police. *La revanche*, or the thought of recovering Alsace-Lorraine, hardly entered into the mind of the French people, whose only hope was for the preservation of peace. The government had one other concern: what would be the attitude of Great Britain if Germany attacked? The entente, even the military and naval conversations, were far from binding her to intervene. A personal letter from the French President to King George V asked for an assurance that Great Britain would not remain neutral if the Central Powers attacked France, but the British government refused to commit itself. The probability is that the German and Austro-Hungarian General Staffs were already so far determined on war, and that such civilian opposition as there was in high places in Germany had been so effectively stifled, that no action by the British could have prevented war; but it was a reasonable conclusion for the French to draw after the catastrophe that a clear statement of the British position (which unfortunately was far from clear) might have averted it. This was to have much influence on French policy after 1918.

The French government could only wait on the course of events and take such precautions as were possible to safeguard itself from any possible charge of French aggression.

When the French cabinet acceded to the demand of the General Staff that covering troops be sent to the frontier, on 30 July, it was on condition that they be kept ten kilometres behind it, to prevent the development of any incidents. The Commander-in-Chief, Joffre, agreed to this, though he protested strongly against the failure to call up reservists and the order that only those troops who could do so by moving on foot should take up their war-time stations. Meanwhile military preparations for war were rapidly and inexorably proceeding in Central and Eastern Europe. On 1 August the French government issued the order for general mobilization. On 2 August Germany occupied Luxembourg and German patrols crossed the French frontier. Joffre was now given freedom of action, but while ordering the repulsion of incursions into French territory, he instructed his commanders not to pursue enemy troops into Germany. He believed that the Germans would attack France without a declaration of war, as indeed they did, but not from the direction anticipated. In 1914 there was still a general expectation that treaties would be kept until they were formally denounced. It is difficult to think back now to a time when the German disregard of Belgian neutrality was regarded as a shattering blow to normal conventions of international behaviour, something that no other Great Power – or so it was believed and perhaps rightly then – could have done, or hardly so blatantly. On 2 August the German government demanded the right of passage for its troops through Belgium, on the ground of its knowledge of French plans to invade Germany from the same quarter. This was a patent lie. The next day Germany declared war on France, alleging with equal mendacity French attacks on Germany. German policy had achieved what a little earlier would have seemed the impossible – a stubborn if hopeless Belgian resistance to the German army, a declaration of war by Great Britain on 4 August, and the entry of France into the war with total national unity from extreme right to extreme left. The Third Republic in 1914 had no Fifth Column.

In the armed camp that Europe had become in 1914, with the atmosphere of tension created by the irresponsible nationalists of all countries, and given the interlocking and opposed systems of alliances, it is all too easy, and correct in a sense, to present the outbreak of the First World War as the result of an international anarchy to which all countries contributed, and the responsibility for which was so divided that if there were any guilt all were equally guilty. To the French in 1914 this would have seemed nonsense. They understood, for they had been through a struggle over the same issue themselves, that Germany was a country where the General Staff could override the civil authorities, and the executive was largely independent of the legislature; its government had repeatedly used the threat of war as a diplomatic instrument. Other countries had their wild men. France was particularly afflicted by the 'integral national-ist', anti-semitic, war-mongering elements in the conser-vative and Catholic sectors of opinion; but the pacifist and defensive sentiments which prevailed in French policy on the eve of the First World War reflected a general national temper, which had gradually risen to dominance with the triumph and consolidation of the democratic Republic. It was difficult for civilized, humane men of the stamp of Jaurès to believe that the rulers of a great European Power could be so wicked or irresponsible, and their subjects so passively obedient, as to plan and put into operation, or accept without question, a major war. More pessimistically, a Delcassé or a Poincaré had believed in the inherent aggressiveness of the German state; but their contribution to the increase in French defensive capacity, in arms and allies, was in no way intended as a preliminary to starting a war on Germany. This is not to deny that the increasing strength of France and her allies was an important factor in provoking war, for 1914 seemed to the Central Powers perhaps the last moment at which it might be launched with a maximum prospect of rapid success. It is difficult to see what France could have done that would have averted the war, short of repudiating her treaty bonds with Russia and recognizing German military and political hegemony over Europe. This was not contemplated in 1914. No one could have been expected to know that the coming struggle, and even ultimate victory, would be almost as fatal to the ideals and achievements of the Third Republic as defeat could have been.

Though developments in the years before 1914 fore-shadowed the change that was coming, it was the First World War that marked the turning-point in the history of the Third Republic, and in a sense the end of its greatness. Henceforth it was to live in the shadow of war and rumours of war. Social cohesion and political stability were to vanish in the civil discord and social hatreds bred by a climate of international war and revolution. As Marcel Proust had felt, something was indeed coming to an end. Looking back, we can see in retrospect that what was ending was a great age in the history of France.

2. THE FIRST WORLD WAR

ON the outbreak of war Poincaré's call for a *union sacrée* met with practically universal acceptance. All divisions in the nation disappeared. Monarchists and republicans, employers, workers and peasants, rich and poor, united in defence of the *patrie*. The peacetime battle of clerical and anti-clerical was forgotten. Priests joined up and fought side by side with laity. Most remarkable of all, defeat was not followed by the cry of '*Nous sommes trahis*'. There was no Fifth Column; that was an improvement of a later age. The notorious *carnet B*, containing the names of all the supposed dangerous revolutionaries in France, whom it was proposed to arrest and intern in the event of war, was wisely left undisturbed in the files of the Ministry of the Interior. The Socialists sang the *Marseillaise*; Gustave Hervé praised patriotism; the tradition of Jacobin patriotism was invoked by Edmond Vaillant, Communard and Blanquist of 1871.

The man of the moment was the Commander-in-Chief, Joffre, appointed in 1911 as a moderate republican general, rock-like in appearance, stolid and unemotional in manner. The son of a cooper, he was evidence of the possibility of *la carrière ouverte aux talents* even in the army. Not lacking in the intellectual qualities needed to gain a place in the École Polytechnique, he was endowed with a peasant shrewdness that was to enable him to meet and often beat the politicians at their own game. Above all he was a man who gave the impression of being reliable. He shared, of course, the views on the nature of the coming war and the correct policy for the French army that prevailed in the General Staff. Something more than the normal decline of a peacetime army is needed to explain the thrice repeated – in 1870, 1914, and 1940 – failure of the French General Staff to judge correctly the nature of the war which each time it believed to be coming and for which it was preparing. In 1914 it calculated, as also the Germans did, on a short war, which could be won by a sharp, decisive offensive.

The most influential theorist of the General Staff, Colonel de Grandmaison, had inculcated the doctrine of the *offensive à outrance*. In accordance with his strategic teaching, the French army began the war by advancing into German-occupied Lorraine and Alsace, across a hilly and wooded terrain that gave all the advantages to the defensive. For a brief moment Mulhouse was taken, only to be rapidly lost again. The German artillery once more exhibited a crushing superiority. Meanwhile the Germans, recognizing that their direct route into France was blocked by the great French fortresses, took the easier route through Belgium, which in the circumstances they regarded as morally forced on them, and after a brief delay they swept under von Kluck into Northern France.

Before the mounting military threat Viviani strengthened his cabinet and made it truly a government of national

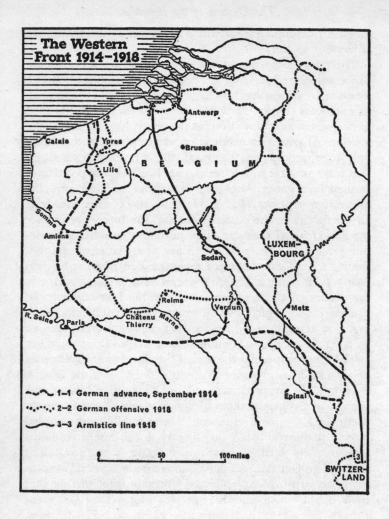

The Western
Front 1914–1918

Antwerp

Calais

Ypres

Lille

•Brussels

B E L G I U M

R. Somme

Amiens

Sedan

LUXEM-
BOURG

Reims

R. Marne

Verdun

Metz

R. Seine   Paris

Château
Thierry

Épinal

〰〰 1–1 German advance, September 1914

•°•°•°• 2–2 German offensive 1918

〜〜 3–3 Armistice line 1918

0   50   100miles

SWITZER-
LAND

union, by calling Delcassé to the Ministry of Foreign Affairs, Millerand to the Ministry of War, Briand to Justice, and bringing in Guesde and another Socialist. The government needed all the strength it could get. Kluck was approaching so close to Paris that, to avoid a repetition of 1870, on 1 September the government left for Bordeaux, where it was to stay for some three months. There was no suggestion of yielding. If any defeatists existed in France they were silent and there were no pro-Germans, so different was the situation from what it was to be in 1940. Again unlike the later campaign, the armies maintained their cohesion, and the general kept his head and never lost control of the situation. On 5 September Galliéni, in command of the troops defending Paris, saw the opportunity to counter-attack. Joffre let him loose on the right flank of the advancing Germans and the battle of the Marne saved Paris. There followed the 'race to the sea', the consolidation of the front from the Alps to the beaches, and the beginning of what no one yet knew was to be four years of exhausting trench warfare. France, in the first four months, had lost in dead, missing, wounded, or prisoners some 850,000 men, and had yielded up some of her most important industrial and agricultural areas to enemy possession.

Despite the experience of 1914 the French General Staff continued to be dominated by the mystique of the offensive. In 1915 the 'young Turks' of Joffre's headquarters adopted the policy of what was called a 'war of attrition' by launching continual petty attacks on the enemy. Since the offensive was invariably more costly than the defensive, it is fairly clear which army was being worn down by this policy. Governmental nerves also were becoming frayed, and in October 1915 internal differences of opinion, and criticisms from outside, brought about the fall of the Viviani cabinet. Briand took over the premiership, still at the head of a broad coalition preserving the *union sacrée*.

But politics was now beginning to re-emerge and affect the conduct of the war. In 1915 Joffre, finding that one of his generals, Sarrail, after an early success, was involved in serious reverses, and moreover was intriguing against his commander-in-chief, removed him from his command. Sarrail was later to be compensated by a command on the Balkan front, where his ill-luck followed him; but unfortunately he was the model of a republican, anti-clerical general, and his dismissal brought the Radicals and Socialists on to the battlefield, politically speaking, in defence of their hero.

The next year, 1916, was the year of Verdun. In February a massive German attack on the Verdun salient was launched. It was a cleverly worked out strategic move. The great fortress was in an exposed situation and would be expensive to defend; but the Germans had studied history and knew that Verdun had a particular meaning for France. By making it their main objective they could practically force the French army to defend it, because of the moral value of its retention and the pessimism that would be engendered by its loss. In spite of this the French High Command had not taken the steps that seemed called for if Verdun were to be treated as a vital position. Joffre, with his usual common sense, was probably prepared to abandon it and shorten the French line when the Germans had paid a sufficient price. Briand, however, knew that the fall of Verdun would not only seriously affect French morale, it would also be fatal to his government. He gave the order to defend Verdun at all costs, and the defence was conducted with a skill, stubbornness, and heroism that made the reputation of General Philippe Pétain. However, the German High Command had achieved its object of enticing the French to sacrifice their manpower for the purpose of holding a fortress of mainly symbolic value. It was the war of attrition in reverse, applied with Teutonic thoroughness. France was to be 'bled white' at Verdun. German losses were also heavy but, starting the war with a population of 66 millions against the French 39 millions, the German Command doubtless thought it could better afford extensive bloodletting. By the time the German attack had worn itself out each army had lost about a quarter of a million men in the fighting. In July, to relieve the pressure, Joffre began a counter-offensive on the Somme, which gained a little territory; the Allied and German armies lost another half-million men between them in this sector.

The continuous and calamitous loss of life, to no apparent gain, inevitably had its effect on the national spirit. By the end of 1916 disillusionment was widespread. A change of leadership was psychologically necessary and a veiled press campaign was launched against Joffre, who for all his cunning was no match for Briand. The responsibility for the carnage of Verdun was gently but firmly placed on the General's shoulders. When his prestige was sufficiently undermined he was promoted chief military adviser to the government, in which post he was ignored and from which he soon resigned. The new Commander-in-Chief of the French armies on the Western Front was to be General Nivelle, who had achieved a number of tactical successes and was affable and popular with the politicians. He was believed, and probably believed himself, to have the secret which had evaded Joffre of breaking the enemy line.

Briand's victory over Joffre did not enable his government to hold out much longer. He fell in March 1917 and was replaced by an elderly, conservative nonentity, Ribot. The first measure of the new government was to approve a great offensive projected by Nivelle. The previous War Minister, Lyautey, the great colonial administrator, whose political maladroitness had in fact brought Briand's ministry down, had not concealed his belief that Nivelle's plans were mad. Lyautey's successor in the War Ministry, the mathematician Painlevé, was himself profoundly sceptical; but Nivelle, asked to modify or postpone his offensive, threatened to resign. Ribot, who saw that this would involve the fall of his government, and Poincaré, who believed in generals, supported him. Although every sane calculation was against it and Nivelle's plan was, in the words of Lyautey, only suitable for the army of the Grand Duchess of Gerolstein, he was allowed to go ahead with it and walk into the trap laid by the Germans, who by now, after all the discussions between politicians and generals, knew the details of the coming offensive almost as well as the French themselves.

The German commander Ludendorff laid his plans for the anticipated French offensive by preparing a defensive line to withdraw to. On 16 April, having been delayed for a week by torrential rain, which reduced the fields to a quagmire and should by itself have caused the offensive to be called off, the misconceived, mis-conducted French advance began. Their peasant armies moved forward across devastated territory, with its houses blown up or booby-trapped, wells poisoned and even fruit-trees sawn off, sights which were not calculated to weaken the increasing bitterness with which the war was being fought, until they came up against the impassable obstacle of the so-called Hindenburg line, against which Nivelle flung his troops in senseless and apparently endless slaughter.

Painlevé, who was struggling to remove the amiable, incompetent, obstinate general from his command and bring the offensive to an end, found himself opposed on all sides. The anti-clerical Minister of the Interior, Malvy, supported Nivelle because he was a Protestant and likely to be succeeded by a Catholic, the British General Haig because the offensive helped to concentrate the fighting on the Western Front where Haig was in command and avoid 'side-shows', Poincaré because he had committed himself, in the face of warnings, to the Nivelle plan. But in the end the evidence of continued and useless loss of life was irresistible. On 15 May Painlevé succeeded in removing Nivelle. He was replaced by Pétain, who was known to prefer the defensive, with Foch as Chief of Staff. The team had been found that, after waiting while waiting was necessary until France's allies had filled the gaps left by a death roll of well over a million men since 1914, was in due course to win the war.

Despite military mistakes, the Third Republic had stood

the test of the most appalling of wars with remarkable cohesion and constancy. Even Verdun and the Somme had not produced more than a demand for a change in leadership. After the pointless massacres of Nivelle's offensive the crack came. In May 1917 scattered mutinies broke out. Pétain dealt with a critical situation with intelligence, tact, firmness, and humanity. He established personal contact with as many units as he could, improved the troops' conditions so far as was possible, limited the military operations that had to be undertaken, minimized losses, and restored discipline at the cost of no more than twenty-three executions of mutineers.

Equally dangerous unrest, developing in civilian quarters, was exposed to the public gaze in a series of political scandals. A campaign against the alliance with Great Britain, against the President, and surreptitiously against the war, was appearing in the press. A minor left-wing journal called *Le Bonnet rouge*, edited by a journalistic adventurer named Vigo-Almereyda, took a prominent part in this campaign. The *Action Française*, with information supplied by police headquarters, in its turn attacked *Le Bonnet rouge*, aided by a league against subversive forces which operated from its offices, to preside over which General Mercier, of Dreyfus-affair notoriety, was brought out of his well-deserved obscurity. Behind *Le Bonnet rouge* the real objectives of the attack were the Radical ministers, Malvy and Caillaux, who were suspected of being prepared for a negotiated peace. In fact Malvy's ministry had bribed *Le Bonnet rouge*, like some other papers, early in the war, to keep it quiet. He stopped his subsidies when it began anti-war propaganda but German money probably took its place. In July 1917 Clemenceau used this connexion to launch an attack on Malvy in the Senate. Almereyda was arrested, and in the curious way that more than once happened with arrested persons who knew too much for the good of the state apparently strangled himself, with a boot-lace or a piece of string, in his cell. Malvy, however, had to resign.

Trouble did not end there. A deputy was discovered with a large packet of Swiss francs, for the possession of which he could give no explanation. There followed the cases of an absurd adventurer named Bolo, supplied with German money to spread defeatist propaganda, and the dramatized woman spy Mata Hari. In November the Painlevé cabinet, tarred with all these scandals and in its turn charged with weakness, was overthrown.

Something more serious was at issue than the machinations of petty German agents and spies. The belief had begun to spread, especially among the parties of the left, that a negotiated peace was the only alternative to endless, meaningless slaughter. The idea of a common humanity and unity among the workers of the world, roughly shaken when the German Socialists wheeled into line behind their government's aggression in 1914, was reviving. The Russian Revolution aroused an idealistic echo in the West; but when an international Socialist congress was called at Stockholm to attempt mediation between the warring nations, the French Socialists were refused passports to attend. They now left the Sacred Union and gave up participation in the government. Industrial strikes, which had hitherto been conspicuously absent, began to develop. Caillaux, re-emerging into political life, with characteristic lack of tact prematurely spoke in public of the possibility of a compromise peace. Even Briand was not unsympathetic to the idea of eventual negotiations with Germany. Reason and humanity suggested that at least the possibility should be explored, though passion and politics prohibited it. The age of slogans had come upon the warring world – the war to end wars could not be abandoned half-won; the propaganda-mongers were caught in their own toils. It must also be recognized that German policy now brought its nemesis: what trust could be put in a régime that had launched a world war by flagrant aggression and justified it by blatant mendacity? Moreover, the recovery of Alsace-Lorraine had now become a war aim for France and only total defeat would bring a German government to envisage this. It might be said that, in spite of all this, nothing would have been lost by allowing the enemy to expose his intransigence, but any willingness to contemplate a compromise peace was interpreted as weakness. Pétain, asked by the President if he could keep his troops under control should there be discussions with the Germans at Stockholm – a loaded question – replied firmly, No. The *Action Française* began to resume its characteristic activity with a charge by Léon Daudet that the ex-Minister of the Interior, Malvy, had betrayed French battle-plans to the Germans.

The lead among those who were determined that there should be no negotiated peace was taken by the old 'tiger' of French politics, Clemenceau, now aged seventy-six. He was an isolated figure, cut off from all parties by temperament and the bitter struggles of the past, and belonging to a different generation. His incessant attacks on the conduct of war, in the Parliament and in the pages of his paper *L'Homme libre*, renamed under war censorship *L'Homme enchaîné*, marked him out in the public mind as the man who could put things right. Poincaré, with his usual clear-sightedness, saw that a choice had to be made, either Caillaux or Clemenceau, and, though he hated Clemenceau, he hated Caillaux and the idea of peace without victory even more. He called Clemenceau to office. The prospect of a compromise peace was at an end, though it is impossible to believe that the German General Staff, now on the eve of its greatest victory in the East, would have contemplated such a peace in the West.

The new Premier turned on the would-be negotiators – defeatists to use the language of the time – savagely. Briand received a fright which sent him into retirement until the war was over; Malvy was put on trial; Caillaux, arrested and charged with intelligence with the enemy, was to stay in prison for two years. Many lesser actual or alleged 'pro-Germans' experienced attacks in which personal enmities were given ample scope, and accusations of treachery were flung about wildly. The right wing welcomed these steps, which brought the needed temporary unity, but also introduced a cleavage into French politics more permanent and deeper than had been known since the struggle over Dreyfus.

So far as winning the war, or not losing it, was concerned, Clemenceau had not come to power too soon. He was his own War Minister and collected round him a cabinet of nonentities: he described them as the geese who by their cackling saved Rome. The situation when he assumed office seemed desperate. In December 1917 an armistice was signed on the Eastern Front and the German Command was free to concentrate its forces on the West, where American reinforcements were only slowly arriving. In March 1918 the Ludendorff offensive drove deep into the Allied lines. An attempt, earlier in the year, to take the first step towards a badly needed unity of command over the Allied armies, by putting the most widely respected French general, Foch, in charge of a Reserve Force for the whole front, had been frustrated by an unholy alliance between Haig and Pétain, concerned with their own prestige. When the German break-through came, Pétain's deep temperamental pessimism seemed likely to prohibit a vigorous reaction; but the situation was now so obviously critical that the political leaders were able to impose Foch as supreme commander over both the jealous generals. From March to July Ludendorff desperately let loose offensive after offensive, penetrating as deep into the Allied lines at Château-Thierry and the Marne. Foch bided his time, stoically supported by Clemenceau. At last, on 18 July, he began the counter-offensive, which was not to stop until the German army had been driven back to its own frontier and on 11 November accepted an armistice.

It was, or it seemed to be, the most glorious hour in the history of the Third Republic. France had borne the brunt of the struggle against the military power of the German Reich and had survived with her national life, her ideals, and her institutions intact. The Republic had emerged triumphant from the severest of all tests, though at a cost that in the moment of triumph was hardly realized. Part of the price of victory had already been paid in some million and a quarter military, and half a million civilian, dead or soon to die, and three quarters of a million permanently injured, in the invaded departments looted and devastated, and in a national debt of huge proportions. The price was to continue to be paid for another generation in the loss of the high hopes which might reasonably have been held in the opening decade of the twentieth century.

In 1918, on the morrow of victory, such pessimism would have seemed absurd. Looking back one can see that a good peace was inconceivable. That the peace was as bad as it proved to be may partly be attributed to the degradation of the public spirit in all the belligerent countries that resulted from the punitive death roll of the war, and the vicious and mendacious propaganda that had been used as a major weapon on all sides; partly to the fact that the common purpose which had united the Western allies inevitably failed to survive victory.

The Peace Conference at Paris revealed their divergent aims and ideals. France, in the person of Clemenceau, knew what she wanted – first the return of Alsace-Lorraine, and on this there was no dispute; secondly, security; and thirdly, reparations. Even with Alsace-Lorraine, France would remain weaker in population and resources than Germany. The main aim of Clemenceau was to redress this balance. He secured the reduction of the German army to a maximum of 100,000 men, without air force or heavy artillery, though, contrary to French wishes, it was, on mistaken British ideas, to be a long-service force, and therefore capable of rapidly providing the trained cadres for a conscript army. To counterbalance the loss of resources in the French devastated areas, the great mining basin of the Saar was put under international control; but this was only for fifteen years, after which it was to decide its future by plebiscite.

Over the terms of the peace a bitter conflict broke out between the chief two French architects of victory, Foch and

Clemenceau. Foch, disbelieving in the efficacy or perman-
ence of treaties of disarmament, insisted that the only solution to the French problem of security was the Rhine
frontier. Clemenceau, as a politician, knew that it would be
impossible ever to extract from Great Britain and from
America, committed to the principle of national self-determination, agreement to such a proposal. He settled for the
best terms he could get his allies to agree to – the occupation
of three bridge-heads on the right bank of the Rhine for five,
ten, and fifteen years respectively, an Anglo-American guarantee against future German aggression, and a demilitarized
zone in the Rhineland.

Foch and the nationalists condemned Clemenceau for his
failure to secure the left bank of the Rhine for France. The
internationalists, such as Léon Bourgeois, put their faith in
an international army. Great Britain and the United States
were unwilling to contemplate either road to security. They
frustrated one French plan after another, and although
Clemenceau obtained a joint Anglo-American guarantee of
assistance to France if Germany should make an unprovoked
attack it was to be repudiated by the United States and the
repudiation used as an excuse for cancelling her obligation
by Great Britain. Clemenceau was certainly no Talleyrand
and he tried to make obstinacy do the work of finesse, but
given the American misjudgement of the European situation, and the shiftiness of British policy, it is difficult to see
what more he could have rescued from the wreck of the
alliance. He did at least provide, by clauses which could
have been brought into effect at the critical moment in 1936,
if there had then been the will to do so, for a French re-
occupation of the Rhineland in the event of a German attempt to remilitarize it.

The other great aim of the French negotiators was one
which she shared with all her allies – to make somebody else
pay for the war; the only difference was that whereas Great
Britain and the European allies were determined to make
Germany pay, the Americans were determined to make their

allies pay. Every war cost that could be thought of was added to the bill for reparations in a frantic competition to draw up an astronomical total. In this way it was hoped to avoid the painful necessity of raising money by taxation. The result was that further borrowing was added to the already huge French war debt and the budget was balanced on the promise of German reparations. The inflation that was the inevitable result was to be a powerful factor in undermining the stability of French society.

By the end of the peace negotiations tempers were frayed and the victorious alliance was dead, but somehow a document was produced which was called the Treaty of Versailles and signed in the Hall of Mirrors on 28 June 1919.

3. BLOC NATIONAL

WITH the restoration of peace the normal processes of politics were resumed in France. The Chamber of Deputies, which had been elected in 1914, was dissolved and elections for a new Chamber were held in November 1919. Clemenceau in France, like Lloyd George in England, was determined to let no scruples of any kind stand in the way of dealing the knock-out blow to his political enemies on the home front that he had already dealt to the Germans on the military front. The degradation of national standards, in the victorious as well as the vanquished nations, that resulted from the First World War, was first clearly shown in the general elections in Great Britain and France. The director of Clemenceau's personal 'cabinet', Georges Mandel – destined to end his political career with more honour than he began – managed the French elections in the interests of the parties of the right, allied in a *bloc national* and led by the ex-Socialist Millerand. In the feverish dawn of victory after a night of misery and bloodshed, the right wing, which had stood for the fight to a finish and total victory, was bound to win. The name of Clemenceau – père la Victoire

as the newspapers with a typical touch named him – was itself almost a guarantee of success.

The first signs now appeared, also, of a new trend which
was to exert a sinister influence on French politics during
the inter-war years. Henri Massis, who, as one of two
journalists writing under the name of 'Agathon' before the
war, had purported to show by various pseudo-scientific
inquiries that the youth of France was moving towards
Catholicism and patriotism, and so had played a part in
stimulating such a movement, continued his pre-war propaganda with the issue, in July 1919, of the Manifesto of the
'parti de l'Intelligence', and followed this up in the next
year by founding a review with a Fascist bias. This was
premature. The only political group which as yet went as
far as this in its sympathies was the Action Française, which
had very slight electoral success though Léon Daudet was
elected for Paris.

Behind such literary guerrillas the big battalions of the
right were moving into action. The heavy industries of
France had long been organized in close cartels, the most
famous of which was the Comité des Forges, established in
1864. Closely linked with the big banking interests, and
together largely controlling national finances through the
Regents of the Bank of France, they were able to bring a
powerful influence to bear on the elections. Their principal
aims were, first, to maintain the military power of France
and her armaments, in which patriotism, a wise scepticism
about the stability of the European situation, and a not un-
natural concern for profits were happily combined; and
secondly, to make sure that they did not have to pay by
higher taxation on wealth for the achievement of their first
aim. A third object, which was also the main propaganda
theme, was the defence of civilization against Communism,
symbolized by a brilliant placard of a bandit with a ferocious
countenance gritting a knife between his teeth.

In the cause of electoral victory, the conservative parties
dropped the old struggle of clerical and anti-clerical, with

the aid of a piece of meaningless verbiage: this said that 'Secularization must be compatible with the liberties and rights of all citizens whatever their religion.' The left, on the other hand, was more than usually divided. The Radicals were alarmed at the rise of Communism and suspicious of the Communist sympathies of part of the Socialist party, which was itself split into those who clung to Socialist orthodoxy and those who followed the lure of Leninism. Finally, for this election a system of multi-membered constituencies was adopted. Supposed to give a fairer proportional representation, in fact it exaggerated the swing which would have occurred in any case away from the left-wing and pacifist Chamber of 1914. Grouped in the Bloc National, the parties of the right won 433 seats, against a mere 86 Radicals and 104 Socialists. It was a new *Chambre introuvable*, called the *Chambre horizon bleu*.

One of the earliest actions of the new Chamber was to turn on its creator. When Clemenceau posed his candidature for the presidency on the end of Poincaré's term in February 1920, Briand got his revenge for 1917 by organizing the election, against Clemenceau, of Paul Deschanel, an amiable nonentity who was President of the Chamber of Deputies. The nationalists voted against Clemenceau because they were discontented with Versailles, and the Catholics out of alarm at the thought that if he died in office, as was not impossible considering his age, the presidential funeral would be a secular one. This was an important factor, for in 1919, for the first time under the Third Republic, France had a Chamber in which there was a majority of practising Catholics. It made possible the negotiation of an exchange of envoys between Paris and the Vatican. The pre-war alliance of nationalism and Catholicism was cemented with the canonization by Benedict XV of Jeanne d'Arc, in the presence of a large contingent of French parliamentarians. The sky-blue Chamber played its part by making her fête day into a national holiday. None of this would have been possible under Clemenceau, but after his rebuff in the presidential election he had withdrawn from office, to be succeeded by Millerand. However, in September 1920, only some six months after the election, his successful rival for the presidency, Deschanel, had to retire to a mental home. This unfortunate episode perhaps led the politicians to make the unusual experiment of choosing a strong President, in the person of Millerand himself.

Public attention, immediately after the war, was still largely concentrated on foreign affairs. Into the vacuum left by the collapse of the Central Empires, the forces of Russian Communism seemed to be advancing. The government of Millerand took what might well be considered a decision of major historical importance when, in the summer of 1920, it sent Foch's right-hand man, Weygand, to fight the battle of Warsaw. This turned the tide in Eastern Europe, but though the Communist armies were thrust back the attempt to intervene in the Russian Civil War proved a disastrous failure. The best that could be produced was a *cordon sanitaire* across Eastern Europe, a sort of Iron Curtain, destined to be revived in reverse some thirty years later, when it was the East that feared the contagion of Western ideas rather than the reverse.

Suspicious, and rightly so, of the reliability of American or British guarantees, France looked elsewhere for possible support against an eventual revival of German military power. Since the Russian Empire lay in ruins and an alliance with a Communist state would anyhow not have been contemplated, treaties of mutual support were concluded with the successor states to the Austro-Hungarian Empire – Czechoslovakia, Yugoslavia, and Rumania, united by their common interest in preserving the new territorial arrangements in what was called the Little Entente. A Franco-Polish treaty was subsequently added to the French system of alliances, which looked formidable on paper. What was not realized was that no combination of however many small states could equal one great state. The strength of the French system was the strength of France, no more and no less. It would survive so long as France had the strength and the will to defend her allies and herself. That she would have this hardly anyone questioned in 1920. Indeed, already in Britain and America voices were being raised against the bellicose militarism of a country that had committed the unforgivable crime of winning, at the price of unprecedented sacrifices, a war that had been forced upon it.

While the government was devoting much of its attention to the problem of security, the French people set about the hard task of rebuilding their shattered land and economy. Within seven years the ten depopulated and devastated departments of the North-east had been restored to normal activity. Unfortunately reconstruction, like arms and military interventions, costs money, and the bankers and industrialists of the Bloc National, as well as their lesser clientele in the propertied classes, were determined not to foot the bill. The current expenses of the war had been met by borrowing at home and abroad and by printing notes. It was easiest to continue the same system, putting all that could not be paid for out of revenue into a separate budget, and hoping to meet it by the receipt of reparations from the Germans. These were not finally settled, and the French share of the fairy gold not determined, until April 1921.

Meanwhile there was a weary and fruitless round of international conferences, at which Britain and France, particularly in the persons of Briand and Lloyd George, manoeuvred for financial and diplomatic advantage in the name of justice and international peace. Franco-British relations were also complicated by a little struggle they were waging in the Near East. Having agreed, by the secret Sykes–Picot agreement of 1916, on the partition of the Turkish Empire and implemented the agreement by the Treaty of Sèvres of May 1920, the two Western Allies were split by the resurgence of Turkish power under Kemal Pasha, when Kemalist armies drove the Greeks, who had invaded Asia Minor with British aid and encouragement, into the sea at Smyrna. When the Turks advanced on the Allied lines guarding the Straits at Chanak, the French concluded an armistice and withdrew their troops. Although a settlement was eventually reached in the Treaty of Lausanne in 1923, it was only after Franco-British relations had been strained almost to breaking point.

In January 1922 the strong man of the conservative parties, Poincaré, took office with the task of collecting reparations. When, after a year, he had failed to do so, in January 1923 he sent a French army into the great industrial complex of the Ruhr to collect them on the spot. French attempts to encourage Rhineland separatism, German passive resistance and sabotage, the final collapse of the German mark, all having produced nothing save an as yet unnoticed crop of dragon's teeth, France had to recognize that the Poincaré experiment had failed. The problem was thrown back again on an international conference in November 1923. This produced the Dawes Plan, by which credits were to be extended to Germany for the restoration of her economy in the present, on the strength of which the Germans promised to begin reparation payments at some date in the future. France liquidated the Ruhr adventure and in the spring of 1924 Poincaré accepted the Dawes Plan in principle. The belief that reparations would balance the French budget was now patently an illusion and the national finances were on the point of collapse.

Reflected in these muddied waters the colour of the 'sky-blue' Chamber of 1919 looked a good deal less attractive, and it was due to face the electorate in the course of the coming year. The elections of 1924 were to be conducted in a very different atmosphere from those of 1919, one of disillusionment with the policy of glory and the iron fist. The name of Poincaré was not the vote-catching bait that the name of Clemenceau had been. Of course, we must be careful not to give an exaggerated impression of the change in public opinion. As in all the elections of the Third Republic, an extensive shift in the balance of parties in the Chamber came about without any equally extensive change in the electorate. The transfer of votes from right to left was comparatively slight. The most important development was that the right was now split. The failure of its domestic and foreign policy had, naturally, brought disarray to the ranks of the Bloc National; and there was a revival of the antagonism of Catholics and anti-clericals, the cabinets of the sky-blue Chamber having gone rather too far for the latter in their concessions to Catholic opinion. On the other hand, Radicals and Socialists managed to form for electoral purposes a Cartel des Gauches, which the Communists were not yet strong enough to weaken seriously. Given the electoral system of 1919 a small change-over in votes could bring about a much greater change in the membership of the Chamber. The Cartel des Gauches won 270 seats against 210 to the Bloc National, with about 50 of the Gauche Radicale in the middle, and a flanking group of some 30 Communists. It was not a safe majority but sufficient to enable the Cartel des Gauches to take over the government.

4. CARTEL DES GAUCHES

THE first objective of the victorious Cartel was to drive Millerand, identified with the Bloc National first as its leader and then as President, out of the Élysée. The new Chamber voted, almost as soon as it met, that his continuance as President was a threat to the Republic. To enforce this view the majority went on strike and refused to form a ministry while Millerand remained President. Within a fortnight he had been forced out, though the Cartel failed to replace him with its own candidate, Paul Painlevé, and had to see the moderate President of the Senate, Doumergue, elected. The Radical victims of the purge of 1917, Caillaux and Malvy, were rehabilitated, and as a gesture to the Socialists the ashes of Jaurès were transported to the Panthéon.

The leader of the Radicals, Édouard Herriot, formed the first Cartel government. Solid and serious in mind and body, as befitted a man who was to be elected and re-elected *maire* of Lyon for a whole generation, Herriot had unshakeable patriotism and a genuine desire for the well-being of the ordinary provincial Frenchman, of whom he was so obviously one. Modest in his origins, lacking *panache*, but having a pipe, a friendly smile, and intellectual and artistic tastes, a sentimental turn of mind and real political shrewdness, what he lacked was a cutting edge to his mind and an appreciation of the fact that France had to come to terms with the twentieth century. But even if Herriot had been less of a politician and more of a statesman the political balance of forces in France would have denied success to the Cartel des Gauches. The left was now to show, what was repeatedly to be demonstrated, that it could only hold together during an election, and that the problem of agreeing on a policy in office was more than it could manage.

Politically allied to the Socialists, in basic social ideas the Radicals were far removed from them. Both the strength and weakness of the Radicals can be seen in the writings of the teacher of philosophy who wrote under the name of Alain. Our only programme, he declared in his *Éléments d'une doctrine radicale* in 1925, 'is to have no other ideal than government in conformity with the will of the majority'. 'The *élite* is worthless. . . . Because it is destined to exercise power, the *élite* is destined to be corrupted by power.' 'What I call liberty is the close dependence of the elected on the elector.' 'In a democracy, not only does no party have power, but even better, there is no power properly speaking.' Basically, radicalism believed in reducing government to a minimum, which was a recipe for failure at a time when political and social problems were urgently demanding positive action; but it suited the peasant proprietors, small employers, and shopkeepers who voted Radical and who represented a great vested interest in economic backwardness.

The partners of the Radicals in the Cartel, the Socialists, naturally had a much more positive attitude towards the economic functions of government, though they shared the faith of the Radicals in political democracy. But they were in a weak position because, since the Russian Revolution of 1917, they had to face the growing threat of a Communist party, always ready to outbid them and taking full advantage of the traditional republican *mystique de gauche*, the principle of 'no enemies on the left'.

For the hopes of the left in France, and therefore for the prospect of social reform, the Russian Revolution was a disaster. In the beginning, of course, it aroused strong socialist sympathies. The French Socialist Party, which had been agitating against French intervention in Russia, sent two representatives to the Bolshevik Congress of 1920 in Moscow. There they were presented with Lenin's twenty-one conditions for membership of the Third International. These conditions were bound to exclude a large proportion of the Western socialists. This was their object, for Lenin, in adherence to the blanquist technique he had adopted, was concerned to secure the adhesion of a ruthless revolutionary *élite* rather than the sheep-like masses and their idealistic leaders. When the emissaries returned and presented the terms laid down by Moscow to the Congress of the Socialist Party at Tours in December 1920, they were rejected by the established leadership. The socialism of Jaurès, declared Jean Longuet, cannot go to Moscow with a cord round its neck and ashes on its head. A leading role in the debate was taken by the brilliant Jewish technician and intellectual, Léon Blum. He saw that the Moscow theses represented a reversal of existing Socialist theory and involved the creation of an occult party directory controlled from Moscow. When he went on to declare that Socialists should defend their country against aggression, this provoked an outburst of pacifist sentiment and cries of '*À bas la guerre*'. The pro-Communist faction under the returned emissaries, Cachin and Frossard, carried the day by a three to one majority.

The victorious majority set up the French Communist Party, which retained control of the Socialist Party organization and funds and its daily paper, *L'Humanité*. On the other hand, as an attempt to capture the political *élite* of the Socialist Party the Leninist manoeuvre, though it had been brilliantly executed, missed its mark. Most of the Socialists on local bodies and at the head of the local parties remained faithful to the traditional leadership and policy, and only 13 out of 68 of the Socialists in Parliament joined the Communists. In spite of a concentrated attack, the Communists failed to consolidate their victory. As early as 1924 the situation of majority and minority had been reversed, and by 1932 the Socialists could poll nearly 2,000,000 votes against a Communist 800,000. There was a similar reversal of fortunes in the trade union movement. The Communist Confédération Générale du Travail Unitaire (C.G.T.U.) began with the support of some 500,000 trade unionists, against 370,000 who followed the Confédération Générale du Travail. By the early thirties, however, the C.G.T.U. had only some 300,000 against the C.G.T.'s 900,000. The real significance of the schism was that it created two left-wing parties in bitter rivalry with one another. Henceforth the presence of the Communists on their left prevented the Socialists from cooperating whole-heartedly with the Radicals, for fear of losing their own clientele to the former. The Communists could always employ the emotional appeal to the tradition of revolution, and there was an ample supply of social grievances and injustices in French society to provide motivation for a revolutionary party. In pursuance of well-considered Russian policy they concentrated their fire on the Socialists.

The division between Socialists and Radicals, along with the guerrilla attacks of the Communists on their left, provide the fundamental reason for the failure of the Cartel des Gauches. In addition it had inherited major problems in the colonies, and was to create problems in France for itself which precipitated its collapse.

Since, after they had disposed of Millerand, almost the only other policy that the parties of the left had in common was anti-clericalism, an attempt was made to maintain their cohesion by that rather dried-up cement. The time and the place for applying it were both ill-chosen. The Vatican had just, after several years' negotiation, approved of the setting up of religious associations to operate under the laws of Separation, despite the opposition and delaying tactics of the extremist bishops appointed in France by Pius X. Instead of welcoming this as a step towards recognition of the Republic and its laws, the government of Herriot, under the influence of a rather old-fashioned, dogmatic anti-clericalism, attempted to withdraw the French representation at the Vatican and to extend the laws of Separation to the regained territory of Alsace-Lorraine.

The restoration of the lost province of Alsace to the Gallic bosom from which it had been so roughly torn some fifty years earlier had not proved as easy as had been anticipated in the first flush of patriotic emotion. In particular, language presented an administrative and educational problem, for the language of the province was the Alsatian dialect, supplemented usually by German, but with very little French. Again, in the German Empire Alsace had possessed a decentralized local administration. After its return to France, a High Commissioner was appointed to supervise a cautious reintegration with the French state. The process had been too slow for the parties of the left. They were anxious to introduce the Laws of Separation, to substitute lay for Church schools, and to impose French as the medium of instruction. Local Alsatian opposition to these measures took the form of an Autonomist movement, which seemed for a short period to be assuming dangerous proportions. Fortunately, as difficulties accumulated the government's enthusiasm for forceful assimilation declined and it reverted to more gradual methods.

It is not possible to assess the connexion between the revival of anti-clericalism and the increased militancy, which appeared at the same time, of the Catholics. A National Catholic Federation was founded in 1924 under the presidency of the monarchist General de Castelnau, with the right-wing *Écho de Paris* as its organ. Just as anti-clericalism was identified with the left, so Catholicism was with the right. Among the spokesmen of the Church militant were such future Nazi collaborators as Philippe Henriot and Xavier Vallat. The conflict of Catholicism and anti-clericalism, which had always had strong political overtones, was now largely a cover for social and political enmities.

A major part in the association between French Catholics and right-wing politics was played by the influence of the Action Française, which in the twenties acquired an astonishing domination, which nothing in its intellectual content seemed to justify, over Catholic writers and intellectuals. Its journal was alleged to be widely read in Catholic seminaries, where the anti-semitic racialism in which it specialized was appreciated. At the same time it kept nationalist sentiment at fever pitch, played on xenophobic emotions and did all it could to prevent a Franco-German *rapprochement*. For this, among other reasons, Pius XI, who had aspirations towards international reconciliation, determined to discipline the movement by bringing out of its pigeon-hole the condemnation of 1914. It turned out that this had been mislaid in the Vatican archives, perhaps not entirely by accident; but despite strong opposition within the Church the Pope remained firm in his resolve to deal with the movement. Following the method employed in starting the Ralliement, he used a French cardinal, the Archbishop of Bordeaux, to initiate the attack. Many French Catholics, including the neo-Thomist journalist, Jacques Maritain, sprang to the defence. Polemics between the Action Française and the Vatican became increasingly bitter, until, late in 1926, the condemnation of 1914, now rediscovered, was published. It was reinforced by a ban on the journal, and a declaration from the French Church condemning the leaders of the Action Française as 'men who, by their writings, have put themselves in opposition to Catholic faith and morality'.

Maurras's gladiators now turned their almost unmatched

powers of vituperation against Rome, which retaliated with punitive measures against priests suspected of sympathizing with the movement. In 1928 episcopal regulations prohibited adherents to the Action Française from receiving religious rites, such as those for marriage or burial. All this was less effective than might have been supposed, for many priests, as well as laity, sympathized with Maurras and his ideas and gave only a half-hearted adherence to the orders of Rome. However, the circulation of the *Action Française*, which was the life-blood of the movement, shrank to about half of what it had been before the ban was imposed.

Communists and Action Française as yet had only a nuisance value in the history of the Republic. They were not strong enough to bring down the Cartel des Gauches. That was achieved by its own mistakes. The treatment of Alsace was one of these. A second difficulty, and one which it had inherited rather than created, was presented by the colonies. In Morocco the rebel chief, Abd-el-Krim, had been in arms since 1921; he was only to surrender in 1926. For the disastrous events in Syria, the one French mandate which had emerged from the Franco-British Near Eastern imbroglio, the government of Herriot was largely responsible. Unlucky on the Western Front, unlucky in the Balkans, Sarrail still remained *par excellence* the republican general. As such he was sent to replace the Catholic Weygand in Syria. His bad luck had not deserted him, for a revolt broke out in Syria in 1925 and Sarrail found himself in the position of bombarding his own capital, Damascus. The situation was never more than temporarily redressed and the revolt dragged on until 1936, when France promised the Syrians independence, though not at once.

The crucial difficulty for Herriot's government, however, appeared at home. The illusion that the huge gap in the French budget would be filled by reparations died hard. It provided an excuse for the wealthier classes, represented by the parties of the right, to resist any increase in direct taxation, and the parties of the left to oppose increases in indirect taxation. The only alternative was inflation. As the national debt rose the value of the franc sank. By 1926 the pound sterling, which itself had not preserved its 1914 value, stood at 243 francs. The parties of the right and the big financial interests, which had no desire to see the Cartel overcome its difficulties, waged a violent campaign to discredit its financial policy. The millions of small property-owners and investors saw their savings vanishing, and employees their real wages shrinking. The Herriot cabinet, incapable of agreeing on any policy to meet the crisis, broke up. Caillaux, brought back from political ostracism as the former financial genius of the left, found himself out of touch with post-war politics; Briand employed his skill at building bridges in vain; and the franc continued to fall in value. The public was increasingly restive. There were demonstrations before the Chamber of Deputies. The Cartel, it began to be felt, had shown itself incapable of governing.

The centre groups which had so far supported the Cartel, though not very enthusiastically, now withdrew their support. The Chamber turned again to the one strong man and elder statesman it possessed, Poincaré, who formed a government of national union including a galaxy of leading politicians – Herriot himself, Briand, Barthou, Painlevé, Tardieu, Louis Marin. Poincaré was given power to deal with the financial crisis by decree-laws – the first admission that the French parliament might be unworkable in a crisis. It enabled him to restore confidence by the fairly simple method, which could never have been put into effect by the ordinary legislative process, of increasing taxes and reducing expenditure. The large part played by speculation in the collapse of the franc was shown by its rapid recovery from 250 to 125 to the pound sterling. With the return of confidence in the government, the real wealth of the country was shown by the ease with which the loans issued in 1926 were absorbed. The small property-owners, whose suspicion – not unjustified – of the financial policy of the Cartel had caused the crisis, were reassured by the name of Poincaré.

It was a guarantee of social conservatism, financial orthodoxy, and republican order. To the Socialists and Radicals, constitutionally suspicious of hard economic facts, the financial catastrophe which had brought them down seemed the result of a deep-laid plot. They saw themselves as the victims of the *mur d'argent*, erected as a barrier against social progress. And so in a sense they were; but it was a plot in which the great mass of small property-owners of France were fellow-conspirators. With the restoration of confidence in the government, financial improvement during the next two years, from 1926 to 1928, was amazing. The 3 per cent *rentes* rose from 48.25 to 67.60 francs, the balance of the Treasury in the Bank of France was multiplied by sixty, and the franc was stabilized at 25.52 francs to the American dollar.

Meanwhile the Cartel des Gauches lay shattered in fragments, and only the approach of new elections could put it together again. It reunited temporarily in 1927 to pass a new electoral law, restoring single-member constituencies with a double ballot, which was expected to be more favourable to the left; but the elections of 1928, held under the influence of the financial success of the Poincarist experiment, proved a disappointment. The Communist Party was not yet in a position to secure many seats for itself, but it was strong enough successfully to pursue a wrecking policy. That doctrinaire intolerance which, for example, forbade its members to be freemasons, was called into operation. Under instructions from Moscow, there were to be no electoral pacts. The Party consequently maintained its candidates at the second ballot, securing only 14 seats with over a million votes, but handing over some 60 or 70 seats to the parties of the right, which won 330 seats out of 610.

There was now open war between the Socialists and Communists. The Socialist leader, Léon Blum, was the son of a wealthy manufacturer from Alsace. He had passed into the highest ranks of the French bureaucracy, and at the same time made a distinguished literary reputation with dramatic criticism, a work on Stendhal, and another on marriage which shocked the bourgeois. He entered Parliament in 1919 and almost at once came to the front. Not a great orator, with a shrill and unimpressive voice, Blum held his leading position by his elevation of character and power of intellect. He had played a leading role in meeting the challenge of the Communists at the Tours Conference of 1920, and never ceased to regard them as the confirmed enemies of social and democratic ideals. He believed that the unity of the workers had as its necessary condition the destruction of the Communist cadres. In fact neither Communists nor Socialists were likely to make much headway in the late twenties, when economic prosperity and progress were at last returning to France.

International tensions also were beginning to relax under the careful diplomacy of Briand, who, becoming Foreign Minister in April 1926, was to continue in the same post, apart from a gap of two days, until 1932. The climate of Versailles had now passed away. Belief in total victory no longer survived. French military predominance would evidently not last for ever and the need for another basis of French security was beginning to be felt. Briand looked to the League of Nations for the machinery of a peaceful consolidation of the *status quo*. After the Ruhr episode France did not wish to find herself again, in peace or in war, *tête à tête* with Germany. It was therefore necessary to bring back Great Britain into the European balance. The first attempt to do this, the Geneva Protocol of 1924 and the consequent disarmament plan, was wrecked by the British government of Baldwin; but the Locarno agreements of 1925 led up to the admission of Germany to the League of Nations in 1926. Briand devoted his last years to the noblest work of his life – the attempt at a genuine reconciliation with Germany and the creation of a peaceful international order. The greatest difficulty, the fog of reparations which had spread like a miasma over the international scene, seemed at last to be dissipated when the plan named after the American banker, Young, was accepted by both France and Germany in 1930. It was followed by the French evacuation of the Rhineland, five years before the appointed time.

5. THE HEY-DAY OF THE LEAGUES

BUT already at this high noon of inter-war hopes ominous clouds were gathering. In October 1929 occurred the Wall Street crash, from which all the disasters of the following decades date. This destroyed the recent reparations settlement even before it had been put into practice. Under pressure from the American President Hoover, a moratorium was imposed on the payment of reparations by Germany, while at the same time Hoover insisted on the payment of the war debts that France owed to the United States. Another cloud also darkened the prospects of Franco-German reconciliation. In 1930, hard on the heels of the last French soldier leaving the Rhineland, 107 Nazi followers of Hitler took their seats in the Reichstag. The failure of Briand's efforts was already written in the realities of the international scene and nothing he or France could have done would have prevented it. In 1931, with Doumergue's term as President ended, Briand had hoped to crown his long service to the state with the highest of its offices. Once again the most distinguished was rejected. Paul Doumer, who was chosen, was to be assassinated by a mad Russian in May 1932. Briand, disappointed, worn out, and ill, was already dead. He was replaced at the Quai d'Orsay by Pierre Laval, not yet seen as quite the significant figure he was later to appear.

By 1932, when a new Chamber was elected, the world slump had not yet seriously affected France, nor had the deterioration of the international situation become a major factor in domestic politics. The reversal of electoral fortunes was therefore to be attributed to different considerations. Four years in opposition had brought the Radicals and

Socialists together again, while the Communists, obedient to the policy of isolation and *poing brandi contre le parti socialiste* continued to lose support. Right and left were still, in votes, extraordinarily evenly balanced, but given the system of a second ballot a small change could alter the complexion of the Chamber drastically. Radicals and Socialists, along with their smaller partners, now held 334 seats, while the right won 257 and the Communists, benefiting from no electoral alliances, a mere 12. The Radicals and Socialists had again won an election. Their misfortune, during the inter-war years, was that each time they achieved an electoral victory – in 1924, 1932, and 1936 – the swing against the right occurred, naturally enough, when its policies, or world conditions, had brought France to the eve of a grave economic or financial crisis. The left was thus repeatedly presented with the need for taking decisions which either it could not take, or which, if taken, almost inevitably destroyed its naturally weak cohesion.

The majority of 1932 came to power in a France which had resisted the effects of the world economic crisis better than most countries. The apparent immunity of France from world economic diseases was however an illusion. By 1933 there were 1,300,000 unemployed and both agriculture and industry were in difficulties. Herriot, called to office by the new President, Lebrun, a worthy political hack who had replaced the assassinated Doumer, had once again to face economic problems of the kind with which his majority was least fitted to deal. This time, with his former unhappy experience to warn him, he made, as is customary, the opposite mistake. Determined not to be swamped by the flood of inflation as in 1926, he chose a rigidly orthodox Minister of Finances, who drew up a budget on the homeopathic principle of orthodox finance, by which the remedy for the evils of deflation was yet more deflation. Expenditure was to be reduced by cutting the salaries of civil servants, reducing ex-service pensions, and closing down public works, and revenue increased by taxing consumers' goods. The whole policy amounted to a direct attack on the interests of the electoral clientele which had voted the government into office. This was more than the parliamentary majority could stand: it therefore rejected at the outset of the new parliament the financial proposals of its own government. The right, on the other hand, thoroughly approved of the policy of deflation but had no intention of helping Herriot to apply it; far better to allow the left to sink in a morass of its own making, and the national finances along with it, so creating a situation to which the Radicals and Socialists would almost inevitably react with opposed policies. After the left was hopelessly split, the right might regain its influence in the Assembly, and finally return to power on a wave of public disillusionment with the left. This programme was almost too successful. Despite his failure to secure the passage of his government's budget, which at least represented a policy even if a mistaken one, Herriot continued in office, though for what purpose was not very clear since he now had no policy.

It was a financial question, though of a different nature, which brought down his government before the year was out. Reparations, which had been troubling the international scene and causing periodic disturbances on the national stage since the end of the First World War, now made their final appearance. The Young Plan, which came into operation in May 1930, had scaled down reparations to what was believed to be a practicable level. The world economic crisis made it an impracticable one. In June 1931 Germany had declared her inability to pay the forthcoming instalment of reparations. President Hoover announced in the following month a moratorium for one year on international debt payments. France, which had just paid a half-yearly instalment on her war debt to the United States, was not quite convinced that the timing of Hoover's proposal was all that might have been desired on the highest principles of international justice, but under American pressure acceded to it. Many Frenchmen suspected that this was a way of ending reparations, and it turned out that they were not wrong. Inter-allied debts still remained, and with the conclusion of the moratorium in 1932 France was called on to pay another instalment on her debt to the United States. Herriot invited the Chamber to authorize the payment. This was to fly so obviously in the face of a bitterly anti-American public opinion, as well as of the views of the majority in parliament, as to lead one to speculate whether he was simply seeking an excuse to get out of office without exposing the fundamental divisions in the left which had in fact made his position untenable. Inevitably he was defeated and resigned.

His successors were no luckier, for French politics had now reached an *impasse*. The cabinet of the independent Socialist, Paul Boncourt, lasted barely a month. Another Radical, Daladier, survived from January to October 1933 by abandoning the attempt to get any financial proposals through the Chamber. When, in the autumn, he at last had to present them, and tried to insist on plans which included a six per cent reduction in official salaries, the Socialists overthrew his government. The government of another Radical, Albert Sarraut, was brought down a few weeks later for the same reason and in the same way. Yet another Radical, Camille Chautemps, succeeded Sarraut, and under him Daladier's not very drastic proposals were at last agreed to, the Socialists walking out of the Chamber before the vote to avoid the responsibility for either supporting the proposals or else overthrowing yet another government.

The repeated slaughter of cabinets had already provided an opportunity for Communists and Fascists to concentrate their fire from left and right on the incompetence and corruption of republican politics. The calendar seemed to be turning back to Boulanger and Panama. Indeed, at the psychological moment, in the autumn of 1933, a new affair did in fact break on the political world. A shady financier named Stavisky, who for years had kept one step ahead of the law, not without the aid of influential acquaintances in the world of high society and politics, at last overreached himself. He floated a loan of millions of francs worth of bonds, allegedly to finance the little municipal pawnshop of Bayonne. This was too ambitious a trick for one who was not really in the first class of financial wizards, and as the bonds began to appear, Stavisky had only one recourse left, to disappear. Tracked to the other side of France, he shot himself in January 1934. Continuing the traditional pattern the Radical premier, Chautemps, tried to hush the matter up. The parties of the right, equally traditionally, alleged that Stavisky had been murdered to prevent him from betraying the names of his influential protectors. Compared with château-bottled affairs like Panama or the Union Générale, the Stavisky affair was small beer, or at least *vin ordinaire*, but circumstances allowed it to develop, or be built up, into a major political crisis. Under the lead of demagogues of the right such as Philippe Henriot, deputy for Bordeaux, the forces of anti-semitism and the old Catholic suspicions of Radical freemasonry were evoked. Ministers who had been connected with Stavisky were driven from office, and Chautemps, himself not the purest of the pure, had to resign.

His place was taken by Daladier, another Radical. Son of a small-town baker in Provence, Daladier, who before entering politics had been a history teacher, had the appearance and manner of a real Jacobin of the Midi. Throughout his career he appealed to, and had the support of, the socially conservative but politically advanced peasantry of the South. Short and solidly built, with a Napoleonic frame and cast of countenance, he seemed a strong man; and a strong man was needed, for the situation was rapidly getting out of hand. The police had been as uncertain and divided in their handling of the Stavisky affair as the politicians. Indeed there were grounds for suspicion that the Sûreté itself had been partly responsible for Stavisky's long immunity from prosecution. When, however, the police official charged with the investigation was found dead on a railway line, tied up and poisoned, the papers of the right attributed his death to murder at the hands of politicians whose complicity with Stavisky he had uncovered. A more probable hypothesis is suicide, arranged for personal reasons to look like murder.

However, the Paris Préfecture of Police, the great rival of the Sûreté, was safely on the other side of the fence. Its head, the Corsican Chiappe, was notorious for his right-wing sympathies. He was suspected, not without reason, of having tolerated or even encouraged demonstrations against the government. One of Daladier's first acts, therefore, was to dismiss him, though the effect of this gesture of strength was somewhat weakened by offering him as a consolation prize the Governor Generalship of Morocco. To reduce matters to the level of a farce, Daladier then dismissed the director of the Comédie Française, who had just produced *Coriolanus* with its patent incitement to anti-democratic demonstrations, and replaced him by the police chief of the Sûreté Générale. Whether at Chiappe's instigation or not, this proved the signal for an attempt at a right-wing *coup* on 6 February.

Of the leagues that joined in this Blanquist-type *putsch* from the right, the Action Française – still dragging its ever-frustrated followers like a long, attenuated snake through the Paris literary and political jungle, its leaders, Maurras and Daudet, still spitting poison from the head – deserves to be mentioned first, at least on grounds of seniority. Though ideologically the Action Française looked to the past rather than to the future, in its methods it set the pattern for the Fascist leagues that were proliferating in the thirties. Its supporters included many of the old gentry, or of those who aspired to be regarded as such, and it still kept the support of clerics whose political commitment exceeded their loyalty to Rome; but it also drew recruits from the professional classes, especially lawyers, doctors, and chemists, and from small businessmen, shopkeepers, and artisans, whose social and economic status was declining under new social pressures and who saw themselves as an *élite* under attack from the forces of egalitarian democracy and unegalitarian fin-ance. Jewish pre-eminence in the world of finance, joined to traditional religious prejudices, made anti-semitism the chief bond uniting these diverse groups. Cultural *snobbisme* drew literary aspirants to the *Action Française*, which provided a training-ground for the more vicious Paris journalists, many of whom, having served their apprenticeship with Maurras and Daudet, moved on later to the pro-Nazi papers. It still had some appeal to the University student population, which in France was traditionally polarized between ex-treme left and extreme right. But though it still attracted new generations of adherents, the Action Française belonged to the past rather than the future. It had shown throughout a remarkable inability to produce new leaders, and now Maurras at 66, Daudet at 67, were rather old to start a revolution. Indeed, the secular canonization of Maurras, and the recognition that he was not, after all, a literary genius, may be said to have been effected a few years later, in 1937, when he was elected to the Académie Française. The purely destructive nature of his propaganda had been demonstrated once again by the ineffectiveness of the Action Française in the elections of 1932. Moreover it now no longer stood alone as the representative of the revolutionary right.

After the First World War rival movements had begun to appear, though they did not crystallize until the victory of the Cartel des Gauches in 1924 offered a specific political challenge. Then Pierre Taittinger founded the Jeunesses Patriotes, wearing a blue raincoat and a beret, and drawing from the University some of the students who in an earlier generation would have been Camelots du Roi. The new model was provided by the Fascist movement of Mussolini. Coty, the perfume and cosmetics millionaire who used his wealth to promote French fascism, financed an anti-demo-cratic journal to which this would-be Marat of the right gave the name *L'Ami du peuple*, and founded the Solidarité Française. A smaller league was the anti-semitic Francistes.

Much the biggest was the Croix de Feu, an ex-serviceman's organization headed by a retired lieutenant-colonel, de la Rocque, who with a gift for mob oratory and wealthy if occult backers, turned it between 1931 and 1933 into a mass movement against socialism and internationalism.

Besides the agitation of the leagues, right-wing opinion was whipped up by the Paris press. In addition to the usual popular journals of the right, such as *Le Matin* and *Le Journal*, there sprang up a crop of venomous weeklies like *Candide*, xenophobic and anti-republican, which dated from the early twenties, *Je suis partout*, founded in 1930, and edited at first by the historical writer Gaxotte, and somewhat later *Gringoire*. These specialized in slandering politicians of the centre or left and outdid even *L'Action Française* in indecency and invective. The part played by the journalists of the right, many of whom ended as collaborators of the Nazis in the Second World War, in sapping the moral fibre and powers of resistance of the Third Republic can hardly be exaggerated.

The strength of the anti-republican movement lay in the concentration of so much of its strength in Paris, its weakness in its divisions and lack of any real constructive programme. The feverish excitement which the leagues and their journalists could whip up was itself fatal to the possibility of a cool calculation of tactics and chances, such as was needed for political success. Why they chose to act on 6 February must always remain a little mysterious. Certainly the projected revolution went off at half-cock. Perhaps the leagues themselves believed in the legend of Daladier as the strong man and felt a need to prevent his government from consolidating itself when it met the Chamber on that day; perhaps they thought they could capitalize on the dismissal of Chiappe and use him as a martyr; perhaps they were just carried away by the wave of emotion they themselves had stirred up. An organized attack on the Chamber must have been planned, for the forces of the various organizations were summoned to meet on the evening of 6 February at varying rallying-points and at times which would enable them to converge simultaneously on the Chamber of Deputies. What was especially sinister was the presence, among the assault groups, of the Communist-controlled Association Républicaine des Anciens Combattants, summoned to the fray by an appeal in *L'Humanité*.

There was nothing secret about the preparations either for attack or defence. Police had been massed across the bridge leading from the Place de la Concorde and on all the other routes of access to the Chamber of Deputies. As the forces of the leagues gathered, pressure on the forces of law and order built up. The confused history of some six hours of street-fighting between thousands of demonstrators, who lost 14 killed and over 200 sufficiently seriously injured to be taken to hospital, and about 800 police, whose corresponding losses were one dead and just under a hundred injured, need not be traced here. By midnight yet another Parisian *journée* had failed.

It is not possible to say whether the threat might or might not have been renewed. What we can say is that it could not have been as serious as it seemed at the time, for no more was needed than the resignation of Daladier and the formation of a centre government, including the leading parliamentarians, under the former President, Doumergue, for the agitation to collapse. The Communists organized a bloody street affray of their own on 9 February at the other end of Paris, but the object of this could not be ascertained, except in so far as it was intended to efface the memory of 6 February when they had fought side by side with royalists and fascists in an attempt to overthrow the Republic.

The new government restored confidence but it restored nothing else. The economic crisis continued. Doumergue, aged, vain, and mediocre, rapidly demonstrated that he was not another Poincaré. He began a series of wireless addresses to the nation which discontented his colleagues, whose disillusionment was completed by his attempts to promote constitutional changes which would increase the powers of the Premier. In principle this was badly needed, but Doumergue was not the man to exercise such powers, nor were the political parties ready to concede the measures that might have strengthened the executive. His cabinet of national union collapsed under the strain, and the usual shift to the right that occurred in the latter years of the life of a Chamber continued with the accession of Laval to the premiership.

6. POPULAR FRONT

THE most important consequence of 6 February was the traumatic effect it had on the French left. At any time after the sky-blue elections of 1919 France ought, if the balance of social forces and political opinion had been adequately represented, to have had a government of the moderate left. The conflicting social ideals of Radicals and Socialists, as well as the differing sectional interests they represented, along with the wrecking policy of the Communists, stood in the way of this. It is tempting to say that the shock delivered by the attempted *coup* of 1934 brought the parties of the left to their senses and forced a broad collaboration on them, but this did not happen at once. The French Communist Party continued its bitter attacks on the 'criminal policy' of the Socialists, and rebuffed attempts at a *rapprochement* from the Socialist left. The change when it came was the result not of internal but of foreign developments. The triumph of the Nazis in Germany belatedly aroused the Russians to a realization of the international consequences of the line they had laid down for foreign Communist parties. It is, of course, rarely possible to say of a switch in the policy of any Communist party how far it was the result of a directive from Moscow, or how far the local party may have taken the initiative. In practice this was not a matter of much significance. Wherever the change in the party line originated, the fact is that the Communist policy of treating the

Socialist Party as the first enemy was tacitly suspended. In June 1934 the French Communist leaders proposed joint action against Fascism. Despite Socialist suspicions an agreement was reached in July for common political action.

From February 1934 to April 1936 French politics seems to bifurcate into two distinct and separate streams. On the one hand the parties of the left were struggling to rebuild on a broader basis, taking in the Communists, the twice-shattered Cartel des Gauches; on the other, a series of governments leaning to the right had practically given up the attempt to cope with the internal social and economic problems of France, but were still attempting, though with almost total lack of success, to stem the rapidly advancing tide of international disaster.

The process of uniting the left was slow and painful, but the Communists were now as persistent in wooing the other parties of the left as they had formerly been, and were later to be again, in vilifying them. The hand of friendship was extended to include the Radicals. In July 1935 Daladier, Blum, and Thorez addressed a combined meeting of their three parties. The great Bastille Day procession of 14 July 1935 saw three or four hundred thousand Socialists, Communists, and Radicals marching together through the streets of Paris. With that concentration of attention on the problem of political power that Lenin had taught them, the Communists were pressing for a working political alliance as the first step. Blum and the Socialists, on the other hand, insisted that the formulation of a common policy must precede such an alliance. By January 1936 it was possible to publish the programme of the Popular Front. This called for a return to the system of collective security and the consolidation of the recently concluded Franco-Soviet pact; for the dissolution of the Fascist leagues, along with other internal political changes; and for an extensive programme of economic and social reform. Its slogan was 'bread, peace, and liberty'; and its enemy was identified as the 'two hundred families' – the reference being to the Regents of the

Bank of France, taken to symbolize, or indeed to embody in fact, the power of organized wealth.

The long weary years of economic depression had prepared the country for drastic political change. Governments of the centre and right were obviously unable to cope with the economic difficulties of France. Laval, after the failure of Doumergue to repeat the success of Poincaré, had been given authority to restore the economic situation by decree-laws. He sent Parliament on holiday and engaged on a thoroughgoing policy of deflation, which naturally increased unemployment, decreased the wages of those who remained in employment, and disillusioned even many of the small property-owners who were the natural electoral clientele of the right. It is only fair to record that the Popular Front, fearful of antagonizing the small proprietors, also pledged itself against devaluation of the franc. Among leading politicians, Paul Reynaud was practically alone in being prepared to draw the logical conclusion to a generation of inflation by accepting the idea of devaluation, which merely won him vituperation from both right and left as the tool of international finance.

The continued appeal of the right to violence, which since February 1934 had been alarming moderate opinion, was responsible for an incident that occurred shortly before the elections of 1936. Léon Blum, on his way back from the Chamber, had the misfortune to encounter the funeral cortège of the Action Française historian, Jacques Bainville. Recognized by the mourners, he was seized on, and saved from probable lynching, though not from injury, only by the intervention of near-by building workers. Even the French courts could not ignore this, and Maurras, who had quite recently reminded his readers of what was their duty in such circumstances, was tried for incitement to murder and given a short prison sentence, which made him more of a hero to his supporters than ever.

While the right was continuing to demonstrate its irresponsibility and trying to create a revolutionary situation,

Thorez was cooing like the dove of peace, stretching out his hand – over the national broadcasting system – even to the Catholics, as brothers oppressed with the same burdens. The Communists' appeal was above all national and patriotic – '*Pour une France libre, forte, et heureuse.*' Only the leaders can have known how odd the appeal to liberty was from the followers of Stalin and presumably they did not care.

The new political alliance of the left had been well cemented by the time when the Chamber was dissolved. The elections of April 1936 were marked by a remarkable coherence among the electors of the Popular Front, and a corresponding disarray among the supporters of the right. The result was a shift of seats from right to left, which gave the Popular Front about 380 deputies against 237 on the right. Within the Popular Front the Communists were the principal gainers, with an increase of some 62 seats; the Socialists gained 39 and the independent Socialists 12. On the other hand the Radicals lost 43 seats, which was not calculated to ensure their continued loyalty to the Popular Front.

In spite of this big swing in representation, once again it must not be supposed that there was an equally marked change in the balance of political forces in the nation. In actual votes the parties of the right and the centre had only lost some 200,000 votes. The uneasy balance of strength which condemned the nation to permanent political instability therefore still survived. Indeed the omens for political stability were worse than ever. The right, baulked at the polls, began to turn even more to the thought of extra-constitutional action. The Action Française, in the person of a former Camelot du Roi, Eugène Deloncle, was to give birth to the Comité Secret d'Action Révolutionnaire (C.S.A.R.), whose members became known later as the 'Cagoulards' or Hooded Men from their cult of secrecy. In this respect they achieved more notoriety than success for it seems likely that the police had planted informers in their ranks from the beginning.

The largest of the leagues, the Croix de Feu, underwent a

series of curious changes. It had already, in October 1935, become a para-constitutional organization under the name of Mouvement Social Français. When, in June 1936, the new government of the left decreed the dissolution of the leagues, it formed itself into the Parti Social Français, aiming to gain power by electoral methods. This was equal to an acknowledgement of the failure of the revolutionary agitation of the leagues, made by the biggest and most powerful of them. The P.S.F. swelled in numbers – by 1938 it claimed three million members; but as it grew in size it diminished in significance. The failure of the leagues to achieve more than a nuisance value – admittedly very considerable – must however not be taken as evidence of the strength of the Third Republic in its last years; the weakness of French politics and society was a conservative clinging to the past, not an irresponsible adventuring into new ways.

The same lesson can be drawn from the failure of an attempt to organize the farmers for revolutionary action. Badly hit by the fall in agricultural prices, peasant discontent had been given leadership by Henri Dorgères, who founded in 1935 the Front Paysan, with a spear-head of Greenshirts as its fighting force. For a moment the Front Paysan seemed to present a serious danger to the régime, but it was only a transient one. A modest rise in prices in the autumn, a reaction against the outbreak of violence, and the traditional conservatism of the peasantry came into play again and Dorgères and his movement faded out.

What was more serious was the general discrediting of parliamentary institutions. Tardieu was writing a series of books against them. The cult of Péguy from one point of view represented the search for a *mystique* in place of *politique*. The left was not immune from these tendencies. Indeed in the long run the dissident and crypto-revolutionary movements of the left were to prove more dangerous than those of the right. A group of disillusioned Socialists, led by Marcel Déat and the mayor of Bordeaux, Adrien Marquet, proclaimed the bankruptcy of Marxism before the problems of the twentieth century and formed a schismatic party of neo-Socialists. Their appeal to nationalism, call for the restoration of authority, and hostility to parliamentary methods, would indicate, even if we did not know of their later record as collaborationists with the Nazis, their kinship with Fascism and National Socialism.

The blue-eyed boy of the Communists, Jacques Doriot, mayor of Saint-Denis and leader in the Chamber of Deputies, impressed by the rise of Hitler, was also looking for a new path. In 1934, after a premature demand for an alliance of the parties of the left, which was then still anathema to the Communists, he split with the party. Instead of accepting the official policy he began a campaign to change it. Summoned, with his chief opponent, Thorez, to the arbitrement of Moscow, he refused to go. Thorez returned with authority to deal with Doriot, who was expelled. In the elections of 1936 he managed to hold his fief of Saint-Denis against his former party, in rivalry with which he founded the Parti Populaire Français. The new Chamber was to contain ten dissident Communists under Doriot, and twenty-six neo-Socialists.

As leader of the largest party and also of the middle party in the coalition, the premiership in the new government naturally fell to Léon Blum. He came into a troubled social situation as well as a depressed economic one. The victory of the Popular Front aroused hopes that the agitation for social reform, frustrated for over a generation, was at last to reap its fruits. In a sense the workers of France might be said to have staked out their claim to a share in the rewards of society, as well as its labours, over a century earlier, in 1792. After nearly a century and a half of frustration, they were determined, to adopt the words of Carlyle, not to have their pockets picked, once again, of a millennium – though indeed their demands were more modest and more practical than that. Some impatience was natural and no political agitation need be hypothesized to account for it.

The elections of April–May 1936 were immediately

followed by an outburst of strikes in the aircraft factories of the Paris region. They were a spontaneous reaction to the electoral victory of the left and took the Communists themselves by surprise. Though the Communist Party had declined to share in the responsibility of the government it had played so large a part in making, it was not prepared to smash it at the outset. The traditions of the French industrial workers, not Communist propaganda, were responsible for the utopian belief of at least the more militant among them that the factories were to be handed over to them to run. Until this happy consummation they proposed to occupy them passively. As sit-down strikes spread from industry to industry, the economic life of the country was brought almost to a standstill. The first task of the new government was therefore by the restoration of industrial peace to start the wheels of production turning again.

A conference of representatives of employers and trade unions was held at the Hôtel Matignon, the Premier's official residence, where alarm at what seemed a revolutionary situation extracted revolutionary concessions from the employers. The larger industrial enterprises, of course, were those that were mainly represented and these were more prepared to recognize economic and political realities than the smaller propertied classes. On 9 June the Matignon agreement was signed. By this there was to be a rise on an average of 12 per cent in wages, which was to be accompanied by an increase in the pay of civil servants; armaments works were to be nationalized and government control extended over the Bank of France. Perhaps the most valuable and permanent gain, and one which in the long run was to have far-reaching social consequences, was the achievement of the *congés payés* – holidays with pay. The most risky was the introduction of the forty-hour week. The employers recognized the right of the trade unions to represent the workers and in return the unions withdrew their claim to direct action, which was tacitly to repudiate the occupation of the factories. Both sides agreed to start discussions for collective agreements. The Matignon settlement was a triumph for Blum; the workers rightly believed that they had made great gains, though spasmodic strikes continued into 1937, and the propertied classes were relieved to have escaped from a threatening situation.

The new reforms were rapidly put into effect. The only problem that remained was how to pay for them. The answer was by the expansion of government borrowing, the full extent of this being concealed by the old expedient of putting part of the deficit into an 'extraordinary budget'. The parties of the left had so often in the past attributed the inflationary result of government policies to the machinations of the men of wealth who knew how to escape from its consequences or turn them to their own advantage, that they had come to believe that this was the only cause of inflation. Blum had tied his hands in advance against effective remedial measures by committing himself to maintaining the gold value of the franc. Consequently the increasing disproportion between internal and external prices, combined with the continuance of industrial unrest though on a less massive scale, and fear of Communist influence on the government, began another flight from the franc. On 1 October 1936 the government swallowed its pledges and reconciled itself to what had been inevitable from the beginning, and would have been much more efficacious if done then: it devalued the franc in terms of gold. This did not have the stimulating effect on French economy that was expected. Production – partly because of the introduction of the forty-hour week – was much lower than it had been in 1929 and unemployment remained high. The financial crisis continued to be acute.

By March 1937 Léon Blum had come to feel that the only way to restore confidence was to proclaim a 'pause' in the reforms of the Popular Front. This merely encouraged the attacks of its enemies, who were determined to drive it out of power at whatever cost and so to have their revenge for the fright they had been given and the concessions that had been forced from them. The bitterness of the opposition to Blum's government was shown in the vicious attacks on the Minister of the Interior, Roger Salengro, mayor of Lille and deputy for the Nord. An old Communist slander against him, of desertion in the First World War, was taken up by one of the most venomous of the journals of the right, *Gringoire*, and the subsequent press campaign drove him to suicide. At the same time, the international situation, which must be dealt with in the next section, continued to exacerbate the domestic situation.

Blum had trouble from his nominal supporters as well as from his opponents. The 'pause' gave the Communists, and even more the militants of the Socialist left, an excuse for attacking his government. In the usual way the extreme left and right played into each other's hands. A party of some 200 Croix de Feu, with their women and children, attended a demonstration at a cinema, held rather unnecessarily in the working-class suburb of Clichy. They were attacked by a Popular Front counter-demonstration. Police opened fire and the resulting casualties gave the now re-united and Communist-controlled C.G.T. a reason for calling a twenty-four hour general strike. Apart from this, industrial peace was still very unsettled. Sporadic strikes continued to break out, like a smouldering heath-fire, in town and country. The middle classes, already bitterly resentful at what seemed to them the arrogance of their inferiors in a country where consciousness of class distinctions was acute, found their usual seaside and country resorts swamped by hordes of workers in the summer of 1937, leaving for the first time on *congés payés*. It seemed like a new barbarian invasion.

To complete the troubles of the government, despite the devaluation of the previous year there were renewed signs of a flight from the franc. The leaders of industry and finance were recovering their confidence. Influential papers like *Le Temps* and *Le Journal des Débats* were largely under their control, and the state of public opinion made a counter-attack on the weakening and divided Popular Front possible. The rumour began to spread, 'better Hitler than Blum'. Even apart from this agitation, it seemed to Blum that some assertion of governmental strength was needed to redress the economic situation. The index of industrial production, 140 in 1929, was still only 101 in 1937; and unemployment remained at the level it had reached in 1934. Since he knew that his majority would never vote the measures he thought necessary, in June 1937 Blum resorted to the old expedient of decree-laws with the intention of establishing control of the exchanges. The Radicals in the Chamber of Deputies accepted the proposals, knowing that they could rely on the Senate to emasculate them. In the upper chamber, the old president of the Financial Commission, Joseph Caillaux, launched a bitter attack in the name of financial orthodoxy, thus performing the last public act in a career marked throughout by an extraordinary capacity for political misjudgement. The Senate, by excluding exchange control from the scope of the decree-laws, delivered the *coup de grâce* to the government of Blum, as it had to that of Herriot in 1925, so far had the upper house risen from its insignificance in the early days of the Third Republic. Blum resigned. For the third time an electoral victory of the left had been reversed within two years of the election.

With the forces of organized wealth thus conciliated, and the left once again shattered by its own internal stresses, weak Radical governments were able to take over, while the financial sky brightened and the propertied classes basked in a final and imbecile euphoria. Unfortunately finance was no longer what mattered most. The economy of France remained in a state of chronic weakness and needed drastic treatment. Even if they had been prepared to give it or the country to support them, the last governments of the Third Republic had little time left in which to attempt a reform and little attention to spare from the international situation.

It is tempting to trace the economic malaise of France between the wars to the effects of the First World War. Approximately 1,300,000 Frenchmen had been killed, apart from the injured, and France seemed a nation of old men, widows, and *mutilés de guerre*. This was partly the reason why, by 1938, it had 140 persons in 1,000 over 60, compared with, say, Holland's 94; and why the death rate was 150 in 10,000 as against 107 in the United States and 117 in the United Kingdom. By 1939 the population of France was practically what it had been in 1913, and even this figure had only been reached with the aid of massive immigration. By 1936 the foreign immigrants numbered 3,000,000, bringing needed, though usually unskilled, labour with them but also creating serious social stresses. The decline in population was most obvious in the countryside, especially in the agriculturally poorer areas of the Massif Central, South-east and South. The balance of population, which at the beginning of the century had been roughly 42.5 per cent urban to 57.5 per cent rural (i.e. living in communes of under 2,000 inhabitants), had changed by 1936 to 52 per cent urban and 47 per cent rural. Although the social consequences were bitterly deplored, the decline in the numbers of small uneconomic farms was little loss, but the productivity in proportion to the number of agricultural workers was still only half what it was in Great Britain. The number fed for each agricultural worker was 5.1 in France as against 14.8 in the United States. French farming was preserved in its state of inefficiency, and prices were kept far above the world level, by a long-standing policy of protection. In the summer of 1939 the price of wheat in France was three times its price in London. The electoral pressure that could be exercised by the rural constituencies prevented any attempt to allow French prices to come closer to the world level. One of the most powerful pressure groups was that of the sugar-beet growers, whose surplus production the state had to purchase at an uneconomic price for conversion into fuel alcohol.

In industry, as well as in agriculture, the small scale of production was a cause of economic backwardness. For each active worker British industry commanded nearly three times as much horse power and American nearly five times as much as French industry. There were, of course, signs of modernization appearing here and there. Hydro-electric power was being developed, though it was not as yet put to much industrial use. André Citröen had introduced American methods of mass production into the manufacture of motor-cars, but this was practically an isolated example. The powers of finance and industry, gathered in great associations such as the Comité des Forges or the Bank of France with its fifteen Regents and Council of 200, formed great monopolistic groups, which operated behind the cover of the mass of small employers whose inefficiency helped to keep prices up and wages down and whose numbers provided a political clientele for use against left-wing governments. Even when reforming legislation, such as the social insurance laws of 1928 and 1930, was passed, the employers' associations were able by working up a press campaign against them largely to nullify their application.

In elections the left might win its victories, but the real power in the state remained in the hands of its enemies, not only in industry and finance but also in the professions and administration. Higher education, in lycées or universities or institutes, was expensive and scholarships were few. The Faculties of Law and the École des Sciences Politiques, the almost essential gateway to a career in the higher ranks of the administration, were conservative, Catholic, Action Française, or even Fascist in their sympathies. Economic backwardness and acute class conflict produced the political instability which repeatedly threatened the Third Republic between the wars with total collapse. Yet the danger must not be exaggerated. Neither economic nor political weakness brought the Third Republic down. This was the result of defeat in war and foreign occupation. All through the thirties a ground swell of international trouble had been rising and diverting attention from domestic problems, until it finally overwhelmed them and drowned the nation in the tide of war.

III

THE FALL OF THE REPUBLIC

I. THE QUEST FOR PEACE

BY 1937 French foreign policy lay in ruins about a nation that was divided in everything except the desire to avoid a second world war. Whatever the blame that may be attached to individuals and parties or even whole classes for the failures of French domestic policy, an air of fatality can be seen, in retrospect, to surround the development of international relations from the high hopes of 1918 to the total despair of 1939.

The peace of 1919, it was said at the time, was one that passed human understanding. It started badly, with American repudiation and British evasion of the guarantees promised to France at the Conference of Paris. In exchange the French fell back on their treaties with the Little Entente and Poland. For some years reparations dominated French policy. Conference followed conference round the more desirable resorts of Western Europe. The Ruhr adventure brought no gain. With the defeat of the Bloc National in 1924 more rational international policies emerged; but by this date the possibility – a real one in the years immediately after the war – of integrating a peaceful Germany into the structure of Western society had largely been dissipated, though it was another six years before this was to be inescapably evident. The Dawes Plan of October 1924 represented the first attempt to reduce reparations to serious economic proportions, and between 1924 and 1930 Germany paid nearly £400,000,000.

Reparations might have been more easily dealt with if the problem had not been tied up, practically if not logically, with the basic French search for international security. The ostracism of Bolshevik Russia, the isolationism of the American Republican party, and the weakness and folly of British Conservative governments, prohibited any solution. In September 1923 a draft treaty of Mutual Assistance was rejected by Great Britain. In 1924 the Labour government negotiated the Geneva Protocol. Generally welcomed by European statesmen, it collapsed with the defeat of the Labour government and the return of the Conservatives to power. The British rejection of the Protocol, for which the French press and statesmen had been passionately pleading, left France determined to maintain the practical safeguards she still had in the form of occupied territory and the allied mission of control over German armament.

Meanwhile German foreign policy came under the control of Stresemann and French under that of Briand. Perhaps for different reasons, they both desired a *détente* in Franco-German relations, and as the British Foreign Minister, Austen Chamberlain, was also prepared for a European solution to the international impasse so long as the commitment was not too high, the three powers signed a Pact at Locarno in October 1925. This was followed by the evacuation of the occupied zone of Cologne and the admission of Germany to the League of Nations with a permanent seat on the Council.

Even after the elections of 1928 had strengthened the French right, Briand remained at the Quai d'Orsay, attempting to build international peace on a Franco-German *rapprochement*, set – to guard against the undue predominance of Germany – in a broad European cadre. It might be argued that Briand carried the country with him for so long only by means of a calculated ambiguity, allowing the right to see in his policy a strengthening of the French system of alliances, and the left an extension of the Locarno treaties. That Briand was sincerely working for the preservation of international peace cannot be doubted; and he can hardly be criticized if his policy was also in the interests of French security. In September 1929 he proposed a European

Federal Union. In the same year a final attempt was made to put reparations on a practical basis. This was the Young Plan. In return for German agreement to the plan, France offered to evacuate her occupied zones of the Rhineland. In May 1930 ratifications of the Young Plan were completed. In June the last French troops left the occupied territory. Three months later the German elections were marked by sensational Nazi gains which carried the representation of the National Socialists in the German parliament from 12 to 107.

The French government, while not abandoning its pacific intentions, now began to turn back to more positive ways of strengthening its position. Military service had been reduced in 1928 from one and a half to one year, but to make up for the consequent decline in manpower the Maginot line had been begun, as a continuous defensive line from the Belgian to the Swiss frontier. These works were now pushed on more energetically. There was a move towards greater friendship with Soviet Russia, which, however, had the effect of weakening the Polish alliance; attempts were made to conciliate Italy; and the states of the Little Entente huddled closer together for protection. In 1931 France was still strong enough to veto a proposed Austro-German customs union. It was almost a last demonstration of strength.

The international Disarmament Conference, opening in February 1932, could not have begun under more unfavourable auspices. Briand's noble and far-seeing struggle to bring France and Germany together in friendship had obviously failed with the rise of the Nazis. He still struggled for an international solution, but this was just what his enemies on the right did not want. At the beginning of 1932 they drove him from office and robbed him of the reward of the presidency. Worn out and disillusioned, the cynical old roué who had given his last years to the noblest of illusions died. Neither he, nor anyone else, could have guessed that he had laid foundations which, after another generation of bloodshed and ruin, were to prove the only ones on which a tolerable future could be built.

He was replaced at the Quai d'Orsay by Pierre Laval –
only briefly, for Laval's day had not yet come – but it was a
symbol of the passage of France from an age of coherent
policies and ideals to one of temporary devices and oppor-
tunism. If circumstances in the coming years were too great
for the men who had to deal with them, the men were also
too small.

By a curious but quite natural reversal of positions, it was
henceforth to be on the left that the policy of resistance to
Germany was to find support, and the right that was increasingly to favour concessions. On neither side was there
any confidence in the future, though much of the kind of
facile optimism that was ready to seize on any straw. When,
in January 1933, Hitler became chancellor of the German
Reich and did not immediately declare war, fears momentarily faded. The Nazi leader, with his genius for telling the
right lies at the right time and his understanding of human
psychology, knew that, if people wanted to believe, the big-
ger the lie that gave them what they wanted the better. He
hastened to announce his devotion to peace and readiness to
sign any international agreements that would guarantee it.
Many on the French right, thus reassured, began to feel that
the Nazi accession to power might even be a good thing.
After all, they shared many of the same ideas. They had
been anti-semitic and opposed to democratic government
long before Hitler. They had the same enemies – Jews,
Communists, Socialists, democrats, internationalists. They
were equally prepared to use violence in domestic politics to
eliminate an 'ignoble parliamentarism'.

The French government was therefore prepared to accept
the Four-Power Pact, which Mussolini, playing on the
British Prime Minister's vanity, had sold to Ramsay Mac-
donald. By it, France, Germany, Italy, and Great Britain
were to form a sort of condominium of Great Powers to settle
the affairs of Europe. This was a way of by-passing the
League of Nations. It was also equivalent to delivering
notice to the smaller states of Europe that their fate was

likely to be settled over their heads. It is extraordinary that the French right should have been so ready to come to terms with the Fascists and Nazis, and so anxious to deliver a blow to the hated League of Nations, that they failed to appreciate that they had also gone a long way to undermine their own cherished system of alliances. The Four-Power Pact was signed in July 1933. In October Germany walked out of the disarmament conference. Still the French right, which had never wanted disarmament, refused to see the writing on the wall, while the left pathetically continued to believe that Nazi Germany was only a transient phenomenon which could not really survive in the twentieth century.

A strong and coherent foreign policy could hardly have been expected from the series of weak Radical cabinets which followed one another in 1933. The following year, opening with the crisis of 6 February, promised no better; but in the government of National Union under Doumergue a new Foreign Minister began a revival of French diplomacy. Louis Barthou was a politician of the right, but he was also a statesman of the old school, author – twenty years earlier – of the three years law of 1913. In a diplomatic tour of Eastern Europe Barthou reinvigorated the Little Entente and took the first steps towards a revival of the old Russian alliance. The new threat from Germany obviously demanded some such reply, even though it involved a danger of alienating Poland, which was already playing with the suicidal idea of saving herself by a separate arrangement with Germany. On the other hand Mussolini, alarmed at Nazi-instigated movements for a German *Anschluss* with Austria, showed signs of moving into the anti-German camp. The ground plan of a grand alliance was being sketched out by which a reborn aggressive Germany might yet be contained. Whether it could ever have been more than a sketch must remain in doubt, for in October 1934, when, as part of Barthou's plan, King Alexander of Yugoslavia paid a state visit to France, he and the French Foreign Minister were both assassinated by a Macedonian terrorist at Marseille. The hope of a revived French foreign policy was ended.

The successor to Barthou at the Quai d'Orsay was Laval, hardly the man to have become a dominant figure in the greater days of the Third Republic, but in his element when the fabric was rotting and crumbling on all sides. Son of a small-town butcher in poverty-stricken Auvergne, he came to the Faculty of Law in Paris, itself a great achievement for a poor boy. In Paris, before the First World War, Laval was a left-wing Socialist, his humanitarian ideals finding expression in voluntary service as a 'poor man's lawyer'. In 1914 he was elected as deputy for the Paris working-class suburb of Aubervilliers; and during the First World War one of the permanent motives which ran through his life appeared. This was the desire for peace at any price. As a young Socialist deputy he opposed the military service law. In 1917 he was a member of what was labelled the defeatist group in the Chamber, and in the nationalist elections of 1919 he lost his seat. Now began a gradual move to the right, which characteristically, aided by his natural camaraderie, he effected without losing his personal links with the left.

Laval's first move away from the left brought him into association with Caillaux and the Radicals. He supported Briand's attempts at a Franco-German *rapprochement*. He claimed, and probably genuinely believed, that ideologies or forms of government were irrelevant to foreign policy – '*les régimes se succèdent, les révolutions s'accomplissent, mais la géographie subsiste toujours.*' When he became Foreign Minister, however, although he continued the negotiations, begun by Barthou, for a Franco-Soviet pact, he delayed ratification as long as he could. In fact, although the negotiations were concluded in May 1935, the treaty was only ratified by France, after the fall of Laval, in April 1936. The other side of Laval's indifference to ideologies and ideals was his respect for strength, or what he took to be such, and it is probable that he already saw European peace as dependent on agreement with Nazi Germany.

Meanwhile Hitler was progressing from strength to strength. In January 1935 the Saar, under French rule for the past fifteen years, held the plebiscite prescribed by the Peace Treaty to determine its future and voted overwhelmingly for return to the Reich. In March compulsory military service was re-established in Germany. France was now facing the 'lean years' of 1935 to 1939, when the annual number of recruits, as a result of the First World War, would be halved. The period of compulsory military service was therefore extended to two years, in spite of the opposition of the Socialists led by Blum, who denounced the militarism and aggressive spirit of what was probably the weakest and most defensive-minded General Staff that France has ever had. If the Germans attacked, Blum declared, the workers would rise as one man to defend their class and country in a far stronger force than any conscript army – so completely was a most intelligent man humbugged by his own wishful thinking and historical legend. A young officer named de Gaulle, who was at this time trying to persuade both soldiers and civilians that tanks might be a better defence than either bare arms or big battalions, merely earned denunciation as a Fascist for having such dangerous ideas.

The imputation would not have been an insult to Laval, who was already negotiating with that other ex-Socialist, Mussolini. In April 1935 the conference at Stresa united France, Great Britain, and Italy in a declaration of resistance to any unilateral repudiation of the treaty agreements on which the European *status quo* was based. This might have been little more than a pious gesture if two months later the British government, living up to its reputation of *perfide Albion*, had not signed a naval agreement with Germany without consulting its allies. The line where stupidity merged into treachery in British policy was naturally a difficult one for the French to draw.

Meanwhile, however, the Italian dictator, looking for a little cheap glory, had decided on Abyssinia as a foe he could measure his troops against without undue risk, having prepared his rear in advance by the Stresa agreement. The Italian army invaded Abyssinia in the autumn of 1935. In spite of the reluctance of the Great Powers, the League of Nations could hardly avoid decreeing sanctions against such a flagrant international aggression. Opinion in France was hopelessly divided. The left saw in Mussolini's action yet one more example of the international menace of Fascism. Yet its pacifism was so deeply rooted that when British battle-ships were sent to the Mediterranean, Blum wrote an article under the heading 'England's Error', in which he made it plain that he was not prepared to go beyond economic sanctions. Even these were too much for the parties of the right, which, partly by natural affinity, and partly as a result of Italian propaganda and bribes, had adopted Mussolini's cause as their own. In September 1935 the *Action Française* published a list of 140 deputies who favoured economic sanctions against Italy, with the warning that if war resulted their blood would be the first to flow. The extent to which Fascist ideas had permeated the French intelligentsia was shown by a manifesto of solidarity with Italy signed in October by over 850 intellectuals. Laval, one of nature's go-betweens, persuaded the British Foreign Minister, Sir Samuel Hoare, to do a deal with Italy. Revealed to the British public, which looked upon right and wrong in the international scene with a less impartial and sophisticated eye than its government, the Hoare–Laval agreement produced an outburst of indignation. To save his government, the Prime Minister sacrificed Hoare in December 1935, and in January Laval himself fell, bitterly resenting what he regarded as yet another British betrayal.

A caretaker government took office to see out the last few months of the Chamber, and it was this government which was faced with what was perhaps the most critical decision in the whole of the inter-war period. In March 1936 Hitler denounced the Locarno Treaties, proclaimed the remilitari-zation of the Rhineland, and sent in a token force of German troops. Even at the time there were many who realized that this was a moment of destiny. The French premier, Albert Sarraut, a typical professional politician of the Radical Party, rather surprisingly favoured a military reaction by France. The Foreign Minister, Flandin, was intelligent enough to see the real importance of the crisis and also at first thought of positive action, in spite of the fact that the right was certain to shriek to the skies if there were any attempt to resist the Nazi move, to such a pitch of pacifist defeatism had their perverted nationalism reached. This reaction might have been discounted. More serious was the fact that the General Staff was not only imbued with right-wing ideas and ideologically more in sympathy with the Fascists and Nazis than with its own Radical government, but its military thinking and preparations, under the influence of Marshal Pétain, had become purely defensive. The lessons of the First World War, and the temperament of Pétain, both dictated a policy of defence, which had been given concrete form by the construction of the great Maginot line. Yet, though the French army in 1936 could only have taken the offensive by a drastic readjustment of its plans and redeployment of its forces, there is little doubt that the small army Hitler had committed to the Rhineland could have been thrown back, and that France still had a sufficient military superiority over Germany to defeat any possible German resistance.

The Sarraut government might have disregarded the opposition of the right and the unpreparedness of the military but for another and decisive obstacle. This was the attitude of the British government. Anthony Eden, who had taken Sir Samuel Hoare's place at the Foreign Office, might have been willing to support military intervention. The cabinet as a whole was unprepared for action; it seems probable that the decisive influence at this crisis, when the inevitability or avoidance of a Second World War hung in the balance, was that of Lord Halifax. Ambiguities in the Locarno Treaties provided the British government with a way of evading, with legality if not with honour, the action which even at the time some saw as the only hope of checking the rush to the Second World War. Though Sarraut and Flandin have had to bear the blame for their tame acquiescence in the remilitarization of the Rhineland, the greater responsibility lies with Pétain and the French General Staff for decisions taken years before, and with the British cabinet for the decisions it evaded at the time.

Hitler had succeeded in his greatest gamble. The result of the remilitarization of the Rhineland was the crumbling of the whole French system of alliances. The eastern allies drew the logical conclusion that henceforth France neither could nor would do anything to defend them if Germany attacked. Consequently they tried to come to terms with the Nazis. Belgium attempted to shelter from the coming storm by a declaration of neutrality, apparently having forgotten what was the value of its neutrality in 1914. The Versailles settlement lay in ruins. The French strategic position had been turned. During the next three years a steady retreat was to degenerate into rout and end in final collapse.

The Popular Front came into power when it was probably already too late to redress the situation. It is doubtful if it had the will to do so in any case. The Socialist Party, which was the dominant partner in the new government, had inherited deep-rooted pacifist instincts from Jean Jaurès, to whose memory Léon Blum constantly appealed. He was faced with a less decisive but more long drawn out crisis in the second half of 1936, in the shape of the civil war that had broken out in Spain. The left pressed for intervention to aid the Spanish republicans, the right passionately supported General Franco. Blum later declared that his reason for not helping the Spanish government in 1936 was that it would have brought about a civil war in France. This was perhaps to avoid the admission that the pacifism of the left was as strong a factor behind the policy of neutralism as the pro-Fascist sentiments of the right. British influence was also brought to bear on the same side. The result was that France watched passively while with German and Italian aid a new

Fascist dictator established himself on her Spanish frontier. Mussolini, who had flirted with Laval while it seemed to his advantage, now saw on which side lay the strength and concluded the Berlin–Rome axis.

Frustrated in its domestic policy and paralysed in foreign policy, the government of the Popular Front collapsed in June 1937. The natural history of left-wing majorities in the Chamber prescribed a gradual move to the right. The place of Blum was taken by Camille Chautemps, well fitted to follow a policy of hesitating compromises, while the international situation boiled up to its next crisis. In March 1938 Hitler achieved the *Anschluss* with Austria, when momentarily Blum was back in office. In the desperate state of affairs he envisaged a government of national union, but this was a weapon of the right, repeatedly used to block social change, not one that they were prepared to hand over to the leader of the left. All the long-nourished enmities of the right against Blum burst out and he was driven from office. His place was taken by the Radical Daladier, with a government now including Paul Reynaud and three other moderates. Once again Daladier could appear as the strong man of French politics, heading a government of national defence in a mounting domestic and foreign crisis. The Popular Front was a thing of the past.

2. THE DRIFT TO WAR

THE German *Anschluss* with Austria was followed by a Nazi agitation for the annexation of the German minority areas of Czechoslovakia. The weakness of France, and the inability of the government of Daladier to take any firm line of its own, were shown by the passivity with which it followed the British lead throughout 1938 and 1939. It is true that the Chamberlain government was providing France with an excuse for a policy to which it was condemned anyhow by the state of French politics. The level to which

Western diplomacy had now been reduced was demonstrated by the fact that it was being mainly conducted personally by Neville Chamberlain. On 15 September 1938, at Berchtesgaden, Chamberlain, under the pathetic illusion that he was purchasing peace, agreed to the cession of the Sudetan areas of Czechoslovakia to Germany. At Godesberg, soon after, he discovered that the price of the Danegeld he was prepared to pay – at the expense of another country, it is true – had suddenly been doubled. The patent treachery of Hitler produced a psychological shock and for the first time there were signs that Britain and France might, however unwillingly, be driven into resistance.

But now the mixture of pacifism and pro-Nazi sentiments in France emerged as a major influence over French policy. The Socialist Party was hopelessly split over the issue of resistance to the Nazis. Its secretary-general, Paul Faure, who led the pacifist wing, wrote articles against resistance in *Le Populaire*, while René Belin carried the C.G.T. and the trade-union journal, *Syndicats*, on to the same side. *Le Canard Enchaîné*, spoilt child of left-wing journalism, echoed British politicians in asking, 'What do we care if 3,000,000 Germans want to be German?' On the right the nationalists, fearing above all the menace of social reform and conscious of their ideological links with Fascists and Nazis, had completely abandoned the foreign policy of the twenties. The Action Française found itself in the happy situation of being able to combine '*À bas la guerre*' with 'Down with the Jews'. Flandin had a manifesto against war posted up in Paris. In the French cabinet a strong pacifist group included the Foreign Minister, Georges Bonnet.

In this situation the initiative was again left to the British government, which had no better idea than to propose another four-power conference. Chamberlain, Daladier, Mussolini, and Hitler therefore met at Munich on 29 September. The Western Powers once more yielded to threats and accepted the partition of Czechoslovakia. The Versailles settlement and the French system of alliances lay in ruins;

but when Daladier, who unlike Chamberlain knew what he was doing, stepped off the plane that brought him back to Paris, half-expecting to be greeted with hisses and brickbats, he was cheered by crowds who believed the menace of war had been lifted from them. Léon Blum wrote in *Le Populaire* that every man and woman in France would pay their just tribute of gratitude to Chamberlain and Daladier. In the Chamber the whole Socialist Party, with one exception, voted for the government. The Communist Party, which denounced the 'treason of Munich' – Russia having been excluded from the negotiations – thereby only saddled itself with the onus of being the war party. In December the German Foreign Minister, Ribbentrop, came to Paris to sign a Declaration of Friendship. All was well.

Meanwhile, though foreign affairs occupied the centre of the stage, there were still economic difficulties for the French government. In October Daladier had obtained plenary powers to deal with them. He appointed the dapper and self-confident little Paul Reynaud, a politician of the centre and opposed to the Popular Front, but also one of the anti-Munich section of the government, as Finance Minister. Reynaud produced plans for new taxation, a reduction in the number of government employees, and an increase in the length of the working week, with the object of restoring international confidence in the French franc. The C.G.T. proclaimed a one-day General Strike on 30 November in protest against these measures, and the Communist Party seized on it as an opportunity for a great demonstration of protest. But the life had gone out of the left wing, which was now also torn by bitter differences over Munich. Public opinion was against the strike. The railways and public services were requisitioned by the government to keep them working. When workers at the great Renault car works attempted a stay-in strike, *gardes mobiles* were sent in and cleared the factory by midnight. The strike was a total failure for the Communist Party, which had led it. The wealthy classes and international finance being thus reassured, the financial situation showed a marked improvement. Economic recovery still lagged in France, but of the social gains of the Popular Front not all had been lost. France thus entered 1939 with the appearance of restored social stability and under what seemed a strong government. In April 1939 Daladier secured the re-election of the mediocre but safe Albert Lebrun as President.

True, this optimism could only be preserved by scrupulously shutting one's eyes to everything that was happening outside France. Hitler and the Nazis were momentarily quiescent: experience should have suggested (yet to many it did not, to such a pitch had the habit of cultivating illusory hopes reached in the Western democracies) that this would not be for long. Mussolini was looking for more cheap colonial conquests, now at the expense of France. The Spanish Civil War was in its last throes, with France as hopelessly divided in its sympathies as ever. The left was still ignorant of the deeds of the Communist commissars against their political rivals in the republican ranks; and if a few Catholic writers, such as Mauriac, and Bernanos in his *Les Grands Cimetières sous la lune*, had raised their voices in protest against the deeds of Franco and his men, the French right as a whole rejoiced when Barcelona fell in January 1939 and the war was over. The rule by which French Chambers beginning on the left ended on the right was demonstrated when the same Chamber that had set up the government of the Popular Front voted by 363 to 261 for the recognition of Franco. France's most famous soldier, Marshal Pétain, was sent as ambassador to conciliate the new Spanish régime.

This Indian summer of the Third Republic was all too brief. The euphoria engendered by Munich lasted a bare five months. In March 1939 German troops occupied the rump of Czechoslovakia in disregard of the undertakings at Munich, while Great Britain and France watched helplessly. Daladier, true to his conception of himself, and the popular image of him, as a strong man, whereas in fact he was merely a well-intentioned one, had himself voted plenary powers. The British government of Chamberlain, at last beginning to understand dimly something of the situation into which it had led its country, tried to stem the rush to war by guaranteeing to support Poland against aggression. It was a sign of the state to which the French government had been reduced that Chamberlain had to speak for France as well as for Great Britain, though France was, of course, committed to go to the help of Poland by its treaty of 1921. Marcel Déat in *L'Œuvre*, the former Radical paper which was now subsidized secretly by the Italian government, asked if Frenchmen were to die for Danzig. Daladier cancelled this by issuing a statement supporting the Polish position in Danzig and French pressure forced Chamberlain to adopt a similar position. Meanwhile, his Foreign Minister, Bonnet, was negotiating behind the scenes with Italy.

Belatedly and reluctantly Great Britain and France came to realize that the only possibility of preserving peace lay in redressing the European balance by bringing in Russia. They sent a military mission to Moscow in August, but it was already too late. On 21 August the conclusion of a German–Soviet Non-aggression Pact was announced, but not the secret agreement for the partition of Poland. Bonnet was now feverishly trying to prevent war in the only way that remained, by persuading Poland not to resist. Daladier, on the other hand, was prepared in the last resort to accept the inevitability of war. On 1 September the Germans invaded Poland, and on 3 September Great Britain and France declared war on Germany.

The minister under whom France entered the Second World War was conscientious and intelligent, but, like his country, for the last five years Daladier had been following events without the power to control them. His vice-premier, Chautemps, a typical political middleman, had not emerged unscathed from the Stavisky scandal. The Foreign Minister, Georges Bonnet, had clung to appeasement as long as he could; he was moved to another ministry but remained in the cabinet. From the beginning it can hardly be said that the government was united on the conduct of the war, and the optimistic propaganda with which it concealed its own doubts did little to prepare the country for the trials to come. The pro-Nazi opposition was comparatively subdued at the beginning, though biding its time. The Communist Party also, discredited by the Hitler–Stalin pact, was not able to take strong action against the war at first; indeed, there were signs that patriotic sentiments were struggling with party solidarity. *L'Humanité*, in a confiscated issue of 26 August, carried the leader 'Union of the French nation against the Hitlerian aggressor'. However, the temptation of patriotism was largely removed from the party by the actions of the government itself. On 2 September the Communist deputies voted for the military credits; but on 26 September the Party was dissolved by law and all its publications banned. In January 1940 all the Communist deputies, many of whom had already fled or gone into hiding, were declared to have forfeited their seats. The indignation of the politicians and journalists of the right, many of whom were only too anxious to do a deal with Hitler, that Stalin, with world Communism behind him, should have done the same, rescued the party from the impossible task of trying to justify Russian policy to the country. It was able to go underground and prepare for the day when the last imperialist war would have ushered in the awaited revolution.

. The war, launched by a German *blitzkrieg* on Poland, began very differently in the West. In the Franco-Polish military conventions of May 1939 Gamelin had promised that, if Poland were invaded, France would attack Germany with the main body of her forces within fifteen days of mobilization. Even if the promise had been kept it would have been of little avail to Poland. The German armies were at the gates of Warsaw at the end of the first week, Russia invaded Poland in the middle of the month, and by the end of September Warsaw had surrendered. Meanwhile France had garrisoned the Maginot line and manned the Belgian frontier; and the British, moving more slowly than in 1914, had landed a small force of 80,000 men at the ports of western France, and were gradually organizing long lines of communication to the north-eastern frontier. France, which called up its conscripts rapidly, was even more backward than Great Britain in its material preparations for the war. Daladier had refused to set up a Ministry of Munitions in peace time, perhaps because it would have involved keeping industrial workers out of the army and so once more allotting to the peasants their traditional role as the major source of cannon-fodder. When such a ministry was set up, after the war had begun, it had to recall between 100,000 and 150,000 men from the armies. The 'business as usual' mentality also prevented preparations for rationing, which Reynaud as Minister of Finances urged while the Minister of Agriculture, Queuille, in the interests of the peasants, opposed.

Even those who were not defeatists believed that somehow or other the war would be a bloodless one for France. Safe within the Maginot line, the French troops would let the enemy army bleed itself white in fruitless assaults, while the Anglo-French blockade excluded the vital raw materials and slowly strangled the economy of Germany. The French and British armies, which had done practically nothing to assist the Poles, passively sat on the defensive waiting to be attacked. It was a *drôle de guerre* all that winter. After the Russian attack on Finland, on 30 November, there was more enthusiasm for aiding the Finns against the Russians than for fighting the Germans; and when the Finns, after a stubborn resistance, capitulated in March 1940, the outcry against Daladier brought his ministry down. He was replaced by Paul Reynaud, dapper, dynamic, optimistic. Daladier, with the Radical-Socialist party behind him, clung to the Ministry of Defence and saved the Commander-in-Chief, Gamelin, in whom he had implicit confidence, but Bonnet was at last eliminated from the cabinet. On the other hand, Paul Baudouin, who had been used by Bonnet in negotiations with Italy before the outbreak of war, was brought in as Under-Secretary to the Prime Minister. With the support of 268 votes, as against 156 opponents and 111 abstentions, Reynaud had a bare majority. To improve his position he obtained from Great Britain an agreement that neither state would initiate separate peace negotiations.

On 10 May 1940 the German army invaded the Low Countries. The French and British, abandoning their prepared positions, moved into Belgium to meet them. Reynaud took the opportunity to broaden his government by taking in more representatives of the right. It was the beginning of a trend that was to go much further than he expected. In spite of the strategic writings before the war of a minor French officer, de Gaulle, which had been passed over, like their author, by the French General Staff but carefully studied by the Germans, and the subsequent lessons of the Polish campaign, the *blitz* campaign that now descended on the allied armies took them by surprise. Holland and Belgium were rapidly overrun. The German offensive against France developed on the Meuse, south of Sedan, where the nature of the ground was supposed to prohibit it. By 15 May the debris of the French army of the Meuse was everywhere in retreat, the defences of France had been breached, and the Panzer columns were ranging the French countryside.

The disaster gave Reynaud the chance at last to eliminate his enemy Daladier from the Ministry of Defence, though, conducting a stubborn retreat, the Radical leader only moved to the Ministry of Foreign Affairs. Reynaud, who took over the Ministry of Defence, at once removed Gamelin, who in the depth of his bureau had progressed from slow motion to almost total inaction. Weygand was called back from Syria to assume command of the lost battle, and Pétain from Spain to become vice-premier and chief military adviser to Reynaud.

In calling back these distinguished if aged figures from the past, Reynaud was aiming to restore the morale of the country, and in this he had a momentary success; but more than morale was needed to hold back the German onrush. The military situation was already out of the control of any general. Practically all trust between the French and British commands had disappeared. Politically, disillusionment was degenerating into recrimination and despair. The Western alliance was breaking up. The Belgian armistice let loose a flood of bitter invective against the Belgian king. In the Dunkirk evacuation the French troops found themselves left to the last on the beaches while the British were evacuated first; it was taken as a sign of British desertion. On 9 June the Council of Ministers moved from Paris to scattered châteaux in the Tours area and on 4 June the German army entered the capital.

Weygand and Pétain were without hope from the beginning; they had come in as liquidators of a bankrupt régime, to bring hostilities to an end. For them the architects of ruin were the politicians of the Third Republic; but however devoutly they believed this, the defeat of France, it must be emphasized, was a military defeat. The French army had been launched into a war it was quite unprepared to fight, against a weight of armour and an air force that outclassed it, and tactics it did not know how to cope with. The military disaster gave their chance to the defeatist and pro-Nazi elements – Georges Bonnet and the 'Munichois', Faure and the Socialist pacifists, the Fascist and Germanophile groups strong in Paris and among the journalists, and the Communists demanding the end of an imperialist war. The new Minister of the Interior, Mandel, who had worked with Clemenceau and inherited some of his spirit, for the first time took strong action against the Germanophiles. But it was clear that the military defeat of France was total. The only question before the cabinet was how and by whom the fighting in France should be brought to an end.

Weygand was determined that France should leave the war and that the government and not the Army should have the onus of concluding an armistice. Reynaud, and those who supported him in the cabinet, wanted the military command to take the responsibility for the armistice, and were prepared to remove the government to North Africa and continue the struggle from there. On the other hand, Weygand, like Bazaine in 1870, was concerned to preserve an army in France to maintain law and order and repress the anticipated Communist rising. Both he and Pétain were also determined that the government should not leave the soil of France, and this was undoubtedly the view of the majority in both official and political circles. It would probably have been shared by the great masses of the people if, bewildered, harassed, overwhelmed, pouring in endless streams along the roads of France, or despairingly awaiting the next blow and not knowing from which direction it would come, they had been capable of having an opinion. Their one hope was in the man who had been summoned in the extremity to save France. Pétain, with the aloofness from immediate concerns and the impassive reaction to misfortune of extreme old age, was already thinking of the future, and the task, to which he believed himself called, of regeneration of a France weakened and corrupted by the ideologies of the left. Defeat was almost to be welcomed if it could bring this about.

On 14 June the government moved to Bordeaux, where the last scene in the tragedy was to be enacted. Relations with Great Britain, in a state of mutual misunderstanding and general confusion, were steadily deteriorating as the pressure for a separate peace increased. A group of ministers behind Chautemps now joined in the demand for an armistice. Outside the cabinet, Laval and his clique, including many who had belonged to the pro-German propagandist organization France-Allemagne, were intriguing. Reynaud yielded to the pressure and resigned on 16 June. Pétain was the obvious successor, and the next day the old Marshal broadcast to the nation a message in which he said that it was necessary to end hostilities and seek an honourable peace with Germany as between soldiers. This completed the demoralization of the Army.

It had still not been settled whether the government

should transfer itself to North Africa and continue the struggle from there. Twenty-four deputies, including Daladier and Mandel, sailed in the *Massilia* with the intention of doing so, only to be prevented from landing in North Africa, sent back ignominiously, and condemned as *fuyards* by official propaganda. De Gaulle, promoted general after a successful armoured engagement, and called back from the fighting to join the government as Under-Secretary for War on 5 June, made a dramatic escape to England and appealed for continued resistance, but only a handful joined him. On 22 June the armistice was signed with Germany in the same railway-carriage, at Compiègne, in which Foch had presented his terms to a German delegation in 1918. And on 24 June Italy, which had entered the war on 10 June when it was quite clear that France was safely beaten, and had conquered the outskirts of Menton, also concluded hostilities.

By the terms of the armistice France was divided into Occupied and Unoccupied Zones. The former covered the whole of the Atlantic and Channel coasts and included all the richer areas of western, northern, and eastern France. The French army was to be disarmed and demobilized, and the navy to be demobilized under German supervision. The latter condition aroused intense British suspicion that it would be handed over to, or seized by, the Germans. This suspicion, though natural, was unjust, for the Admiral, Darlan, was determined to keep the last card in his hand and sink the navy rather than give it up; but it was to lead to a British attack on the fleet of their so-recent allies at Mers-el-Kébir.

The two clauses in the armistice which gave Germany a stranglehold over France were the agreement for the payment of unlimited costs of an undefined army of occupation by France; and the retention in German hands of the great army of French prisoners of war until the conclusion of peace. No one – not even the Germans – saw the significance of these clauses, for no one believed that the war could last

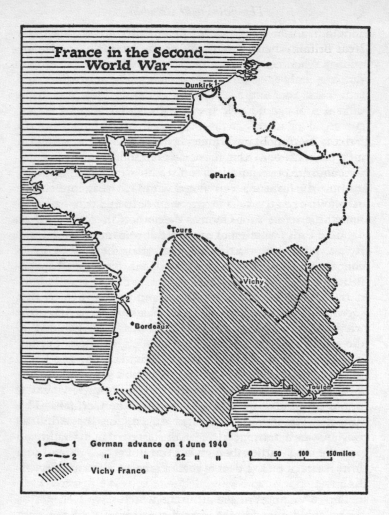

France in the Second World War

Dunkirk

Paris

Tours

Vichy

Bordeaux

Toulon

1 ——— 1 German advance on 1 June 1940
2 –––– 2   "   "   22 "   "

////// Vichy France

0   50   100   150 miles

more than a few weeks, or at most a month or two, now that Great Britain was left alone to face the irresistible German military machine.

3. VICHY FRANCE

WHILE metropolitan France lay plunged in a state of numbed confusion, the first reaction to the armistice of generals and governors in the French overseas possessions was one of refusal to accept defeat. Perhaps this represented an inability to face facts rather than determination to continue the struggle, for as soon as the news of the formation of a government under Pétain reached the colonies, with very few exceptions their authorities, both military and civilian, came into line. The most notable resister, General Catroux in Indo-China, was immediately dismissed. The tradition of hierarchical subordination to Paris, and the spirit of defeatism with which the French upper classes were permeated, prohibited any different reaction. This was also shown by the absence of response to General de Gaulle's broadcast appeal from England. His military career before the war had been injured by the publication of a prophetic book, *Vers l'armée de métier*, in which he had shown the conditions in which a future war would be fought. He seemed destined to be the advocate of lost causes. '*La France a perdu une bataille!*' he cried, '*mais la France n'a pas perdu la guerre.*' It fell on deaf ears. Pétain's authority was accepted inside France and throughout practically the whole of the vast French Empire. By a tacit but nation-wide plebiscite he was entrusted with the task of taking France out of the war.

The government of the Armistice, seeking for a suitable capital in the Unoccupied Zone, but fearful of exposure to popular pressure in a large town, moved to the health resort of Vichy, there to await the moment, which it believed could not be long delayed, when, the Germans having defeated Great Britain, the war would be over and Pétain and his ministers could transfer their authority back to Paris. They did not guess that Vichy was to be their home for far longer than they conceived possible, to become the symbol of many hopes and fears, and the visible centre and name of the ailments of a nation.

It would be a mistake to suppose that the Vichy régime began in the spirit of benumbed despair which was that of the average Frenchman after the military collapse of France. On the contrary, while some of its supporters, particularly among the right-wing journalists, even rejoiced in defeat because it had brought the end of the Republic, many more found at least a consolation in this consequence. Even the parliamentarians themselves were prepared fatalistically to accept what seemed to be the verdict of history. Convoked at Vichy in extraordinary session, the Senate voted with a single dissentient (the aged Marquis de Chambrun, descendant – perhaps he remembered – of La Fayette), and the Chamber of Deputies by 395 out of 398 present, for the revision of the constitutional laws. And now Laval came into his own. His feverish activity secured the almost unopposed suspension of the constitutional laws of the Third Republic and the establishment of the new régime. '*Laval*,' Pétain said of this period, '*a été inouï.*'

The first act of Pétain was to declare himself *Chef de l'État français*, thus avoiding the use of the term 'republic', a dirty word to his more ardent supporters. With the headship of the state he combined the headship of the government. In two days France passed from a parliamentary to a personal régime, reminiscent rather of Bonapartism than of royalism, despite the enthusiastic support from the Action Française which the Vichy government received. The essential and only cement of the new régime was loyalty to its head. We need waste no space over its constitutional arrangements; they were of no significance. The titular head was the Marshal, and the real government, from beginning to end of the Vichy episode, was the bureaucracy. The heads of the ministries were for the most part, since Pétain was suspicious of politicians, high officials. The problems they had to face were enormous – not least those created by the division of France into two zones. Their technical ability kept the machinery of state in operation, even in appalling conditions, though on a lower level of administration a deplorable collection of rogues and adventurers flocked into the ranks of Vichy, while at the centre there was only, in the words of the American ambassador, 'a feeble, frightened old man, surrounded by self-seeking conspirators'.

Many of the hangers-on of politics and fashionable society, who gathered at Vichy in the first winter, soon returned to Paris where the money was, as well as the Germans, leaving Vichy to pursue its dream of a National Revolution. This was conceived in terms of the campaign so long conducted against the Third Republic by the Action Française and more recently by the Fascist leagues. For many of the upper bourgeoisie, the officers of the army and navy, and high officials, defeat was the price paid for the sins of the Republic and at least it provided an opportunity for the creation of a new and better social and political order. A memorandum by Weygand called for an end to be put to the masonic, cosmopolitan, capitalistic state, to class war, demagogy, and the cult of pleasure, and a return to the principles of Religion, the *patrie*, and the family. In place of an egoistic individualism, the National Revolution put forward the corporative idea. This involved the dissolution of the trade unions and an attempt to replace them by professional corporations, in which the interests of employers, workers, and the state would all be represented and reconciled. Though, in practice, this never amounted to more than the bureaucratic control of industry, it would be unfair to deny the existence of a genuine desire for social reform. It found expression in laws, only very partially applied, introducing old-age pensions and physical training of the young, and penalizing alcoholism. Decrees making divorce more difficult and favouring large families reflect the increased influence of the Roman Catholic Church, which provided strong support for

Pétain's government. An attempt to restore religious control of education ran into serious opposition, and a labour charter was also of very limited practical effect.

Vichy was more successful in destroying than in rebuilding. The ending of the parliamentary régime was followed by the abolition of elected local councils in all communes of over 2,000 inhabitants. The leading politicians of the defunct Republic, including Daladier, Blum, Vincent Auriol, Jules Moch, Reynaud, and Mandel, were interned; but when a small group, including Daladier and Blum, was, after many postponements, tried at Riom in the spring of 1942, the defendants were able to turn the hearings into a debate over the causes of the defeat of France. So much discredit was cast on Pétain and the General Staff by the evidence, that the trial was stopped and the case never reached a conclusion.

The anti-semitic tendencies of the French right found expression, as early as October 1940, in a law excluding Jews from all positions in government service, teaching, and state-subsidized industries, from managerial positions in the press, radio, and cinema, and fixing a quota for their entry into the liberal professions. The Action Française had been relieved of the papal condemnation on the eve of the war. Pius XII, almost as soon as he ascended the papal throne, in February 1939, began negotiations and the ban was lifted in July. This made little difference to its influence and none to its policy. The defeat of France and the fall of the Republic should have seemed to Maurras as though, at the end of his life, the gates of the Kingdom were being opened; but the old man had lived too long with his hates to forget them now. Published in unoccupied France, the *Action Française* intensified its campaign for the exclusion of Jews, freemasons, and 'metics' of non-French parentage from the state services. Anti-semitic legislation gradually became severer, though it lagged far behind the standard set by the Nazis.

All this hardly amounted to a policy. Indeed, Vichy was too preoccupied with urgent economic and administrative problems to have much scope for applying one. Hordes of refugees and demobilized soldiers had to be returned to their homes, in spite of which nearly two million prisoners of war remained in German hands. Raw materials, machinery, and supplies of all kinds were requisitioned by the Germans and payment left to the French authorities. An artificial rate of exchange enabled the occupying troops to go through the French shops like an army of locusts. The cost of the occupation was assessed at the colossal figure of 400 million francs a day, while the division of France left the richer half, with 60 per cent of the cultivated land and 65 per cent of the industrial works, in the hands of the Germans. A British blockade closed the Atlantic and Channel ports. A bad harvest, made worse by the chaos of the summer of 1940 and the absence of labour, reduced the country, in the winter of 1940–1, to the verge of starvation. Faced with these conditions, Vichy had to introduce economic controls of a severity that France had not known since the government of the Committee of Public Safety, including rationing and strict control of wages and prices.

The greatest, indeed the only real asset of the régime was the name of Pétain, and the cult of the Marshal was promoted by all the usual devices of totalitarian propaganda. His photograph, in all sizes, was omnipresent. The *Marseillaise* of the National Revolution – *Maréchal, nous voilà* – was chanted all over the country by bands of youths and girls. Pétain made personal tours through the Unoccupied Zone in the autumn and winter of 1940–41. But though his cult was stimulated it was not created by propaganda. The country had greeted him, wrote *Le Temps* in December 1940, as a saviour. It believed he had saved the nation from revolution and social chaos. The Church surrounded him with an almost religious aura of respect. 'He is the incarnation of suffering France,' declared the Archbishop of Lyon, one might have thought a little blasphemously.

The personal qualities of Pétain in no way explain this almost mystical adulation. His name was linked with the defence of Verdun in the First World War and he had earned a reputation for humanity by his treatment of the mutinies in the French army. His disastrous influence on the General Staff during the inter-war years and his responsibility for the weakness of the French army were not known. The right-wing parties had had some success in building him up as a potential leader in the thirties, when the Fascist leagues also tried to make use of him. He was honest, unpretentious in his way of life, calm, and dignified, with an almost royal capacity for impassivity. Above all, he supplied the need that the average Frenchman felt in the hour of total defeat for someone to believe in, a saviour of society. His own mediocrity helped to fit him for the role, for he had neither positive qualities to stand in the way, nor the self-critical faculty which might have inhibited his adoption of it. 'I offer France the gift of my person to assuage her ills,' he declared in his first broadcast, revealing the vanity which was a marked feature of his personality. Apart from the normal prejudices of an army officer and a man of the right, Pétain had no political ideas; nor had he the mental capacity to control his cabinet or frame its policy. His actions were those of the group or individual which influenced him at the moment, though there were to be limits beyond which he could not be pushed in the direction of collaboration with the Germans.

The first illusion of Vichy was the belief that France, by accepting the Armistice, had succeeded in withdrawing herself from a world at war and creating a little oasis of peace. The conclusions drawn from this varied. There was a conflict between those, like Laval, who wanted France to enter the German camp at once and earn the reward for her prompt recognition of the new order in Europe, and those, like most of the supporters of the Action Française, who believed a policy of independence was still possible. While Laval's star was in the ascendant, Vichy propaganda was violently anti-British. The British attack on the French fleet at Mers-el-Kébir on 3 July 1940, under the belief that it might be handed over to the Germans, intensified the wave of anglophobia. Laval gave the impression of having been deterred from declaring war on Great Britain only by a total lack of the resources necessary for waging it. It is difficult, in fact, to believe that he was unaware of this, or that it was other than a manoeuvre to impress the Germans. His more serious plan for a reversal of alliances culminated in the famous interview which he arranged in a railway-carriage at Montoire, on 24 October, between Pétain and Hitler. The apparent triumph of Laval's policy was marked by his appointment, a few days later, as Foreign Minister, while Pétain, in a broadcast speech, proclaimed a policy of sincere collaboration with the Germans. Attempts have been made to present this Montoire policy as a subtle Machiavellian scheme for bringing about the defeat of Germany. This is nonsense; even after the failure of the German air attack on England, doubts about German victory hardly existed at Vichy. Collaboration was no deep-laid scheme for bringing France back into the war on the British side: it was what it called itself, collaboration.

The first blow to the hope of Franco-German reconciliation was dealt by the Germans themselves in their treatment of Alsace and Lorraine. Ruthless germanization of the two provinces was accompanied by the expulsion of up to 200,000 of their inhabitants, who were regarded as unassimilable. In spite of this Laval did not turn back. Under cover of the negotiations with the Germans, he was extending his influence over the government. To complete the process of capturing it, a plot was concocted in which the essential element was the return of the remains of Napoleon I's son, for burial at the Invalides. It was proposed that Pétain should go to Paris for the ceremony; and once there, it was not intended that he should be allowed to return to Vichy. Laval and the germanophiles would instead set up in his name a French government at Versailles under German control. The Marshal might have fallen into the trap, but the rest of the government, who had no desire to hand over control to Laval, organized a cabinet plot against him

and secured his dismissal. The first attempt at total collaboration had failed.

A struggle now began between the neutralists at Vichy,
conservative and Catholic in bias, and the ardent collaborationist politicians and journalists of Paris, drawn largely
from the extremist left- and right-wing politicians of the pre-
war Fascist leagues. Among these the most prominent were
the former Communist Doriot and the former Socialist,
Marcel Déat. In January 1941 they founded the Rassemblement National Populaire to advocate full cooperation with
the Nazis in the creation of the new European order.

At Vichy a period of governmental confusion after the fall
of Laval was succeeded by the rise to the chief position,
under Pétain, of Admiral Darlan, Commander-in-Chief of
the French navy from the beginning of the war. He had
managed to keep control of the navy. Undefeated, with its
prestige increased by exploits against the Germans before
the Armistice and against the British after, the French navy
was in good shape and morale. It supplied governors for
many of the colonies and administrators for Vichy France,
who provided an effective backing for Laval. In politics
Darlan was a complete opportunist. Like Laval, he had
decided that since the Germans had won the war, an understanding with them was the best policy, possibly for France
and certainly for his own personal ambitions.

The most important decisions with which Darlan was to
be faced in the course of 1941 were those affecting the
future of the French empire. The French West Indies and
Jibuti had remained under the control of governors who
supported Vichy. Indo-China, nominally governed by Vichy,
became perforce practically a Japanese base. In Syria a
High Commissioner of doubtful loyalty to Vichy was dismissed in 1940 and the former police chief Chiappe, who had
played such an equivocal role in the attempted *coup* of 6
February, was sent out to replace him. Chiappe was killed
when his plane was shot down and his place was taken by
General Dentz, who had to deal with the consequences of

the temporary success, in April 1941, of a pro-Nazi *coup* in Iraq. This made it necessary, if aid was to be sent to Iraq, for Germany to obtain the use of Syrian airfields. It was also desirable in the interests of the Axis campaign in North Africa for the Germans to be able to use French North Africa for supplies and transport. Darlan saw in this situation the possibility of a deal with Germany. In May 1941 he was received by Hitler at Berchtesgaden and out of the discussion emerged the May Protocols, giving the Germans military facilities in Syria and North Africa. What France got in return was so insignificant that the agreement can only be explained as an attempt by Darlan to buy German support for himself by showing that he could produce better results for them than Laval had been able to. The consequence was a British and Free French attack on Syria, which expelled Dentz and his troops. The other members of the Vichy government, alarmed at Darlan's apparent willingness to sell out completely to the Germans, called Weygand back from his governorship in North Africa to oppose him; and after Weygand's influence had been thrown into the balance the Protocols became a dead letter. The Germans had their revenge in November 1941, when they secured the dismissal of Weygand. They did not deal more firmly with the growing spirit of *attentisme* at Vichy – which was encouraged by continued British resistance, Axis defeats in the Mediterranean area, and the opening of a second front in Russia – because they were unwilling to pay the price of more effective French collaboration, and as yet unready to impose it by further exercise of force.

4. COLLABORATION AND RESISTANCE

FOR a year the situation in France remained essentially static, despite frequent changes in the personnel of Pétain's cabinet, in which Vichy seemed to be perpetuating the governmental instability of the Third Republic. What altered the situation was the German invasion of Russia in June 1941. Vichy was divided in its reaction. Pétain, in a broadcast, described the Nazis as the defenders of civilization against Communism. The Paris collaborationists were vociferous and organized an Anti-Bolshevik Legion, which received little active support. For the first time, however, a large body of opinion, even among the adherents of Vichy, now became doubtful of ultimate German victory.

The most important consequence within France of the German invasion of Russia was the development of the Resistance movement, which had hitherto operated on a very limited scale, though small resistance networks had been formed, mainly in the unoccupied zone. From the time of the Hitler–Stalin pact the French Communist Party had been the tacit ally of the Nazis. After the Armistice it called for fraternization with the occupying troops, denounced economic sabotage in the factories, and advocated collaboration on the basis of the German–Soviet alliance. The Nazis had not received these advances in the friendly spirit with which they were put forward and the Communist Party had to remain underground, but it continued to attack de Gaulle and the British imperialists. The outbreak of war between Germany and Russia changed the situation overnight. Former enemies now became allies. The Communist Party launched its militants into the Resistance with the advantage of possessing a widespread underground organization. They began with attacks on individual members of the occupying forces, to which the Germans replied by taking hostages, especially Jews, and shooting them in batches of fifty at a time.

Meanwhile, the stalemate between the Nazis, trying to get something for nothing, and Vichy, only willing to sell its aid at a price, continued. Both sides were becoming increasingly discontented with Darlan. Pétain himself was jealous of the Admiral's prominence and the pomp with which he surrounded himself. Laval, who had been negotiating with the Germans for his own return to power, at last convinced them that he could serve their purposes better than the Admiral. On 18 April 1942, therefore, Darlan was moved down to the post of Commander-in-Chief, and Laval became the head of a government which represented a more pro-Nazi orientation though it did not go as far in this direction as the Paris collaborationists desired.

Laval was still convinced of the inevitability of German victory. He had the intellectual limitations and the inability to escape from fixed ideas that often go with a capacity for successful intrigue. Before the Armistice he had made up his mind that the fate of France was bound up indissolubly with that of Germany, and that collaboration was necessary to the salvation of France and the restoration of peace. The one thread, apart from devotion to his own career, that runs through his life is a sincere and almost unqualified pacifism. This was what made him an ideal instrument for the Nazis. Moreover, convinced of the invincibility of the German military machine, he was determined that a Laval should not be found on the losing side. Back in office again, and more convinced of his own astuteness than ever, he picked up the threads of his policy where he had dropped them in December 1940. In a broadcast of June 1942, he burnt his bridges behind him with the notorious words, '*Je souhaite la victoire de l'Allemagne.*' That this was not a mere uncalculated gesture was shown by the phrase with which he concluded the sentence – '*car sans elle, le communisme s'installera partout en Europe.*' He saw the future of the world as determined either by Nazism–Fascism or by Communism and had thrown in his lot with the former.

The next turning-point in the history of wartime France came not in France itself but in North Africa. There, Weygand had been succeeded by General Juin, who continued the same policy of loyalty to Pétain. The Americans, meanwhile, had been preparing for a landing. Their representatives in North Africa had persuaded themselves, and the American government, of the existence of effective support for intervention. When the Anglo-American force reached

North Africa on 8 November 1942, it therefore expected to
be welcomed by a strong body of supporters. These hopes
proved false, and what at first sight seemed worse was that
Darlan himself happened by chance to be in Algiers. In fact,
his Machiavellian traits proved the salvation of the American expedition. Telegrams passed between Algiers and
Vichy. Their real import has never been established but it
seems probable that Pétain gave Darlan full powers to deal
with the emergency, though not necessarily expecting him
to do what he did. Impressed by the size of the American
armada, he switched sides and, followed a little belatedly by
General Juin, proclaimed a cease-fire. Opposition at Casablanca led to a short but sharp bout of fighting, after which
Morocco followed Algiers. Tunis, on the other hand, was
seized by the Germans. Darlan himself was not to profit long
by his change of sides. Some six weeks later he was shot. The
assassination seems to have been connected with a royalist
intrigue, but its motivation remains obscure.

The Germans reacted to the invasion of North Africa by
putting into operation a long-prepared plan for the occupation of the whole of France. What they wanted above all was
the French fleet, riding at anchor in the great naval harbour
of Toulon. On 27 November, after a promise that so long as
the French pledged themselves to defend the port and the
navy against Allied aggression it would be immune from
seizure, the German army pounced. Laval and the admirals
at Vichy played the German game loyally by sending orders
to Toulon to avoid resistance. But now at last Darlan was to
be justified. For two years the orders he had signed in 1940
for the sabotage of the French fleet to prevent it from falling
into German hands had rested in inviolable secrecy. Now at
last they were put into effect, and even faster than the German mechanized units could speed through Toulon, explosion after explosion sounded the death-knell of the last
great French navy.

November 1942 was the real end of Vichy and the
'National Revolution'. It was already little more than an

agency for the Nazi exploitation of France. This took many forms. Occupation costs were raised, after the invasion of North Africa, from 300 to 500 million francs a day. The vast amount of credit which the German authorities accumulated in this way was used for the acquisition of raw materials and food stuffs, French securities and works of art, for payments to the dependants of French workers recruited for labour in Germany, and to finance all the civil and military services of the occupying power. To prevent the French from following the precedent set by the Germans at the time of the occupation of the Ruhr and using inflation as a weapon of economic defence, the Germans insisted on a policy of controlled wages and prices. This resulted in the growth of a vast and nation-wide black market, which the occupying authorities themselves tolerated and used with an appropriate rake-off.

Behind the financial exploitation of France, which was largely a matter of book-keeping, there was the reality of systematically stripping France of raw materials, food stuffs, and manufactured products. In addition, the German war machine required an ever-increasing supply of foreign workers. Up to the summer of 1942 the exportation of French labour was kept down to the fairly low figure of about 70,000. After Laval returned to office stronger pressure, combined with his need to retain Nazi support, brought greatly increased numbers. Laval, characteristically, tried to win German favour and popularity in France at the same time by negotiating an agreement for the release of French prisoners of war in return for an increase in the supply of French workers for Germany. By the autumn of 1943 it was estimated that French workers constituted one fourth of all foreign male workers in Germany and amounted to 605,000 men as well as some 44,000 women. The conscription of this great mass of labour was not effected, of course, without much evasion and opposition; and in the last stages of the occupation the flight of workers to avoid compulsory transfer to Germany was one of the chief sources of the Resistance.

After November 1942 it is difficult to regard Pétain and Laval and their little group of ministers, operating in increasing isolation at Vichy, as a government. Laval remained in office, perhaps because the Nazis could find no one more serviceable to put in his place. Moreover, up to an extraordinarily late date he appears to have clung to his long-standing belief in the invincibility of the German war-machine. He had the stupidity in big things that can go with excessive cleverness in little ones. Much of his energy had to be devoted to defending his position from the Paris collaborationists, still trying to outbid him for Nazi favour. In September 1943, led by Déat and Darnand, they produced a plan for a French *parti unique* on the Nazi model, to bring France into full alliance with Germany. This alarmed the more moderate advisers of Pétain, who was induced to prepare a constitutional amendment transferring power, after his death, back to the National Assembly. Laval, who did not intend to be by-passed in this way, informed the German authorities who blocked Pétain's proposal. After some delay they moved against those who had counselled him. Laval was instructed to re-form the government 'in a sense which would guarantee collaboration'. This meant that he had to accept as his colleagues the whole gang of extreme collaborationists from Paris, with the exception of his bitterest personal enemies and rivals, Déat and Doriot. Even Déat was able to force his way in soon after, in March 1944.

Long before this, France was in a state of virtual civil war, as the Resistance movement, from inside and outside France, grew in size. French North Africa had passed out of the German sphere of control with the Allied landings and the subsequent defeat of the armies of Rommel. It was not at first clear into whose hands it had passed. Darlan's hour there, as we have seen, was a brief one. If the royalists were implicated in his murder, they gained nothing from it. The claimant to the throne, the comte de Paris, spent the war hanging about behind the scenes, occasionally making a tentative approach to one of the leading players, but never succeeding in getting on the stage himself. If, even in this crisis, he was to be pushed on one side and ignored, it was clear that for all the sound and fury of the monarchists their cause was dead.

Darlan was succeeded as civil and military head of the North African government by General Giraud, who, after a picturesque escape from Nazi captivity, had been chosen by the Americans as their candidate for authority over the regained colonial territories. There was, however, another candidate, who, it might almost be said, had chosen himself. This was General de Gaulle. His initial appeal from Great Britain had only rallied the governors of French Equatorial Africa and the French Cameroons to his cause. A small Gaullist naval expedition to Dakar in September 1940 had been repulsed rather humiliatingly. The Free French Movement, as the small body of supporters who had gathered round de Gaulle called themselves, made a very poor start.

Although the British government welcomed de Gaulle and provided him with moral support and material facilities, it was not sure of the wisdom of committing itself to the Free French Movement, and relations were often difficult, while the Americans were profoundly suspicious of de Gaulle and his ambitions. However, by means of wireless propaganda from his Free French movement in London, his was becoming the one name that was associated in France with continued resistance to the Germans. In January 1942 the Free French sent the former prefect, Jean Moulin, into France to coordinate the small resistance movements that were growing up. He became the first head of a National Council of Resistance, which met in Paris in May 1943; but Moulin himself was arrested, tortured, and killed a month later. His successor was Georges Bidault.

The Allied conquest of North Africa had meanwhile provided an opportunity for de Gaulle to measure his strength and assert himself as the single leader of resistance outside metropolitan France. To begin with Giraud held apparently all the winning cards in North Africa. His total lack of political capacity, combined with the skill with which de Gaulle played his own weaker hand, determined the outcome. Giraud was gradually eliminated and de Gaulle remained in sole control as the acknowledged leader of the Free French (now called La France Combattante) movement outside, and the Resistance movement within, France.

In France Nazi repression kept pace with resistance. The first high-ranking German officer was assassinated in October 1941. Fifty hostages were killed in retaliation. When, a few days later, a German major was shot, fifty more were destroyed. Vichy and the Nazis agreed that the acts of assassination or sabotage must be the work of Jews or of Communists. One result of this was to restore to the Communists the patriotic reputation they had lost at the time of the Nazi–Soviet alliance.

The campaign of the occupying forces against the Resistance was partly misdirected because of the lunatic Nazi preoccupation with the Jews, who were singled out for seizure as hostages, and for execution, whether they were implicated in the Resistance or not. The French anti-semites also were now given their chance, and after the Germans had moved into the Unoccupied Zone this ceased to provide a partial refuge for Jews. In the last stages of the occupation the extremist factions and the French Militia under Darnand joined enthusiastically in the hunt. The most effective French aid in repression did in fact come from this Militia, founded in January 1943 by Joseph Darnand, which was in the end to be more feared and hated than the SS troops themselves.

The first triumph of the Resistance was the liberation of Corsica in September 1943 by a force from North Africa. From the Corsican Resistance groups, operating in wild country, came the name of *maquis*. In France the numbers of coherent groups in the *maquis* and the membership of the Resistance greatly increased in 1943 and 1944, though on the eve of the Allied landings in France the Allied Supreme

Command had little faith in their military value. Equally, the Allies refused to believe that de Gaulle had become a name to conjure with in France. His influence was, in fact, at this moment to be of decisive importance for the future history of France. The Communist influence in the Resistance had become increasingly strong, and the Communist leadership never forgot its ultimate aim of converting liberation into a Communist takeover. The effective, if subtle, preparations for countering the Communist plan were taken by de Gaulle. He set up, parallel with the Council of the Resistance inside France, a Délégation Générale, which was to represent the interests of the state and be above the parties. A committee headed by the future Fifth Republic Premier, Michel Debré, drew up a list of *préfets* and *commissaires* to take over the administration of France as it was freed from the German occupation. The effectiveness of these preparations is shown by the fact that out of 80 future *préfets* on the list as many as 45 in due course assumed that office. On the military side, in April 1944 General Koenig, hero of the defence of Bir-Hakeim in the North African campaign, was appointed Commander-in-Chief of the French Forces of the Interior. The captain of engineers who took the *nom de guerre* of Colonel Passy, and a former professor of anthropology named Jacques Soustelle, headed the organization of secret agents which provided intelligence from France for both the Free French and the Allies.

It cannot be pretended that the Free French preparations were taken seriously by their Allies. Throughout the war American policy towards France was strongly influenced by the reports of Admiral Leahy, the ambassador to Vichy, and Robert Murphy, special envoy in Algiers, who both felt some affinity with the Pétainist régime. New York and Washington had also their quota of French exiles, politicians of the defunct régime like Camille Chautemps, who presented de Gaulle to the Americans as a would-be military dictator. Alternatively, or at the same time, he was treated as a mere British puppet, which could hardly have been further from the truth. He was certainly a difficult ally and was not taken into serious consideration in Allied plans for the organization of France after liberation. Instead, it was proposed that an Allied Military Government should assume responsibility for the liberated territories.

The reckless gossip, as a result of which the ill-fated Dakar expedition had practically become public knowledge before it even set out, made the Allied higher command reluctant to communicate its plans to its French allies. Moreover, the Americans in particular were sceptical of de Gaulle's authority over the internal Resistance. So it was that he was not informed of the imminence of D-day until the eve of the invasion. In spite of this the Allies called the forces of the Resistance into action by broadcast messages, summoning them to start general guerrilla activity and sabotage. This led, inevitably, in parts of France, to premature risings, with serious loss of life and much subsequent recrimination. The need for a general call, if the specific areas of invasion were not to be revealed to the Germans, was accepted by Koenig and the French command, though it involved such a tragedy as the revolt of Vercors, where some 700 *maquisards* out of 3,500 were lost in pitched battle with 20,000 Germans. In the whole of France it has been reckoned that 140,000 *maquisards* were armed by the Allies in parachute droppings, in addition to those who captured arms from the Germans; 24,000 were officially reported as killed in battle. The *maquis* of Brittany, about 30,000 strong, distinguished itself by the military effectiveness of its operations in a strategic zone on the flank of the invasion. Everywhere the cutting of railways and destruction of bridges hampered German movements.

The Anglo-American command intended to set up a military government of French territory as it was liberated, and an informal arrangement was negotiated in advance between representatives of General Eisenhower and General Koenig. In spite of the past difficulties in their relations, the British Foreign Office had long realized the power that the name of de Gaulle had come to represent in France. On the other hand Admiral Leahy, as late as spring 1944, was advising Roosevelt that the French could be rallied to the Allies after the landing in the name of Pétain. However, on 14 June de Gaulle visited the bridge-heads, and when he departed left behind him his representatives, who proceeded to take over the sub-prefectures peacefully from the Vichy incumbents. Where Gaullist administrators appeared on the heels of the invading forces or revealed themselves in the midst of the population, the transition was free from excesses. Elsewhere things were very different. Particularly in the South-west, when the German troops withdrew, a Communist and Resistance terror followed the Nazi and collaborationist one.

Vichy, of course, was not even a name now. On 17 August, when his German masters ordered Laval to transfer the French government to Belfort, for the first time he refused to obey. Pétain also refused to leave Vichy but the Nazis were determined that those who had served them so well in the past should not escape them now. The Marshal, Laval, and as many of the ministers as they could lay hands on were carried off, first to Belfort and then to Germany. The ultra-collaborationists needed no compulsion. In a general *sauve-qui-peut* the less conspicuous ones tried to sink into obscurity or insinuate themselves into the ranks of the Resistance. The more prominent collaborationists fled with the retreating German armies to Germany. At Sigmaringen they set up, still in the name of Pétain, the last French government of the war, achieving, on German soil and under the defeated and disintegrating régime of the former all-powerful Nazi conqueror, the object for which they had intrigued and agitated during five years of occupation and war.

5. CONSTITUTION-MAKING

IN the Second World War republican France passed from the humiliation of total collapse to the moral ambiguity of divided allegiance. Sabotage and rebellion were the needs of patriots, loyalty and obedience the virtues of defeatists and collaborators, murder and torture part of the normal machinery of government, and assassination the method of opposition. On more than one side honour was rooted in dishonour and faith unfaithful kept men falsely true. It seemed impossible that anything but civil war and chaos could appear when the Vichy administration collapsed and the German armies retreated. The immediate setting up of an independent and coherent government, and the restoration, within a reasonable time, of law and order all over France, was due to the existence of de Gaulle. His name had become identified with the idea of French national independence for millions who knew no more than his name. But if he was a symbol he was also a symbol who knew very well what he was doing, and he was determined that a liberated France should be free and united and independent.

Of course, there was inevitably some settling of accounts by private action. In areas like the South-west, where local Resistance bodies, particularly the Communists, were able to take control temporarily after the German withdrawal, there was a good deal of this, both private and public. How many of the more prominent collaborators were summarily executed, and how many other persons were disposed of in the pursuance of local feuds, cannot be estimated. The official figure of some three or four thousand is a gross understatement which must be multiplied by at least ten. Where the new Gaullist authorities were set up at once the summary executions of collaborators, stripping and shaving of female associates of the Nazis, dispossessions and expulsions, were held in check. Everywhere, sooner or later, courts created to deal with collaborators formally handed out penalties ranging from deprivation of civic rights through fines and imprisonment to death. A High Court was established to try the more notable collaborators. The reports of a series of *causes célèbres* provide valuable source material for the historian, though they do not shine as bright models of the judicial process at work. The trial of Laval, in particular, was conducted with such miserable pettiness by the prosecuting lawyers, and senile incompetence by the presiding judge, that it merely provided the greatest of the collaborators with a platform for turning the accusers into the accused. With scant regard for the forms of law he was silenced and sentenced, allowed to poison himself in the night, and ignominiously resuscitated for the sake of being hauled out at dawn and shot. Pétain, in the remoteness of great age, did not, or perhaps could not, deign to pay more than momentary attention to his own trial. He was sentenced to detention in a fortress for the rest of his life.

In place of the defunct authorities of Vichy, the government in exile, set up by General de Gaulle in Algiers, came to Paris. A Consultative Assembly, formed out of the advisory body constituted at Algiers together with representatives of the Resistance movements within France, was joined to it. For all effective purposes the government of France for fourteen months after his entry into Paris on 26 August 1944 was in the hands of General de Gaulle. There is a tendency to regard this as the lost year, when vital opportunities were missed. The speed with which France returned to normal, peaceful conditions is really the more remarkable phenomenon. To blame de Gaulle, in his capacity as head of the provisional government, for lost opportunities, is to exaggerate the extent of his personal authority. It is not possible to praise him for his abstention from setting up a dictatorial régime and at the same time blame him for not imposing solutions of the many problems pressing on the country. It should also not be forgotten that a war was still being waged on the soil of France. Even when most of the territory had been liberated, fighting continued round the Atlantic pockets of German resistance and in the eastern frontier region.

Looking back, it is easier now than it was at the time to see that de Gaulle had one prime object – to contain the Communists – which he pursued with characteristic subtlety and indirection. Because the Communist Party did not aim –

it was not in their tradition nor was it possible in the circumstances – to seize power by a military *coup*, it must not be supposed that they had no hope of capturing the citadels of authority by the methods of infiltration that – aided by the benevolent proximity of Soviet armies – were to prove so efficacious in Central and Eastern Europe. They came out of the war with many advantages. The memory of the Hitler–Stalin pact had been washed out in the blood of Communist Resistance fighters. The Communists were the one party that had retained its identity and its cadres intact throughout the underground struggle. Its leader, Maurice Thorez, former miner and trade-union organizer, one of the few genuine sons of the people to rise to the top in French politics, implacable in devotion to the strategy of the party line laid down by Moscow, yet conciliatory and flexible in the day-to-day tactics of political life, returned from Russia, where he had fled by some unknown route in 1939, to lead the party. Their victory seemed to the Communists a foregone conclusion. Many of their opponents in France would have agreed with them, all the more because General de Gaulle seemed to be playing their game for them. Looking backward, or possibly farther forward than was justifiable at the time or perhaps for long to come, he made a bid for a renewal of the old Franco-Russian alliance. He went to Moscow to sign a treaty with the Soviet government. This bid for support for his new and shaky régime from Stalinite Russia rather than America seemed to many misguided in foreign policy. It made better sense in domestic affairs, if it was conceived as the first step towards drawing the teeth of the French Communist Party. De Gaulle's ultimate objective was never easy to judge from his immediate actions. He knew that the prospect of a Gaullist military dictatorship was being used by the Communists to gather the support of the left behind them, and by his conspicuous moderation gradually dissipated this fear. The failure of the Communist takeover bid was all the more remarkable in the atmosphere of French politics during the first years after the war, which were marked by the strength of the left, the political annihilation of the right, and the discredit of the centre.

The first positive decision that had to be taken concerned the future régime in France. Given the general desire for a new beginning, the result of the referendum of October 1945 was a foregone conclusion. By an overwhelming vote of 96 per cent the French people rejected the idea of continuing, or reviving, the Third Republic. The Assembly that was elected in the same month was therefore a Constituent Assembly, with the task of making a new Constitution. It was naturally one in which the left was overwhelmingly represented: many collaborationists were disenfranchised and the memory of Vichy was too recent to allow its known adherents to influence the voting. There was, however, one new and major factor on the other side. The franchise had now been extended to women, and this, as the left-wing parties which had opposed it had always believed, meant a great accession of strength to the Catholic interest. The result of the election was what might have been expected from the combination of these factors. The vote for the right wing fell from its customary strength of something just under 50 per cent to a mere 16 per cent. The once great Radical centre, socially conservative and anti-clerical, suffered on both counts and was now a mere 10 per cent. The parties of the old left, Communists with 25 per cent and Socialists with 23 per cent, came near to winning an absolute majority. Their success was natural and expected. What was not anticipated and was a new phenonemon was the rise of a large and progressive Catholic party, born out of the small pre-war group of Popular Democrats. It had the prestige of possessing, in the person of the pre-war history teacher, Georges Bidault, the president of the Resistance Council at the end of the war. Catholic organizations had survived better than any others, except the underground Communist Party, during the occupation. The new party, the Mouvement Républicain Populaire, was that which was closest to General de Gaulle in its political outlook, and could therefore draw on the prestige of his name, even though he himself kept rigorously out of party politics. It was headed by a group of able Catholic intellectuals, little dreaming of the success they were about to achieve. Many from the right, whose support for its ideals was less than lukewarm, undoubtedly voted for the M.R.P. as the least of three evils. Support snowballed and the M.R.P. emerged from the election with some 24 per cent of the popular vote.

With the meeting of the Constituent Assembly, de Gaulle became the head of a parliamentary government, a role for which he was suited neither by his nature and training nor by his political beliefs. However, he used his position to take the next trick from the Communists by excluding them, in the tripartite ministry which he formed, from the three key ministries of Foreign Affairs, Interior, and Defence, to one of which, at least, they seemed entitled as the largest party in the Assembly. This was only the beginning of a series of conflicts between the head of the government and his Communist and Socialist ministers. Even with the M.R.P. Foreign Minister, Bidault, de Gaulle's relations were strained and the seeds were sown of a resentment which was to produce bitter fruits later.

The basic issue was whether there was to be a unified policy determined by the head of the executive, or whether policy was to emerge, as in the past, from party compromises in the legislature. In January 1946 de Gaulle recognized that he could not govern on the lines in which he believed with parliament; he was unwilling to attempt to govern against it, and so resigned. Tripartism continued, the Socialists, as the middle party, providing the Premier, while the Assembly set about the task of constitution-making.

The most important constitutional issue had already been tacitly settled before the Fourth Republic began. General de Gaulle had stood for a presidential as against a parliamentary executive. When his views were rejected he resigned. There was a strong tradition of personal government in France, which had only been broken by the defunct Third

Republic. The strength of the tradition was the measure of the hostility to it, which made it certain that a left-wing Assembly would react against it. De Gaulle said ironically that the Assembly was determined to make the President a mere figurehead for fear that Charles de Gaulle might one day become President. The first President of the Fourth Republic, the Socialist Vincent Auriol, was in fact, because of his personal prestige and political skill, able to play an important role behind the scenes, but it was still, like that of presidents of the Third Republic, mainly one combining the functions of prompter and scene-shifter. His successor, René Coty, was even closer to the presidential tradition of the Third Republic.

The left-wing majority in the Constituent Assembly, if it was agreed that the government should be a parliamentary and not a presidential one, was far from agreed on anything else. The Communists, anticipating a new Popular Front majority through which they might turn tripartism gradually into one-party rule, and the Socialists, clinging to their old Jacobin traditions, stood out for a single, omnicompetent legislative chamber. This was included in the terms of the first constitutional draft, which Communists and Socialists carried in the Assembly by 309 to 249. It was submitted to the country for ratification in May 1946. The triumphant Communist Party swept the country in a great political campaign with the cry, ' *Thorez au pouvoir!* ' and the country replied with a vote of nine and a half million for the Constitution but ten and a half million against it, nearly six million not voting. Even at a time when the right was discredited, its leaders in prison or disenfranchised, and its supporters in total disarray, the French people, or at least a majority of them, set their sails against the dominant winds of the left and veered back to the centre.

A second Constituent Assembly was elected in June 1946. The Socialists lost votes because of their association with the Communists. The M.R.P., which had led the campaign against the first Constitution, now became the largest party, with a popular vote of 28 per cent. Only time could show whether its predominance was to be a permanent feature of the political landscape, but for the present it had the gravitational force which drew the unwilling Socialists, as in the previous Assembly they had been drawn by the Communist Party, towards it. The new constitutional draft established a second chamber, to be called the Council of the Republic, while the lower house retained the name of National Assembly by which the whole parliament had traditionally been known. The second chamber was, to begin with, more a symbol than an effective political force. It was described as a chamber of reflection and in its first years did indeed do little but reflect the views of the other house.

The new constitution, though closer to that of the Third Republic than the first draft had been, would, it was hoped, avoid the major weaknesses of the old régime. Specific provisions were introduced to deal with governmental instability. To prevent the use of *interpellations* to upset governments at a moment's notice, it was laid down that a government could only be overthrown by a formal vote of no confidence, for which twenty-four hours' notice had to be given. To rob deputies of their power of destroying governments one after another without running the risk of a dissolution of parliament, some rather complicated arrangements, intended to provide for compulsory dissolution after the fall of a government on a vote of no confidence, were included. Thirdly, by weighting the constitutional arrangements in favour of large parties it was hoped to escape from the group system with its built-in bias towards instability. For a time, indeed, the three great parties practically monopolized power: they behaved, it was complained, more like orchestras under a conductor than the cacophony of political virtuosos which France seemed to have preferred in its public life. The three parties naturally were not averse from proposals calculated to perpetuate their own monopoly of power. Indeed they subsequently organized the electoral system with the specific object of preserving it.

All this was well and effectively contrived on paper, but it was to prove easier to change a nation's laws than its political habits. The demise of the Third Republic may have been voted: its successor was to follow so closely in its steps that the observer might well feel that it had merely changed to remain the same thing. In one way or another governments fell without having received the fatal vote of no confidence and the first parliament of the Fourth Republic was to last nearly its full term, from December 1946 to June 1951. Its eight ministries averaged just under seven months each; and, as in the past, while governments changed, their personnel remained much the same. Those who were regarded as *ministrables* appeared and reappeared in successive ministries, often in the same office. Thus year after year the Quai d'Orsay witnessed a *pas de deux* in which the two M.R.P. ministers, Bidault and Schuman, replaced one another in turn. The group system gradually re-emerged. Of the three great parties, only the Communists succeeded in retaining their monolithic character, while in the centre and to the right smaller groups began to reappear.

None of the three major parties felt very enthusiastic about the new constitution they had made; but if a poor thing it was the best they could manage. With muted voices and little enthusiasm they recommended it to the country, to the accompaniment of a blast of denunciation from de Gaulle and opposition from an extra-political Gaullist Union set up in his name. The constitution won the acceptance of the country in the referendum of October 1946 by the narrow margin of nine million votes to eight million; but one wonders if the real voice of France were not better expressed by the eight million who abstained. It cannot be said that the Fourth Republic had got off to a flying start. General public opinion was perhaps illustrated by the advertisement which was familiar on Métro walls in those days: it represented four painters inscribing the figures I to IV respectively on one another's backs, and bore the inscription, 'Republics pass but so-and-so's paint stays'.

While the politicians had been debating the terms of the constitution, the French had somehow or other been putting their shattered country together. The essential first step was the restoration of the railways. In proportion as this was accomplished so economic life gradually revived. As after the First World War, though the problem was now a nation-wide one, reconstruction proceeded at a remarkable pace. The political dominance of the parties of the left provided an opportunity for it to be accompanied this time by a programme of social reform. Laws of social insurance voted in April 1946 were added to the *Code de la Famille* of 1939. One result was a dramatic rise in the birth-rate.

In the Resistance movement, as well as the ideal of social reform the whole economic ideology of the Popular Front had been reborn. The powers of finance and capitalist industry had been discredited by collaboration, and the left-wing coalition which came to power in October 1945 was determined to carry through an extensive programme of nationalization and workers' control. The latter amounted to no more than an increase in the powers and responsibili-ties of the trade unions; and while de Gaulle was in office the policy of nationalization was pursued with calculated slow-ness. However, the state took over the great Renault motor works, the North-eastern coalfield, and Air France. The first Constituent Assembly carried the policy a good deal further by adding the Bank of France and the larger private banks, insurance, gas, electricity, and the whole coal-mining indus-try.

Except in so far as they helped to weaken the hold of big business on national life, the nationalizations were really less significant than either those who supported or those who opposed them expected. The development of a system of social security affected national life more widely and deeply. But perhaps the most important of the economic decisions in the period immediately after liberation was taken in the field of finance. During the war German policy had simul-taneously swollen the supply of paper money by the demand for occupation costs, and prevented the inflated note circulation from having its natural effect by enforcing, with the cooperation of Vichy, a rigid policy of wage and price controls, to which the accompaniment had been a nation-wide black market, especially in foodstuffs. With the disappearance of the Vichy authorities the system of control, such as it was, collapsed; and at the same time new and heavy obligations – for the support of an army in the field, the reconstruction of transport and industry, the import of raw materials and other supplies of which France had been starved – pressed on the French economy. The Minister for National Economy, the Radical Pierre Mendès-France, proposed a policy of *blocage* of the notes, combined with a tax on capital gains, control of wages and prices, and strict rationing. This policy was supported by the Socialists. It was challenged by the Minister of Finance, Pleven, who, with a background in business, believed in the free play of economic forces to cure economic ills. De Gaulle, with little technical economic knowledge, accepted the arguments of Pleven, and Mendès-France resigned. Both men were justified in the event, Pleven by the remarkable speed of reconstruction, and his opponent by the even more remarkable speed of the inflation which accompanied it.

Whether political pressures would have allowed even the simple step of blocking the circulation of occupation notes is doubtful. The rivalry of the three main parties stood in the way of the adoption of a policy which was bound to be unpopular with important sections of the electorate. The peasants, who had accumulated such quantities of notes during the war that they were said to keep them not in the traditional stockings but in *lessiveuses* – washing coppers – would have resented their formal devaluation by the government bitterly, and the result might have been a reduction in the much-needed agricultural production. The Communists, who were alleged to have accumulated great quantities of hot money during liberation, were also opposed to a policy of monetary control. Perhaps, also, they were not unaware

that inflation can be a great revolutionary force. The circulation of notes, which had been about 100 milliard francs
in 1939, had risen to 600 milliard by 1944. By the end of
1947 it was 900 milliard. In the two years from December
1945 to December 1947 the value of money was divided by
three, and the process was to continue. In so far as inflation
was a running sore of the Fourth Republic, as it had been of
the Third, and one which was a basic cause of its political
weakness, it could be said that the death-warrant of the
Fourth Republic had been written before its birth. However,
for the time inflation did not hamper, and may even have
assisted, material reconstruction. The necessary foreign imports, which the weakness of French currency might have
prevented, were made possible by massive American aid.

6. THE FOURTH REPUBLIC

GENERAL DE GAULLE was neither by training nor disposition a politician. Therefore he did not play the game
according to the established rules. Instead of flinging himself into opposition to a constitution which he believed to be
unworkable, a course of action which would have compromised him irretrievably and made impossible for the
future the role of national leader that he had reserved for
himself, he withdrew from active political life. When his
admirers, in the spring of 1946, formed a Gaullist Union, he
took no part in it. Only a year later, in a speech at Strasbourg on 7 April 1947, did he issue a call for the formation
of a Rally of the French People – Rassemblement du Peuple
Français, or R.P.F. This was, paradoxically, to be a party
against parties. It rapidly gathered support. Gallup polls
assessing the proportion of the electorate that was prepared
to vote '*de Gaulle au pouvoir*' produced results rising from 31
per cent in spring 1946 to 36 per cent in January 1947, with
the aid of the faults of the existing parties, the skilfulness of
Gaullist propaganda, and avoidance of positive proposals.

The Gaullist policy was an attractive one. It demanded that the taxes should be paid, but without specifying who should pay them. It proposed 'associations' in industry and a paternalist organization which for its critics was reminiscent of the ideals of Vichy. It appealed in non-committal terms to the Army, the peasants, the bourgeois, the workers, the industrialists, for a great national union. De Gaulle's campaign was reminiscent in many ways of that conducted between 1848 and 1851 by Louis Napoleon Bonaparte, particularly in its concentration on the provinces, where the General made a series of major speeches. It is true that Paris is only one-fifteenth of France, and that since 1871 the provinces, and not Paris, have decided the government of the country. Like Louis Bonaparte, also, de Gaulle had a profound belief in his destiny. His career provided a Gaullist mystique to take the place of the Bonapartist legend. At St Étienne, in 1947, a miner's lamp, presented to the General, bore the inscription, 'To General de Gaulle, who lightened us in our darkness'. Unfortunately, the success of the R.P.F. was fatal to his ambitions. The combination of progressive and conservative forces within the Rassemblement undermined its unity. When it won a considerable body of seats in the Assembly it became difficult for it not to behave as yet one more political party. Realizing that his time had not yet come, de Gaulle disassociated himself from the movement, leaving its members divided and leaderless and its future uncertain.

However, he had established his claim as a potential residuary legatee of the Fourth Republic if it had the misfortune to die. Meanwhile, the Communist Party had not abandoned its own hope of taking over the state. The general election of June 1946 revealed two new factors in the political situation – first, that the Socialist Party was beginning to suffer the usual fate of middle parties by attrition from both sides, losing its supporters to Communists on the one side and M.R.P. on the other; and secondly that the pendulum had already begun to swing back to the right, which (if the

M.R.P. is included) now obtained 53 per cent of the votes, against 47 per cent for the Communists and Socialists.

For the first months of the Fourth Republic, in 1947, an uneasy truce was maintained and the three big parties shared the government. Inflation, however, produced an agitation for wage increases, and in May 1947 strikes, which the Communist Party, at first somewhat reluctantly, supported, although they were directed against the government to which it belonged. The Socialist Premier, Ramadier, instead of resigning, took the bold and novel step of dismissing the Communist ministers. It was the end of tripartism and the beginning of the open war of Communists against Socialists and M.R.P. Communist-led strikes in November–December 1947 provided a critical test of the Party's power. Their failure showed not merely that France could be governed without the Communists, but that it could even be governed against them, despite their hold on the trade-union movement – they had recaptured the C.G.T. in 1946 – on the majority of the industrial workers and on about one quarter of the whole electorate. The result of their use of the strike weapon for political ends, which went against the French syndicalist tradition, was to blunt it in their hands.

Perhaps the turning-point in France, and indeed in the history of the whole world after the Second World War, came with General Marshall's speech of June 1947 on economic aid. The Communist Party rapidly moved into the attack with a denunciation, in December, of French acceptance of American aid. It was 'the subjection of France to the aggressive designs of American imperialism', they said, and the preparation for a new world war in which France would be the battlefield. In the course of the autumn strikes, the Communist Secretary-General of the C.G.T. announced the plan of his party: the denunciation of all military agreements, dissolution of the Gaullist Rassemblement, rejection of Marshall aid and the development of economic relations with the U.S.S.R. Unfortunately, France badly needed economic aid, which only America could give. The general public must vaguely have felt this, or perhaps it felt that Communist warnings were not entirely disinterested. In any case the strikes failed and their only effect was to assist a swing to the right.

Since the Gaullist Rassemblement had won some of its national support as an insurance against the danger of a Communist takeover, the apparent weakening of the Communists brought about a corresponding weakening of the Gaullists. Between them there was room for a Third Force, which was formed, in January 1948, by an alliance of Socialists, Radicals, and M.R.P. Shortly before, a breakaway from the Communist-controlled C.G.T. had formed a Force Ouvrière among the trade unions.

The basic problem of the Third Force, as of previous governments, remained inflation, and the Third Force was as powerless to deal with this as the Cartel des Gauches before the war. The laissez-faire traditions of the Radicals prohibited them from accepting measures of state intervention in economic matters which the Socialists put forward; and the M.R.P. was increasingly divided between its more reactionary and more progressive supporters. Disunity in the Third Force was increased by the conflict between Radical and Socialist anti-clericalism and the attempt of the M.R.P. to protect the interests of Catholic education, and by the reluctance of the Socialists to vote for the army estimates. In such divisions it was becoming ever more apparent that the traditions of the Third Republic lived on in the Fourth.

As the centre of gravity of French politics moved towards the right, so M.R.P. and Radical replaced Socialist Premiers. The pre-war Radical Minister of Agriculture, Queuille, formed a ministry in September 1948 which was to survive till 1949, with the aid of his Socialist Minister of the Interior, Jules Moch, who defeated new Communist strikes in October–November 1948; also with the aid of a good harvest and some measures of price control. The cost of living remained stable throughout 1949. By the autumn of 1949, however, there were signs that this economic miracle was only a temporary one, while the old conflicts between the partners in the Third Force were becoming acute once again. The Queuille Ministry fell in October 1949. The Third Force reverted to the worst habits of the past and the last eighteen months of the first Assembly of the Fourth Republic witnessed a sorry procession of weak and short-lived ministries.

The one point on which the three government parties managed to agree in the last days of the parliament was in passing an electoral law intended to keep both Communists and Gaullists out of power. By a complicated arrangement combining proportional representation where it suited them with a majority vote where that was likely to be favourable, the parties of the centre hoped to achieve this result. Their calculations were not mistaken. When the elections were held, in June 1951, the parties of the Third Force obtained 62.5 per cent of the seats with 51 per cent of the votes, while the Gaullists had 19.6 per cent with 21.7 per cent, and the Communists, with 900,000 votes more than the R.P.F., had only 17.8 per cent of the seats to represent an electoral vote of 25.9 per cent.

In spite of this electoral victory it was apparent that the Fourth Republic could rely on the support of barely half the nation, and that those who did support it were too hopelessly divided among themselves ever to be able to form a strong or stable government. The Third Force was still split over the question of state aid to Catholic schools and a proposal to allow their pupils to be eligible for scholarships. The shift to the right continued. In March 1952 the new Assembly produced, in the person of Antoine Pinay, the first Premier from the right since the war. In May Pinay fell, and there was a gap of five weeks before a new government could be formed. Reynaud could describe France as 'the sick man of Europe'.

Yet there were elements of stability, behind the political instability, which should not be ignored. For the first ten

years after liberation, up to the summer of 1954, the Quai
d'Orsay was practically monopolized by two ministers,
Georges Bidault and Robert Schuman, both belonging to
the same party, the M.R.P. The re-shaping of the French
economy was largely free from the vagaries of party politics.
It was entrusted to a Commission inspired and headed by
the brilliant technocrat, Jean Monnet. If the political and
financial weakness of the Fourth Republic is stressed, it is
only fair also to give due weight to its positive achievements.
These were particularly in the fields of foreign and economic
policy.

During the Second World War France had practically
been eliminated from the community of nations. The Free
French outside, and the Resistance movement inside, began
the process of recovery while France was still under enemy
occupation. In foreign policy the problem of the Fourth
Republic was not essentially different from that which had
faced the Third. During the centuries when military strength
depended primarily on manpower, France, with by far the
largest population in Europe, was its greatest military power.
The balance of power shifted in the nineteenth century with
the change in comparative populations. The military decline
of France was accentuated by comparative backwardness in
industrial development. To keep in the ranks of the Great
Powers France had to find allies to redress the balance.
Before the First World War Russia, and after it for a time
the small states of Central and Eastern Europe, filled the
gap. The parties of the right clung to a belief in the military
efficacy of the Little Entente up to and beyond the point at
which it had patently become an illusion. But long before
this, after the victory of the Cartel des Gauches in 1924,
Herriot opened a new chapter by appealing for a United
States of Europe. The theme was taken up by Briand in
1929. In the thirties the European idea, transmuted into the
strange dream of a Fascist international, found support from
the right. After the German victory of 1940 a substantial
body of opinion saw France's future as the favourite *Gau* of

the German Führer. At the other extreme, the Communists had, of course, for long dreamed of, and worked for, a Moscow-orientated grouping of what were not yet thought of as satellite states. Thus by the Second World War many sections of opinion in France had come to envisage the future in terms of internationalism, though the nature of the international association envisaged varied through all shades of the political spectrum.

After the war a strong current of neutralism found expression in the influential columns of *Le Monde*; but the experience of the inter-war and the war years did not suggest that France could cut herself off from international affairs and find security in isolation. The creation of the Third Force in French domestic politics naturally led to the speculation whether there might not be a Third Force also in international politics, between the Communist and capitalist colossi of East and West.

In April 1948 the Gaullist Conference called for European federal institutions. 'Economic union,' it declared, 'is clearly the indispensable basis of political union. It is *Zollvereins* which make federations.' The governments of the Third Force put these ideas into practice. As early as March 1948, the Brussels Pact, a Treaty of Mutual Assistance between France, Great Britain, Belgium, the Netherlands, and Luxembourg, was the first step. At the first session of a new Council of Europe, in 1949, Bidault spoke of a possible German accession to the Council. At the same time France had strengthened her ties with the West by the Dunkirk Treaty of Alliance with Great Britain in March 1947 and the North Atlantic Treaty of April 1949; but the memory of their policies between 1918 and 1939 stood in the way of any unqualified reliance on British and American guarantees. A *rapprochement* with a defeated Germany and a real identification of economic and political interests seemed to offer a better prospect for French security.

The prospects of economic cooperation also seemed brighter with European neighbours. Significantly it was the

moderate Catholic M.R.P. leader from Alsace, Robert
Schuman, who put forward, in May 1950, the plan for a
pooling of the coal and steel industries of Western Europe.
In April 1951 a coal and steel agreement was signed by the
governments of France, Germany, Italy, Belgium, Holland,
and Luxembourg.

Political and economic links had now been established in
Western Europe. A military treaty proved more difficult to
negotiate. In October 1950, Pleven proposed the formation
of a European army under the authority of a European
Minister of Defence and the Strasbourg Assembly. Robert
Schuman did not shirk the implications of the Pleven plan.
'States,' he said, 'must reconcile themselves to the abandonment of part of their autonomy to a collective authority in
which they will participate.' However, this proposal had a
more difficult passage than its predecessors. The Communists rightly regarded it as intended primarily to form a
European bulwark against Soviet advance. It also went too
far for the Gaullists, who accepted the idea of Federal
Europe only so long as in making the omelette of federation
the eggs of national sovereignty were left intact. Socialists
and Radicals approved in principle but were suspicious in
practice, not least because the M.R.P. and the Catholic
parties in Germany and Italy had taken the lead in pro-
moting the plan for a European Defence Community. It was
denounced as a Catholic plot, a plan for *la petite Europe
vaticane*. It could even be regarded as a continuation of the
ideas of Albert de Mun and the Christian Socialists at the
end of the nineteenth century, with behind them a long
clericalist ancestry of legitimism, the Austrian alliance of the
eighteenth century, the *parti dévot* against Richelieu, and the
Spanish satellite *Ligue* which fought against Henry IV. This
was going rather far back in the search for a discreditable
ancestry, but French politics have often been fought, like a
Homeric combat, over the dead bodies of former heroes.

On a more practical level, the fear of being dragged into a
conflict with Russia, the prospect, with French troops heavily

committed overseas, of being left in an embarrassing *tête-à-tête* with a more powerful Germany, and resentment at the idea of putting the French army under international control, also produced opposition. British entry into E.D.C. might have resolved these doubts but it was not forthcoming. Because the discussions had been largely conducted by experts behind the scenes, the plan was denounced as the dream of irresponsible technocrats. For nearly three years the controversy bedevilled French politics. No government dared submit the draft treaty to the Assembly in the face of almost certain rejection. Finally, in 1954, Pierre Mendès-France, who himself had little enthusiasm for the Defence Community, submitted the plan to the Assembly, which by 319 to 264 voted for a postponement *sine die*. This was equivalent to burying it.

The collapse of the hopes based on E.D.C. was, however, not the end. There were supporters of the European idea in every political group, with the exception of the Communists. Relations with Germany continued to become closer; the return of the Saar to German sovereignty in 1956 removed the only outstanding territorial dispute between the two countries; and the European idea gradually strengthened.

In the economic life of the nation, also, fundamental change was coming to France under the Fourth Republic. It was to an extraordinary extent the work of one man, Jean Monnet. The coalition of three parties on the left in the Provisional Government, to the exclusion of the right compromised by collaboration and Vichy, provided what in a sense was the fortuitous circumstance which enabled a start to be made on the reform, as well as the reconstruction, of the economy of France. In January 1946 General de Gaulle signed the decree setting up a Commissariat du Plan, under Jean Monnet, with this task. The First Plan dealt mainly with the nationalized industries of railways, mines, and electricity, though it also intended to promote other basic industries, in particular steel, cement, and farm machinery. From 1947 to 1951 the equivalent of some £2,300 million was invested in railways, electrical power plants, coal, shipping, petroleum refineries, and various lesser industries. Hydro-electric plants, which in 1929 had produced only fifteen, in 1951 produced forty milliards of kilowatts. Coal and steel recovered the level of productivity of 1929. The number of tractors on the land was multiplied by five over the pre-war figure. In 1939 sixty per cent of French imports had been paid for by exports: the comparable figure for 1951 was eighty per cent. By 1954 the productivity of fifteen of the twenty main industries had passed that of the boom year of 1929.

Marshall aid – and the flow of credit from America continued in one form or another up to 1955 – played an essential part in French recovery, but much of the capital required for the restoration and modernization of French industry came from domestic sources, not least by way of monetary inflation. One result was an increase, compared with the position before the war, in the proportion of the national income that went to profits and a corresponding decline in the share of salaries and wages. The resulting combination of distressing poverty with ostentatious wealth seemed to be made to assist the Communists, and their failure to exploit the situation successfully is all the more remarkable. To some extent the new forms of social assistance introduced by the Provisional Government helped to redress the balance, and in 1952 wages were tied to prices by a sliding scale.

An exception to the general progress of the French economy was agriculture. The peasants had done well during the food shortages of the Second World War, but inflation wiped out much of the value of their accumulations of paper money. There was a good deal of depression among the poorer peasants, following antiquated methods on uneconomically small farms with scattered holdings, especially in the Centre and South-west. They were protected from world competition by high tariffs, maintained because of the electoral pressures they were able to exert; but although the average yield of the crops was low, there were regular surpluses which the market could not absorb. Even the great increase in the number of tractors, from under 16,000 in 1938 to nearly 630,000 in 1959, did not represent the increase in efficiency that might have been supposed. Often bought on credit as a status symbol rather than for their actual use on many of the tiny farms, their most effective use may have been for blocking roads in the peasant demonstrations periodically organized against the falling prices resulting from over-production, or to dump surpluses of such commodities as beets and artichokes in the towns as a visible protest.

A steady decline in the numbers of the rural population was evidence of economic progress, but naturally not a welcome progress to the peasants who were being eliminated. It is estimated that between 1949 and 1954 over one quarter of the working population in rural occupations left the land. Though France still had a much higher proportion of its population on the land than other large Western countries, urbanization was proceeding rapidly. The Paris region doubled its population in the twentieth century, and urban standards of living were higher than rural, though even the agricultural population was not uninfluenced by changing standards. The expectations of the peasants were no longer essentially different from those of the urban population. France was ceasing to be two nations.

While the population of the rural areas was declining, the general tendency for the birth-rate to fall had been halted and indeed drastically reversed. The process had begun even before the Second World War, with the passing of legislation to favour larger families. The net reproduction rate, which had been only 87 in 1911, and the same in 1935, was 132 in 1953 and 128 in 1959. Improved social services also reduced the high death-rate among infants. In the first ten years after the Second World War the population of France rose by three million.

Despite inflation the Fourth Republic was making remarkable economic and social progress. Whatever the electoral strength of Communists and Gaullists, the Third Force might well feel that it deserved well of the country and was presiding over a period of remarkable recovery and increasing prosperity. True, all progress is bought at the expense of those who cannot go along with it. The France of small employers, small shopkeepers, small peasants, slowly but remorselessly being squeezed out, did not like the process. Electoral pressure could check the passage of legislation unfavourable to them, but could not stop the operation of economic forces. The small shopkeepers found a leader in the person of Pierre Poujade, from the backward Massif Central, who organized a local revolt against taxes, which naturally attracted a good deal of support. He moved into national politics and in the general election of 1956 the Poujadists were to win 50 seats and collect a total vote of three millions; but their leader exhibited a total lack of political capacity. His only programme was the evasion of taxes, and his followers already did that to the best of their ability. When Poujade attempted to revive his movement by contesting a by-election in Paris he was crushed. Those of his followers who had any serious political ambitions transferred their allegiance to other right-wing parties and the movement disappeared.

The fatality for the Third Force, and ultimately for the Fourth Republic, lay not in its domestic or even its foreign policy, but in the problem of the colonies. During the war the policy of the Vichy government, and its powerlessness, had laid the whole of the French Empire open to either enemy or allied occupation. France's allies had promised to respect the territorial integrity of her Empire, but at the end of the war this promise had not been interpreted as requiring active steps for the restoration of French rule in the colonies. The independence of Syria and the Lebanon, promised before the Second World War, was turned into a *fait accompli* by the Allied forces of occupation: it was not forgotten in France that the decisive step had been the expulsion of the

Vichy General Dentz's troops by the British. In Indo-China a temporary occupation by British forces gave the nationalist Viet Minh a chance to establish itself.

Concern about the future of the Empire was perhaps not widespread in France. For the average Frenchman, on the morrow of liberation, the problems of France itself were quite enough. However, some of the opponents of Vichy, and particularly de Gaulle, returned from their overseas bases with new ideas on the colonies, inspired partly by their war-time experiences and partly perhaps by the British example. De Gaulle had the idea of converting the Empire into a Federal Union, for the headship of which his own constitutional proposals would have been more appropriate than a parliamentary executive. The parties of the left envisaged a slower development in the direction of federation, although this went counter to their inherited tradition of Jacobin centralization. The M.R.P. on the other hand, perhaps not without thought for the interests of the Roman Catholic Church in the colonies, wanted the maintenance of French influence.

The constitution of the Fourth Republic proclaimed that the French Union was 'based upon equality of rights and duties without distinction of race or religion', but its constitutional provisions were so soon to be rendered anachronistic by the winds of change that we need not delay over them. The two essential articles were that whereas in France the National Assembly alone had the right of legislation, in the overseas territory the President could decree special provisions; and that organic laws were to determine the conditions of representation in the colonies. The effect was to leave all real power in the hands of the French government. As regards local representation, the crucial case was Algeria, where there were to be two electoral colleges – one including some 900,000 mainly of European descent, the other 7 to 8 million native Algerians, each college being represented equally.

It would be unfair to give a picture which did not men-tion the introduction of social and economic reforms in the Empire – the legalization of trade unions, a labour code, progress in education, plans for capital investment. But the dominant fact was the rise of nationalist movements and the consequent antagonism between European and non-European populations. This was all the more acute because of economic competition for jobs, provoked especially by the French habit of using Frenchmen for even the minor official posts in the colonies.

Changes in the French colonial empire were formal rather that actual. Paris, not unnaturally, had been unable to grasp the extent to which the whole condition of empire had changed in the course of the Second World War. The states of Indo-China – Laos, Cambodia, and Vietnam – were elevated to the rank of Associated States in 1948 and 1949, but already in 1945 Ho Chi Minh, the nationalist leader in Vietnam, had proclaimed its independence. In 1947 a revolt broke out in Madagascar; North Africa was in ferment; but it was Indo-China that produced the first great crisis. There, a state of open war was proving a heavy drain on French military and financial resources. Though the rank and file of the French army in Indo-China included many African troops and many other non-French of the Foreign Legion, the loss of French commissioned and non-commissioned officers was heavy and continuous. Above all there was the psychological strain of an apparently unending war in a country of which the average Frenchman had little knowledge and in which he had little interest. There was also the steady pressure of American anti-colonialism against the French presence in the Far East. Without the brilliance of the French General de Lattre de Tassigny the crisis might have come earlier. When, in 1954, the French strong point of Dien Bien Phu, the defence of which had become symbolic, fell, the balance was tilted decisively against a continuation of the war.

Pierre Mendès-France, most energetic and incisive of the Radical leaders, who had consistently and correctly prophesied the failure of most of the policies of the Fourth Republic, was elected Premier largely because it was believed that he would get France out of the Indo-Chinese impasse. There was no choice but total withdrawal. The relief in France was reflected in the vote of the French Assembly approving the Indo-China settlement by 471 votes to 14. While most Frenchmen accepted the loss of French possessions in the Far East as inevitable, the leaders of M.R.P. opposed what was an abandonment not only of political but also of religious influence; the elements in the upper classes that had interests in colonial investment and government resented their loss; while for the army officers, who had fought on so long, with such inadequate resources, it was the final stab in the back by the mandarins of Paris.

Elsewhere, too, the government of Mendès-France recognized that the colonial age was coming to an end. Autonomy was offered to Tunis, where nationalist agitation was making the traditional method of government through a puppet sultan impossible; and in June 1955 agreement on self-government was reached with Bourguiba, the leader of the nationalist party, the Néo-Destour. Negotiations for a settlement with Morocco were also begun. Algeria remained round the neck of the Fourth Republic, a heavier burden and one much more difficult to cut away, because of its large French, or European, minority.

The ambitions of Mendès-France went much further than finding a solution to the problem of the colonies. He had taken control of the Radical Party out of the hands of older, traditional leaders for the purpose of giving it a new ethos and using it to steer an unwilling France into the twentieth century; but the party was no suitable instrument for such a policy. It soon broke in his hands, a large section following Edgar Faure into opposition. However, it was a coalition of the right and the M.R.P. with the Communists which finally overthrew his government. Its fall showed that the parties of the Third Force could only hold together, and even only maintain themselves as parties, by refusing to face the national problems that demanded a solution. M.R.P. could not accept the colonial policy of Mendès-France; the Radicals could not face the prospect of economic and social reforms that would be contrary to the interests of a large part of their electoral clientele; and the Socialists seemed to belong, more clearly than any other party, to a France that was dying. In their old industrial strongholds of the North and Centre they were in retreat. The industrial proletariat had long since passed over to the Communists. The active membership of the party fell from 353,000 in 1946 to 117,000 in 1956. Its cadres were getting old. It had become a petit-bourgeois, small-town, provincial party, looking for support to backward areas like the South-west or Franche-Comté. Its greatest support came from the lower ranks of officialdom, in both the public and private sectors. Behind the revolutionary verbiage of tradition it had become profoundly conservative and opposed to change.

The disarray of French politics was reflected in the instability of governments. From January 1947, when the Fourth Republic began, to the election of Mendès-France in June 1954, there were fifteen cabinets, keeping up the average rate of change of the Third Republic. The presidential election of December 1953, after the conclusion of Vincent Auriol's term of office, demonstrated strikingly the acuteness of political conflicts. There was an unprecedented delay in the election and only after thirteen ballots did a majority rally round the name of René Coty, a worthy but undistinguished Norman conservative politician. His succession to a Socialist President showed how far the centre of politics had shifted to the right in seven years. The success of the Poujadists in the general election of 1956, which has already been mentioned, also seemed to confirm this swing, though in the same elections there were also Socialist and Communist gains. The centrifugal tendencies of French politics were evidently reasserting themselves.

Immediately after the general election a cabinet headed by the Socialist, Guy Mollet, took office, supported by a

'Front Républicain' of Socialists, Radicals and others, which even included the Communists. This was merely a gesture to the memory of the Popular Front. It had no political future; the fact was already becoming evident that no coherent majority existed in the Assembly or even in the country at large.

7. DOUBTS AND QUESTIONINGS

THERE was a paradox about the situation of France ten years after liberation. Economically and in the international sphere remarkable progress had been made: politically the Fourth Republic was in what seemed a hopeless impasse, which reflected only too well the general frame of mind of her people. The hoped-for recovery and rebirth of the state which was to follow liberation had not come about. Objectively there had been progress; subjectively, to the French people, France in the fifties seemed to be much what she had been in the thirties. Indeed, we can go further back. Two world wars had apparently had little effect on the mind of France. This, at least, is the impression that one obtains from the literature of the twentieth century. The notes that were to be dominant later had all been struck in the years before the First World War. Even the strong pacifist theme, which might reasonably have seemed a consequence of that holocaust, in fact predates 1914. It was continued in anti-war novels, such as Henri Barbusse's *Le Feu* of 1916, or *Les Croix de Bois* by Roland Dorgelès in 1919. And, alongside protests against war, the normal, peacetime habits of the French middle classes were narrated, after the war as before and in much the same terms, by novelists such as Jules Romains, Georges Duhamel, or Roger Martin du Gard. Bridging the gap, the Saint-Simon of the Third Republic, his colours shining with the glory of its great days, and turning in anticipation to the angry hues of the setting sun after the storm of war, Marcel Proust, in 1918 with only a few years to live, was able, dining almost nightly in the Place

Vendôme, to see something of the glow that *À la recherche du temps perdu* was to cast over the declining Republic. The war had brought no break in French literary history. Péguy and the author of *Le Grand Meaulnes* died in it; but the better known literary figures of the inter-war years – Claudel, Mauriac, Bernanos, Gide, Colette, Giraudoux, Maritain, Valéry – were all established writers, before the First World War.

One who looked far back as well as forward, Paul Valéry, provided a link with the Symbolism of the nineteenth century and the rationalism of the world before 1914. *La Jeune Parque* of 1917, and *Le Cimetière marin* of 1922, mysterious and beautiful poems, evoke a world not of the time or place any of his contemporaries knew. On a lower level, the revival of Catholic thought that had begun before the war continued. Neo-Thomism, strongly supported in the Dominican Order, found its most influential advocate when Jacques Maritain passed over from Bergsonism. His *Trois Réformateurs* of 1925 was a powerful denunciation of the three men who embodied what he saw as the three great heresies of the post-medieval world – the Protestantism of Luther, the rationalism of Descartes, and the romanticism of Rousseau. In a different way the cause of religion was proclaimed in the prose-poetry of the former Symbolist poet and diplomat, Paul Claudel, from the medieval *L'Annonce faite à Marie* of 1912 to the sixteenth-century Spanish *Le Soulier de satin* in 1943.

In painting, also, the themes dropped in 1914 were resumed in 1918. Cubism, created about 1907 in succession to an Impressionism that was losing its inspiration, reached its height in the few years after 1918. The greatest of French painters of the time – Picasso, Spanish by origin, Juan Gris, Fernand Léger, Braque – passed through it, and through Cubism Braque attained to a classical serenity which was in striking contrast to the restlessness of the age.

Paris was the Mecca of artists and writers from the whole world in the nineteen twenties. At the tables of the Dôme and the Coupole and Le Select, along the short length of the boulevard Montparnasse, levelled by the Ateliers Nationaux for what purpose they knew not seventy years earlier, gathered the great and the less great, the classic and the romantic and the merely queer. Among the fevered and poverty-stricken exiles of a wartime Paris, but also repeating the experience of pre-war Futurism, developed Dadaism – a philosophy of meaninglessness, a literature of incoherence, an art of destruction. Its adepts would have counted it the supreme irony if they had known that their nonsense was to make all too much sense in the years that were to come. Dadaism, like any other outburst of lunacy, however consciously willed, could not survive, but out of it grew Surrealism, a more methodical madness, and a more sinister, because rationalized, kind of irrationalism. Its manifesto was written by the poet André Breton in 1924 and rewritten by him several times after. The future Communist poets Paul Éluard and Louis Aragon began as Surrealists, and in painting its best advertised exponent was Salvador Dali. The aim of Surrealism was to create shock and revulsion by the association of incompatible and unpleasantly combined images. The Surrealists wanted not to imitate reality but to present the clear-cut representational image in such a way that it had the hallucinatory, frightening reality of a nightmare. Attempting to dredge up its images and associations from the unconscious mind, Surrealism had affiliations with the new Freudian psychology and the methods of psycho-analysis.

The new psychology was, however, less influential in France than elsewhere; perhaps an education in Cartesian rationalism was not favourable to it. But, with or without the aid of psycho-analysis, it was an age of self-questioning, moral uncertainty, and introspection. The Marcel of Proust's great novel, in his agonizing doubts and hesitations, illustrated the times, though in his final achievement of the ultimate certainties he rose above them. André Gide, born two years before Proust and to live nearly thirty years after him, whose productive career stretches for sixty years from 1891 to 1951, is a better representative of the inter-war years.

Protestant by descent and education, beset with religious and moral anxiety, tormented by egocentric introspection, paradoxically finding morality only through the experience of immorality in the *acte gratuit*, the motiveless crime, craving love but unable to concede it, in books like *L'Immoraliste* of 1902, *Les Faux-Monnayeurs* of 1925, and perhaps most of all in his *Journal*, published in 1939, Gide exposed the quivering flesh of a generation that seemed to have lost its protective covering and to have its nerve ends bare to the assaults of a hostile world. Similar introspective anxieties can be found in the Catholic writers of the thirties. For Georges Bernanos man was the victim of original sin; there was no other way, for him, of coping with the agony of the Spanish Civil War, which presented moral problems to both right and left. François Mauriac saw life as a battleground between good and evil, and painted the passions seething beneath bourgeois respectability. To writers without the consolation of religion, like Céline, whose *Voyage au bout de la nuit*, if we did not know that it was written in 1932, might have been thought to reflect the moral chaos of the years of occupation, the world was a cess-pit, portrayed with the disgust but without the humanity of a Voltaire.

Of course this is not the whole picture. There were other writers, perhaps historically less significant, more detached, less imbued with the pessimism of the age: Jean Cocteau, who moved from Dadaism to neo-classicism, was a brilliant amateur of all the arts; Colette was the prose painter of the sensual world, translating the immediacy of sensations into words as the Impressionists seized and put in paint the transience of the seen world.

The other arts often carried the same message as literature. In Picasso, who led the fashion in painting for nearly sixty years, there was a tragic sense of life. Matisse, Braque, and Léger preserved a less committed art. Music set out on a new course with the Swiss-born Arthur Honneger and Darius Milhaud. In the cinema the brilliant, light-hearted, tender comedies of René Clair offered a moment of sunshine in a clouding sky. Politics and violence swept over the scene in the thirties. Henry de Montherlant eulogized war, the bull-fight, physical endeavour. André Malraux sought a solution in political action; and found his way through Communism in China, the Spanish Civil War, and the Resistance, to de Gaulle and office in the Fifth Republic.

Over all, increasingly, hung the cloud of impending war. In 1935 Jean Giraudoux's *La Guerre de Troie n'aura pas lieu* shows Hector, victorious in battle but hating war, struggling for a peaceful solution to the quarrel begun by the abduction of Helen. Success, up to the last moment, is wrecked when a sudden drunken killing makes war inevitable, and the great gates of Troy, opened only in time of war, slowly begin to part. The last comment, on the stupidity of war as well as its inevitability, is the sight of Helen, revealed within the gates in the arms of yet another lover. Here, as elsewhere, we see the intense pacifism, combined with pessimism, of France in the inter-war years.

The Second World War and the occupation seem to have contributed little, at least for the time, to French literature or art. In the clandestine writings of the Resistance, Vercors' *Le Silence de la mer* stood out for its presentation of the dilemmas of conscience created by the enemy occupation. Anouilh's *Antigone* (1942) reflected the conflict between loyalty and obedience to established authority and loyalty to the higher law of the conscience. In his other plays, Anouilh continued the pre-war concern with moral issues, with the same inability to resolve them. *La Peste* (1947), by Albert Camus, could be seen as an allegory either of France under German occupation or of the whole predicament of humanity in the face of unavoidable evil.

The conflict of good and evil, already in Gide becoming so confused that each could assume the character of the other, was intensified by the moral problems of occupation and liberation. Intensified scepticism seemed the main result. The religious revival continued but without any notable intellectual or artistic substance. It was marked by an increased tolerance – the fire of integral Catholicism and the Action Française seemed to have died out – and a corresponding decline in anti-clericalism. The re-admission of the Action Française to the fold by Pius XII in July 1939, the religious adulation with which Pétain was surrounded, and the attempt under Vichy to revive clerical control of education; the collaborationist activities of some clerics, notably of Cardinal Baudrillart, the aged director of the Catholic Institute of Paris – all this was counterbalanced by the anti-Nazi policy of *Action Catholique* and the Dominican Fathers, and the underground resistance of the Christian Democrats. After the war 'worker-priests' went into the factories to revive the Church in proletarian quarters. There was some doubt how far they were converting the proletariat they lived and worked with, and how far the proletariat was converting the priests, perhaps to socially dangerous views, and the Vatican brought the experiment to an end.

After the war Communism, like Catholicism, increased the number of its adherents, and yet somehow seemed to have lost its intellectual vigour, despite all the efforts of such a brilliant leader as Thorez to preserve its militancy. Aragon wrote pleasing lyrics, Picasso continued to bestride the artistic world and designed the dove of peace for Stalin. The memory of the Hitler–Stalin pact had been partly obliterated by the deeds of the Communist Resistance; but later revelations about the Stalinist terror, and the suppression of the Hungarian rising, were daggers in the hearts of many of the Communist-oriented intellectuals. The party militants were better conditioned to accept whatever came from Moscow, as thoroughly as Pavlov's wretched dogs salivating at the sound of the master's bell.

The one intellectual movement which, though it had its origins before the Second World War, seemed for a time to offer something new after it, and to give an answer to a generation that only knew how to ask questions, was existentialism. Its origins were to be found in the religious mysticism of the mid-nineteenth-century Danish writer,

Kierkegaard. It penetrated to France by way of the contemporary German philosophers, Heidegger and Jaspers. The earlier existentialist writings of its chief French exponent, Jean-Paul Sartre, precede the Second World War. They reflect the subjectivism and pessimism of those years. After the war, his titles – *Les Mouches* (1943), *Les Mains sales* (1948) – are a programme in themselves. *Huis clos*, in 1944, is little to do with war, resistance, or liberation. It is a denial of the possibility of liberation from the self-made chains of evil binding man. To be, to endure, is to sin and suffer, each man in his own self-created and self-perpetuating hell. Merely to be is to deny life; to exist is to act, to choose freely; yet freedom of choice is what man cannot have – all he can do is to choose to engage himself in the world, as Sartre himself did in left-wing politics.

The mental confusion of the intelligentsia, struggling with the problems of politics and literature in the left-bank cafés of Paris after the war, is portrayed in less abstruse form in Simone de Beauvoir's *Les Mandarins*. Here, also, and in her *Le Deuxième Sexe*, appears another feature of the post-war scene – the changing position of women in French society, emerging now as individuals capable of playing a part in public life, yet still with all the hesitation of the first steps adding to the uncertainties of the general atmosphere. Existentialism itself denied the possibility of rational choice and preserved the dignity of man only by falling back on irrational choice, such as the choice of rules to break for no purpose other than breaking them. But this was nothing new: it was a return to the *acte gratuit* of the inter-war years. At the end of his search for the consistently anti-social, Sartre found a writer from the underworld, only again to be disappointed, for Jean Genet achieved literary success, which is a very social kind of thing. And twenty years after liberation existentialism had lost its philosophical respectability. If the works of Anouilh, Camus, Sartre, de Beauvoir, Genet continued to have social relevance, it was to a France that might soon belong to history.

8. THE RÉGIME OF 13 MAY

THE political and psychological malaise of France after the First World War was a chronic rather than an acute condition. It took a second war and an overwhelming military defeat to shatter the Third Republic. The fabric of the Fourth Republic was more fragile, but even so only war, though this time a smaller and a colonial war, cracked it. Before this the coherence of the Republic had obviously been weakening. In November 1955, for the second time during the life of the Assembly, a cabinet was defeated on a vote of confidence and the conditions for a dissolution existed. The Assembly was dissolved, and as it had been unable to agree on a new electoral law the system of 1951 still applied. This time it operated chiefly against the parties of the right which lost 40 seats. The Social Republicans (the name adopted by the former Gaullists) lost 46, while the Communists and their allies gained 52. Any possibility that the Communists might consolidate their position and become again a real force in the Fourth Republic was frustrated, first by the Russian revelation of some part of the Stalinite atrocities – the image of the Communist leader Thorez was closely linked with that of Stalin – and secondly by the crisis of conscience which affected many of the Communist intellectuals after the repression of the Hungarian revolution.

The election did nothing to alter the state of paralysis which had stricken the Fourth Republic. The parties retained just enough life to inhibit action by their opponents, but not enough to take any themselves. The nation was the less concerned about this situation because it was losing interest in politics. Even the disastrous and humiliating failure of an Anglo-French adventure in the Near East, provoked by Egyptian nationalization of the Suez Canal, made no profound impact on the national consciousness.

In many ways the Fourth Republic had not served the

nation badly. France was adapting herself to the new situation in Europe. In December 1956 the French government agreed, in return for economic concessions, to the return of the Saar to Germany. This ended territorial disputes between the two countries, and began the real possibility of finding in new European institutions an end to the millennial struggle of West and East Franks, and therefore an answer to the problem of security. In January 1957, rather more than a year before its collapse, the Fourth Republic began negotiations for a Common Market with Germany, Italy, and the Benelux countries. In March, the Rome treaties setting up the Common Market were ratified by the Assembly. Within France, economic prosperity, even if unevenly distributed, was spreading, and social reforms had removed some of the worst social evils.

An important step was taken towards a solution of the colonial problem when, in March 1956, the independence of Morocco and Tunisia was recognized. In June a law extending local self-government in the other African possessions prepared them for a future grant of independence. This left still unresolved the most intractable of the colonial struggles that bedevilled France after the Second World War, the Algerian revolt. It entered the acute stage in November 1954, when the nationalists initiated a campaign of terrorism. By 1955 France had 170,000 troops stationed in Algeria in an attempt to contain the revolt, while another 100,000 were still in Morocco. The General Secretary of the Socialist Party, Guy Mollet, who became Premier after the election of 1956, began with an attempt to apply the Socialist policy of negotiation with the rebels. A visit to Algiers and the hostile demonstrations of a mob of Europeans revealed to him the violence of feelings of the *colons*. This experience seems to have shocked him into a remarkable reversal of policy, from one of concessions to one of resistance. More French reinforcements, many only just back from the Far East, were poured into Algeria until some 350,000 men were there, to contain the activities of some 15,000 active rebels. Despite the size of the French forces, the remoter, mountainous parts of the country remained largely under rebel control, and in the more settled areas continuous terrorist outrages made normal life difficult. Government increasingly passed into the hands of the military. They recruited native forces, settled villages under armed guard, and engaged in a campaign of education and indoctrination. The Algerian nationalists intensified their campaign of largely indiscriminate murder, while the army organized underground counter-terrorist services. Terrorism was met by counter-terrorism and torture by torture. It was becoming increasingly a private war, waged with the utmost barbarism, between the army and the *colons* on one side and the Algerian rebels on the other. The French people as a whole, heartily sick of colonial wars which had never been other than unpopular in France from the time of the first conquest of Algiers in 1830, felt itself committed to the Algerian war only through the army of young French conscripts, sent out to wage the kind of struggle imposed on them by the Algerians, by methods of which the nation, in spite of the censorship, was becoming uneasily aware, and at a price in human life that it increasingly resented. The injury done by the Algerian war to French interests went on mounting. France could not exercise her European influence while the bulk of the army was tied down on the other side of the Mediterranean; the expense of the war was prohibitive of sound national finances; Algerian terrorist outrages were spreading to France itself; and while the struggle continued there seemed no hope of stability in domestic politics.

In autumn 1957 France was without a government for five weeks because of the inability to get any majority together to support one. As governments fell, one after another, the stock of possible Premiers was rapidly being exhausted. When a government fell in April 1958 it was again a month before a new one could be put together. The desire somehow to end the struggle and get out of Algeria was reaching a pitch at which it was an obvious threat to the aims of the

Army and the interests of the *colons*, a few rich but hundreds of thousands of poor whites, who saw no future for themselves in what was the only homeland they had if the native Algerians took control. It only needed the choice of a Premier who was reputed to favour negotiation to fire the explosive atmosphere in the European quarters of the Algerian towns.

On 13 May 1958, when Pierre Pflimlin was to present his cabinet to the Assembly, the extremists struck. The Army was determined that it should not be stabbed in the back yet again, as it believed it had repeatedly been, by the civilians in Paris. The Europeans of Algeria, driven to hysteria by being for years the target of bloody and indiscriminate terrorist attacks, marched and screamed and harangued to the tune of innumerable pots and pans and motor-horns blaring out the beat of *Algérie française*. A mass demonstration in Algiers invaded the government offices and a self-elected revolutionary committee seized control. Paris was powerless to check the revolt so long as the Army was on the side of the *colons*. The question was rather whether the extremists in Algiers, and their sympathizers in the French parties of the right, could extend the movement to metropolitan France. The rebels succeeded, some ten days later, in getting control of Corsica.

For the first time since 1799 it seemed as though a military *coup* might overthrow a legitimate government of France. In fact the position of the Army and the *colons* was much weaker than either the leaders of the *coup*, or the republican politicians, now stricken with terror, supposed. The Army could not invade France without losing such hold as it had on Algeria. Moreover it began to be suspected that the rank and file of the troops, if called into action to overthrow the government in Paris, might refuse to march. The officer class, right-wing in political sympathies, often following a family profession, career men whose loyalties were to their colonels and generals rather than to the politicians of Paris, was ripe for revolt. The Foreign Legion and the parachute regiments might have followed them. The weakness, of which they were probably not aware till it was put to the test, was that the rank and file of the Army were young temporary soldiers, conscripts who, back in France, would be no proper metal for rebellion, and even in Algeria manifested their unwillingness to be used to overthrow the Republic. The leaders of the revolt, therefore, saw no way of following up their success, though the political authorities in Paris were in daily expectation of disaster. For a fortnight there was a stalemate.

The one person who saw what might be done with a situation which he had been anticipating for years was General de Gaulle. He had long been convinced that the Fourth Republic could not survive and that when the crisis came he would be called on to save the state. He had done nothing to bring about the crisis, and even now that it had come his only act was to announce, on 15 May, that he held himself in readiness if he were called upon. At the same time he made it clear that he would contemplate no move that was not strictly legal. Among those who saw the return to power of de Gaulle as the only solution there were three main groups. The Gaullists proper were personally devoted to the General. They believed that only by accepting his principle of presidential government could France escape from the political impasse which seemed to be the inevitable result of government by Assembly. Secondly, there were many – conservatives, Radicals, even Socialists – who were reluctant to accept either de Gaulle's personal authority or his political principles, but who saw the Fourth Republic lurching inevitably towards a condition in which government would become impossible and law and order completely break down: they were prepared to accept the authority of the General as a temporary solution to the crisis, a *faute de mieux.* Finally, there were those of the right, especially the 'colonels' leading the revolt who – with typical political *naïveté* – could not believe that a general could do other than share their views, and, in spite of his

237

whole record and everything he had said, looked to de Gaulle as the man who would establish a more or less fascist dictatorship based on the Army and use it to save an *Algérie française*.

De Gaulle let them, and any other potential supporters, believe what they pleased. He remained in a masterly silence. The situation grew more and more tense and everyone else's nerves gave signs of breaking. The President, René Coty, occupied the strategic position. It was customary for Presidents to negotiate the transfer of government from one Premier to another, less usual for them to arrange for the fall of one Republic and the transfer of power to another; but this is what Coty did. Everything followed the correct formal channels. Pflimlin resigned. De Gaulle was appointed Premier. On 1 June the Assembly accepted him by a majority of about 100. The Communists voted solidly against him, the right generally in his favour, and the Radicals and Socialists were hopelessly divided. The new Premier laid it down as a condition of accepting office that he should have decree powers for six months, and at the end of that time should submit a new constitution to the vote of the whole nation.

From the time of liberation de Gaulle had consistently argued that France could only recover political stability and national strength by means of a government based on a presidential rather than a parliamentary executive. He used the six months of personal rule to put into law a host of badly needed reforms which it had hitherto proved impossible to get through the Assembly, and for the preparation, particularly by his former wartime colleague and future Premier, Michel Debré, of a new constitution. It was submitted to a referendum in September 1958 and accepted by a majority of about 80 per cent of the voters. It changed the whole balance of French politics by transferring effective legislative powers from the Assembly to the Premier, making ministerial office incompatible with membership of the Assembly, and attributing the nomination of the Prime Minister to the President. Despite the deep-rooted prejudice, dating back to the election of Louis Napoleon Bonaparte in 1848, against a popular election of the President, he was made the representative of the sovereignty of the nation by becoming the nominee of a large electoral college of members of local government bodies, with a considerable bias in favour of the rural communes. The general effect of the changes was to weight the constitution heavily in favour of the executive and against the legislature.

The development of a conflict between the President and the Assembly, such as might have been anticipated, was eliminated, so far as the opening stages of the Fifth Republic went, by a surprisingly complete victory in the election of Gaullist candidates. The electoral system of single-member constituencies, with second ballot, produced some remarkable results. The overwhelming majority that supported the new constitution were in effect voting in a plebiscite for General de Gaulle. Immediately after, the nation gave a third of its votes to his main opponents – 19 per cent to the Communists and 15.5 per cent to the Socialists. But after the second ballot the Communists, in electoral isolation, were left with a pitiable 10 seats; the Socialists, with fewer votes, were better off with 44, but even so many of their most prominent men disappeared from Parliament. In the second ballot there was a nationwide swing over to candidates who put themselves forward as supporting de Gaulle, with the result that the new Gaullist party, the Union pour la Nouvelle République (U.N.R.), obtained some 200 seats. The Radicals, with 13 seats, were practically eliminated; M.R.P. survived with about 56; the Independent–Peasant bloc of the right did well with 118. The significant fact was the overwhelming national support for de Gaulle, which unexpectedly gave him not only a large party in the Assembly, but also the means of controlling his own majority if it were to become recalcitrant. A referendum in January 1961 confirmed his hold on the country with 75 per cent for and 24 per cent, mostly Communist, against him. In April 1962 it was 90.7 per cent against 9.3 per cent.

However unrepresentative the membership of the Assembly may have been, the electoral massacre of the old parties, and the appointment of ministers from outside their ranks by de Gaulle, produced a second great political change – a revolution in political personnel. The Fourth Republic had been run by men whose political habits had been formed under the Third Republic, just as the Second Empire had depended on the political management of many former Orleanists. The Fifth Republic, like the Third, began with something more important than a change in laws, and that is a change in men. The *ministrables* lost their monopoly of office, though not to their old enemies of the extreme right and left. Their fault had been their failure to provide France with a government. Both the old left and the old right had been condemned to frustration by their own inherent contradictions. The right, with the support of the conservative, wealthy, Catholic classes, had stood for the overthrow of the Republic, if necessary by force. Too many of the wealthier, more religious, conservative elements in society, who should have served as the ballast of the ship, had spent their time talking, and sometimes even acting, revolution. They had succeeded to the fatal inheritance bequeathed from the *ancien régime* of an irresponsible *noblesse frondeuse*. The parties of the left, on the other hand, Radicals, Socialists, and Communists, depending on the electoral support of *les petits*, were tied to outdated interests and followed intensely conservative social policies, while at the same time they had inherited the historical tradition of Jacobinism and continued to make appropriate revolutionary gestures. As for the extreme right and extreme left, neither was as influential as the size of its electoral support, or the volume of the noise it made, suggested. To interpret French politics in terms of a polarization between extremes is profoundly mistaken. Ever since 1871 the ruling element has been the centre. Continual instability must be seen in terms of comparatively small movements to right or left about an always dominant centre. Within the loose coalitions formed for electoral purposes by left and right, the divergences were always greater than those between the moderates on either side of the dividing line; and in the last resort these would always join to save the state from the extremists. This was what happened in 1958. The Fourth Republic had already dealt successfully with the threat of Communist extremism from the left; it fell, and the nation accepted de Gaulle, because it was unable to deal equally successfully with the Army and the Algerian extremists from the right.

In the light of these considerations it is easier to understand why the break in continuity that was effected as a result of the Algerian coup of 13 May, which seemed so great at the time, especially to those who had ruled France and now found themselves cast into the political wilderness, may appear much less dramatic when it is looked at in historical perspective. To exaggerate the change is to underestimate the achievements of the Fourth Republic. Even in respect of the problem of the overseas territories the Fourth Republic had advanced to the edge of a solution. The abandonment of Indo-China had been a forced one; but the independence of Morocco and Tunisia was negotiated; and the legislation of 1956, endowing the overseas territories with local assemblies elected by universal suffrage, was an important preparation for later developments. When, in the constitution of the Fifth Republic, the last and the boldest step was taken, it only carried to its conclusion the policy that governments had pursued, inevitably if erratically, since liberation. Under the new constitutional laws ten West and Equatorial African territories, and Madagascar, chose to be self-governing member states of the French Community of States, while five smaller and remoter colonies remained as overseas territories. General de Gaulle had added one other possibility, which no previous government could have put forward without being overthrown in the midst of a violent outcry from the right. This possibility, that of total independence from France, was in fact chosen by only one colony, Guinea.

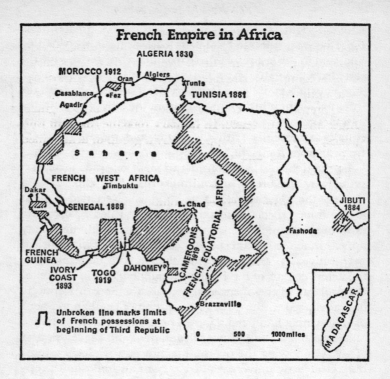

French Empire in Africa

ALGERIA 1830

MOROCCO 1912
Algiers
Oran
Tunis
Casablanca
TUNISIA 1881
Fez
Agadir

S a h a r a

FRENCH   WEST   AFRICA
Timbuktu

Dakar
JIBUTI
1884
SENEGAL 1889
L. Chad

Fashoda

FRENCH
GUINEA
CAMEROONS
1919
IVORY
COAST
1893
TOGO
1919
DAHOMEY
FRENCH EQUATORIAL AFRICA

Brazzaville

Unbroken line marks limits
of French possessions at
beginning of Third Republic

0   500   1000 miles

MADAGASCAR

Meanwhile, in Algeria, the forces of the old right were making their last stand, when it became increasingly evident that the new government of President de Gaulle, instead of upholding the principle of *Algérie française* as those who had initiated the *coup* of 13 May had expected of him, was preparing to complete the process of recognizing Algerian independence. In January 1960 the Algerian Europeans, the *pieds noirs*, supported by a group of army officers and a few old and once faithful Gaullists like Soustelle and Bidault, attempted a second *coup*, this time against de Gaulle himself. His government, this time, did not yield an inch, and the intended revolution rapidly degenerated into a terrorist conspiracy, which was gradually but ruthlessly crushed.

A second major field of national activity in which the Fifth Republic continued and extended the achievements of the Fourth was that of foreign policy. The European idea was already well established before 1958. As the institutions of a federal Western Europe gradually took shape, economic cooperation between France and Germany began to replace political rivalry. While it had been in opposition the Gaullist movement had stressed national rather than European interests: in power de Gaulle made himself the symbol of French national traditions. At the same time he continued the work of reconciliation with Germany begun by the Fourth Republic, in particular by establishing a close personal relationship with the German Chancellor, Adenauer. The economic institutions of a Western European community therefore continued to develop. The stress was now on a Europe of *patries* rather than a federal Europe, but this might be considered a necessary recognition of facts rather than repudiation of the European idea.

In one field, however, in which the Fifth Republic inherited a problem, it can hardly be said to have inherited the line of action on which a solution could be found. This was the problem of national finances. Forty years of inflation had reduced the franc of 1914 to near worthlessness, and in a period of increasing government expenditure such as the twentieth century finance was something which a French parliament was ideally suited not to cope with. The Fifth Republic adopted the method of decree-laws, which the Third Republic had fallen back on in successive financial crises, to increase taxes and reduce expenditure. There was a partial devaluation, though French prices still remained high by world standards. To establish the psychological conditions for a fresh start a metallic coinage was restored for the lower values, and a new franc was created worth 100 old francs. Confidence in the new régime brought out of hiding in France, or back from their flight abroad, great quantities of refugee capital, and even metallic gold, which could now contribute to the growing economic activity in France. Continued increase in economic activity, and more settled government, kept prices fairly stable for a time, though the spectre of inflation still haunted the Fifth Republic.

France emerged from the Fourth Republic in very different shape from that in which she entered it. French economy, so stagnant during the inter-war years, had become dynamic. The genius of a great technocrat, Jean Monnet, turned the French economy into new paths when he inaugurated the first of a series of national plans, drawn up and supervised by a permanent Commissariat du Plan.

The First Plan was remarkably successful in laying the foundations of economic revival, but the secondary sectors did not keep pace with the basic reconstruction, and the economic atmosphere of the early fifties was still one of modified pessimism. After some hesitation a Second Plan, with a broader scope, was drawn up, to cover the years 1954 to 1957. Paradoxically, this period, marked by the instability and decay of the political institutions of the Republic, economically was the time of the real breakthrough. Technically and managerially French industry set out on a process of radical change. Even more important, the habits of the French consumer – for the expansion was still dependent mainly on the exploitation of the home market – underwent a fundamental transformation. There was a marked shift in the direction of mass consumption. The result was an annual rate of growth of the economy, between 1954 and 1959, of five and a half per cent. The total output in 1957 was thirty per cent above that of 1954, and this conceals an even greater rate of industrial progress of forty-six per cent, obscured by a much smaller agricultural growth of nineteen per cent. Most remarkable of all, prices and the balance of payments remained passably stable.

A Third Plan, from 1958 to 1961, brought in more sectors and attempted a comprehensive cover of the whole national economy. Production now began to take more account of the export market. Aided by the devaluation of the franc in December 1958, the balance of exports to imports between 1958 and 1961 was in the neighbourhood of 100 per cent. The preliminary steps in France towards the development of a European Common Market were thus facilitated.

Economic progress was, of course, patchy. The division was largely one of geography. In the West of France the average income was half what it was in the East, where eighty per cent of the industry was concentrated. Ironically, it was the generally more conservative France of the East that was progressive, and the politically advanced France of the Centre and South-west that remained economically conservative. The famous *mystique de gauche*, which kept France politically to the left, also operated to keep her economically backward. It was an inheritance from the time when, in a nation still predominantly made up of peasants and craftsmen, the rights of the individual needed to be asserted against the pressures of authority, the interests of the weaker against the demands of the stronger, and the ideals of the little men against the egoism of the great. Admirable, perhaps, in its day, still carrying into the twentieth century the nostalgic memory of a Rousseauist ideal, imbued with all the sentimentality that the idea of *les petits* can evoke in the French mind, the *mystique de gauche* had become a protective covering for economic inefficiencies and social evils that were tolerated because they worked to the immediate advantage of the mass of petty peasants and small businessmen. They were also a professional interest of left-wing politicians, whose political careers depended on the survival of abuses they devoted their time to denouncing, and they were the basis of the recurrent alliance of left and right against the centre. The interests of *les petits* were not only a stalking-horse for political career-hunters, they were a camouflage for what the Fourth Republic learnt to call *les richesses inciviques*. The *mystique de gauche* was also an indirect means of perpetuating the rule of a *haute bourgeoisie* which still kept its hold on the strategic centres of power.

The very economic success of the first three plans made the survival of poverty, of social evils and class inequalities more patent and shocking, and emphasized the contrast between the prosperous North and North-east and the remainder of the country. The political weakness of the left, which, apart from anything else, the division between Communists and the rest was guaranteed to perpetuate, prohibited any effective political pressure for a change in the distribution of wealth or income. But poverty is inefficient, and under the Fifth Republic the Fourth Plan, which was to cover the years 1962 to 1965, began a war of attrition against it by adding social to economic ends. Private investment was now deliberately restrained in order to promote development in the public sector. Housing, schools, hospitals – none too soon – appeared more prominently on the lists of priorities. Universities were added, not soon enough to forestall violent student demonstrations, though this problem, it is true, was made worse by a tendency to believe that the Sorbonne was the only university in France and Paris the only town where a real education could be obtained.

The problem of the backward regions was tackled by the encouragement of industrial development, for example in Brittany and the Massif Central. The Rhône Valley down to Marseille, and the Côte d'Or, were already experiencing economic development even without government stimulus. Areas untouched by economic progress still remained, but they were slowly being penetrated by the new economic forces. The lowest-paid workers also remained a wretched, unimproved stratum of misery at the bottom of the social structure, but in proportion there were now fewer even of these.

The effect of the series of Plans on France was revolutionary. Within fifteen years France had, in large sectors of her economy, caught up with the twentieth century. It had been done by a means which largely by-passed the normal processes of politics. This indeed was a necessary condition of economic and social progress. Not merely the party politicians, many of whom undoubtedly knew what the country needed but saw no advantage in trying to secure it at the price of political suicide and so failing to secure it anyhow, but the social forces represented by the parties, were irreconcilable with such progress. In fact, the political parties showed themselves extraordinarily disinterested in the Plans, when they were not actively opposed to them. The Communist-controlled Confédération Générale du Travail did its best, unsuccessfully, to sabotage them, and it represented a large majority of the workers. The mass of small businessmen, shopkeepers, and farmers were opposed to any kind of planning, which directly conflicted with their interests and threatened their very survival. Though the Plans began and were well advanced under the Fourth Republic, the latest and more advanced stages of planning, carried out under the auspices of the Fifth Republic, could hardly have survived the political pressures inherent in the previous parliamentary régime, for French society, as has been said, had a built-in resistance to economic progress and social amelioration. The fatality for the Fourth Republic was that its political habits did not keep pace with the demands for social and economic progress.

Scientists, technicians, industrialists, civil servants, experts from *écoles polytechniques*, gathered to provide the extra-political pressure which was needed to force through the reshaping of France's economy. In them might be seen the reappearance of what France had known in the days of Turgot, or of Colbert, of Sully and Villeroy – a great reforming bureaucracy. The task of government was taken over, as in the past, by servants of the state, tracing their ancestry back through *Conseillers d'état* and prefects, intendants, Secretaries, *officiers*, to the royal lawyers of the medieval monarchy. Time and again they had held the country together and provided it with government in a political vacuum. Such were the men who began under the Fourth Republic, and continued under General de Gaulle, what was essentially a technical revolution. Their expertise was remarkable, as was their capacity for dealing, in a pragmatic way, with the problems of national economy. The specialized training in practical economics given to some of the French higher civil servants now proved its value. The ease with which they could move between executive posts in the administration and in private business, while obviously open to abuse, meant in fact that the directors and managers of private enterprise and their opposite numbers in the Commissariat du Plan had the same intellectual background and outlook, spoke the same language, and largely envisaged the same ends.

On the other hand, the political parties, with their commitment to the issues of the past and seeming indifference to the needs of the present, gave the impression of being prepared to leave the task of reform to the bureaucracy. It should perhaps not have been entirely unexpected when the country in its turn rejected the politicians and looked once again for the head of its government to a super-bureaucrat.

The Fifth Republic is already putting the Fourth into proportion. Its politics are sinking into insignificance, a preparation for the revolution of 13 May, which itself now seems of significance mainly as ensuring the continuance of the economic and technical changes that embody the real revolution of contemporary France. The traditional enmity of *les gros* and *les petits* still survives, perhaps more acutely than ever a class war of rich against poor, as does the unholy alliance of parties of the left and right with a vested interest in its perpetuation. It is still an open question whether economic progress, in the absence of a spirit of humanitarian reform, will so transform the social fabric that the older pattern of social strife will cease to have relevance. The least we can say is that under both the Fourth and Fifth Republics the ancient strongholds of anarchy, on left and right, were falling before the pressure of an advancing economy. The Fifth Republic stands as an end, but also as a beginning. Not, indeed, that any historian could venture to anticipate the fate of its political system, or even guess whether an incomes policy will be evolved and the menace of inflation, with its probable political consequences, avoided. The Fifth Republic provides a suitable point at which to end, for a time, a history of modern France. It initiates a new phase in the history of France not because of a dubious and possibly undurable constitution, but because under it the social and economic revolution has been carried to a point of no return. One of the greatest traditionalists of France has presided over a revolution which is none the less fundamental for being peaceful. The conditions of French development in the future will not be what they were in the past. This is the end of one book. Fortunately it is not my task to prophesy what will have to be written in the next.

CHRONOLOGICAL TABLE

1871 18 January. Armistice
    8 February. Election of Assembly
    Government of Thiers
    1 March. Terms of peace ratified by National Assembly
    18 March. Troops fail to remove guns from Montmartre
    28 March. Election of Commune
    10 May. Treaty of Frankfurt
    21 May. Versaillais enter Paris
    28 May. End of the Commune
    5 July. Manifesto of comte de Chambord
    July. Evacuation of five departments by Prussians
    Supplementary elections
    Bishops' petition for restoration of temporal power of
      Pope
    Rimbaud's *Le Bateau ivre*
1873 Death of Napoleon III
    May. Resignation of Thiers. Appointment of MacMahon
    September. End of German occupation
    October. Letter of comte de Chambord
    Foundation stone of Sacré Cœur laid
    November. Law of the *Septennat*
1874 May. Defeat of Broglie's government
1875 February. *Amendement Wallon*
    Constitutional laws passed
    December. Dissolution of National Assembly
1876 Mallarmé's *L'Après-midi d'un faune*
    Election of new Chamber
1877 16 May. Dissolution of Chamber by MacMahon
    De Broglie government
    September. Death of Thiers
    October. Legislative elections: republican victory
1879 Republican majority in Senate
    Resignation of MacMahon
    Grévy elected President
    Death of Prince Imperial

1879 Parliament returns to Paris
Partial amnesty to Communards
1879–82 Educational reforms of Ferry
1880 Full amnesty to the exiles of the Commune
Les Soirées de Médan
September. First ministry of Ferry
1881 May. Protectorate over Tunisia
Legislative elections
Tariff law
November. Fall of Ferry
Ministry of Gambetta
1882 January. Union Générale crash
February. Fall of Gambetta
Anglo-French demonstration at Alexandria
Foundation of Ligue des Patriotes
December. Death of Gambetta
1883 February. Second ministry of Ferry
Death of comte de Chambord
1884 Trade unions legalized
Law of municipalities
1885 Tonkin reverse
Fall of Ferry
Legislative elections: revival of right
December. Grévy re-elected President
Protectorate over Madagascar
1886 January. Boulanger Minister of War
Foundation of Fédération Nationale des Syndicats
1887 Formation of Indo-Chinese union
May. Boulanger loses office
Foundation of *Bourses de Travail*
November. Wilson scandal
December. Resignation of Grévy
Sadi Carnot elected President
1887–9 Building of Eiffel Tower
1888 Boulangist campaign
Foundation of Pasteur Institute
1889 January. Election of Boulanger at Paris
April. Flight of Boulanger
Paris exhibition
September. Elections: republican victory
1890 November. Cardinal Lavigerie starts the Ralliement

1891 May. Encyclical *Rerum Novarum*
     Labour Day shootings
     French fleet visits Cronstadt
1892 Méline tariff
     Encyclical: *Au milieu des sollicitudes*
     November. Panama scandal
1893 August. Elections: moderate majority
     Heredia's *Les Trophées*
1894 Franco-Russian defensive alliance
     Lumière brothers make first film
     June. Assassination of Sadi Carnot
     Casimir-Périer President for six months
     December. Condemnation of Dreyfus
1895 January. Félix Faure elected President
     Establishment of Confédération Générale du Travail
     Repression of Madagascar rising
     November. Radical cabinet of Léon Bourgeois
1896 April. Cabinet of Méline
     Annexation of Madagascar
1897 Barrès' *Les Déracinés*
1898 January. Zola's *J'accuse*
     June. Resignation of Méline
     June 1898–June 1905. Delcassé Foreign Minister
     September. Marchand at Fashoda
     Formation of Comité de l'Action Française
1899 Death of Faure
     Election of Loubet as President
     June. Government of republican defence under Waldeck-
          Rousseau
     September. Court-martial finds Dreyfus guilty of high treason
          with extenuating circumstances
1900 Franco-Italian secret agreement
1901 July. Law on Congregations
1902 Debussy's *Pelléas et Mélisande*
     May. Legislative elections: victory of Bloc Républicain
     June. Resignation of Waldeck-Rousseau
     Government of Combes
1903 Edward VII and President Loubet exchange visits
1904 April. Anglo-French Entente
     Grand Orient scandal. Resignation of General André
     Ten-hour day law

1904 November. Law for separation of Church and State introduced
1905 January. Resignation of Combes
  Foundation of S.F.I.O.
  March. Wilhelm II at Tangier
  June. Resignation of Delcassé
  December. Law of Separation of Church and State passed
1906 Conference at Algeçiras
  Amiens Labour Charter
  May. Legislative elections
  Presidency of Armand Fallières
  October. Government of Clemenceau
1907 Bergson's *L'Évolution créatrice*
1908 Anatole France's *L'Île des pingouins*
  L'Action Française became a daily paper
  Sorel's *Réflexions sur la violence*
  Thalamas student riots
  Affair of German deserters in Morocco
1909 Wave of strikes
  Income-tax law passed by Chamber, vetoed by Senate
  Marinetti's *Manifesto of Futurism*
  Beatification of Jeanne d'Arc
1910 November. Railway strike broken by Briand
  Papal condemnation of Le Sillon
  Legislative elections
1911 July. Government of Caillaux
  The *Panther* sent to Agadir
1912 January. Fall of Caillaux
  Government of Poincaré
  Claudel's *L'Annonce faite à Marie*
  French protectorate over Morocco set up
1913 Proust's *Du côté de chez Swann*
  January. Poincaré elected President
  August. Law of three years' military service
1914 Secret papal condemnation of Action Française
  April–May. Legislative elections: victory of left
  Government of Viviani
  28 June. Assassination of Archduke at Sarajevo
  16–23 July. Visit of Poincaré and Viviani to Russia
  23 July. Austrian ultimatum to Servia
  28 July. Austrian declaration of war on Servia

1914 30 July. Russian mobilization
31 July. German ultimatum to Russia
Assassination of Jaurès
1 August. German declaration of war on Russia
French mobilization
3 August. German declaration of war on France
4 August. British declaration of war on Germany
22 August. French defeated in the Ardennes
23 August. Viviani government re-formed
1 September. French government leaves for Bordeaux
5–12 September. Battle of the Marne
December. French government returns to Paris

1915 October. Fall of Viviani
Briand ministry

1916 21 February. Battle of Verdun begins
1 July–September. Battle of the Somme
Sykes–Picot agreement for partition of Turkish Empire
December. Nivelle appointed Commander-in-Chief

1917 March. Fall of Briand government
Ribot ministry
16 April. Nivelle offensive
15 May. Dismissal of Nivelle
May. Mutinies in French army
Appointment of Foch and Pétain
Trouble among workers
Bonnet rouge affair
Fall of Ribot government
13 September. Ministry of Painlevé
Bolo affair
13 November. Fall of Painlevé
Clemenceau government

1918 March–July. Ludendorff offensive
18 July. Counter-offensive of Foch
11 November. Armistice

1919 28 June. Signature of Treaty of Versailles
November. Election of Assembly: victory of Bloc National

1920 January. Paul Deschanel elected President against Clemenceau
Resignation of Clemenceau
May. Treaty of Sèvres
Government of Millerand

1920 Weygand mission to Poland: Battle of Warsaw
September. Resignation of Deschanel
Millerand elected President
December. Socialist Congress at Tours
1921 Trade union split
1922 January. Government of Poincaré
Le Cimetière marin of Paul Valéry
1923 January. Occupation of Ruhr
Treaty of Lausanne
1924 May. Election: victory of Cartel des Gauches
June. Resignation of Millerand
Doumergue elected President
André Breton's Manifesto of Surrealism
Government of Herriot
September. Geneva Protocol
October. Dawes Plan
1925 April. Fall of Herriot
July. Evacuation of Ruhr begins
Revolt in Syria
October. Locarno Agreements
1925–32 Briand Foreign Minister
1926 July. Government of Poincaré – decree-laws
Papal condemnation of Action Française published
1928 Military service reduced to one year
Decision to build Maginot Line
1929 July. Retirement of Poincaré
September. Briand proposes European Federal Union
October. Wall Street crash
1930 May. Young Plan comes into operation
June. French evacuation of Rhineland
September. Election of 107 Nazis to Reichstag
1931 May. Paul Doumer elected President
1932 May. Assassination of Doumer
Lebrun elected President
Election of Chamber: success of Cartel des Gauches
Government of Herriot
1933 January. Hitler becomes Reich Chancellor
January–October. Government of Daladier
July. Four-Power Pact
Stavisky affair
1934 6 February. Attempted *coup d'état* of the Leagues

1934 9 February. Government of Doumergue. Communist demonstration

   9 October. Assassination of Barthou and King Alexander

   Doriot breaks away from Communist Party

   Laval becomes Foreign Minister

   November. Fall of Doumergue

1935 January. Saar votes for reunion with Germany

   April. Stresa pact

   May. Franco-Soviet pact negotiated

   September. Italian attack on Abyssinia

   Giradoux's *La Guerre de Troie n'aura pas lieu*

   December. Hoare–Laval agreement

1936 January. Fall of Laval. Manifesto of Popular Front

   March. Remilitarization of Rhineland

   April. Ratification of Franco-Soviet pact

   April–May. Election of Chamber: victory of Popular Front

   Government of Blum

   Occupation of factories

   Matignon agreements

   October. Devaluation of franc

   Spanish Civil War

1937 March. Léon Blum announces 'pause'

   June. Fall of Blum government

1938 April. Government of Daladier

   September. Munich

   October. Reynaud becomes Finance Minister

   December. Ribbentrop visits Paris: Declaration of Friendship

1939 February. French recognition of government of Franco

   March. Germany occupies Czechoslovakia

   Daladier voted plenary powers

   March. Anglo-French guarantee to Poland

   April. Re-election of Lebrun as President

   12 August. Anglo-French mission at Moscow

   21 August. Russo-German agreement announced

   22 August. French Communist Party supports Nazi–Communist Pact

   1 September. German invasion of Poland

   3 September. Great Britain and France declare war on Germany

1939 17 September. Russian invasion of Poland
26 September. Daladier dissolves Communist Party
1940 20 March. Reynaud succeeds Daladier
10 May. German invasion of Low Countries
13–14 May. French front broken on Meuse
18 May. Reynaud becomes Minister of National Defence in place of Daladier
19 May. Gamelin replaced by Weygand
Pétain enters government
29 May–4 June. Dunkirk evacuation
10 June. French government moved to Touraine. Italy enters war
14 June. Germans enter Paris. Government moves to Bordeaux
16 June. Resignation of Reynaud. Succeeded by Pétain
18 June. General de Gaulle calls from London for continued resistance
22 June. Armistice with Germany
24 June. Armistice with Italy
1 July. French government moves to Vichy
3 July. Mers-el-Kébir. British attack on French fleet
10 July. National Assembly votes full powers to Pétain
11 July. Vote of constitutional laws
Ministry of Laval
September. Free French expedition to Dakar fails
Japanese forces enter Indo-China
24 October. Hitler–Pétain interview at Montoire
13 December. Dismissal of Laval
1941 January. Foundation of Rassemblement National Populaire
February. Darlan in control of government
May Protocols
June. Syrian campaign. German invasion of Russia
Communists begin resistance
November. Dismissal of Weygand
1942 April. Trial at Riom of Blum, Daladier, etc., abandoned. Laval returns to power
8 November. Invasion of North Africa
11 November. Germans move into unoccupied France
27 November. French fleet sunk at Toulon
24 December. Assassination of Darlan

1943 June. Committee of National Liberation formed at Algiers
    under de Gaulle and Giraud
    September. Liberation of Corsica
1944 January. Paris collaborationists enter government
    Sartre's *Huis clos*
    6 June. Allied landing in Normandy
    20 August. Pétain transferred to Belfort
    26 August. De Gaulle enters Paris
    Ho Chi Minh proclaims independence of Vietnam
1945 21 October. Referendum ends Third Republic
    Election of Constituent Assembly
1946 January. Resignation of de Gaulle
    May. France votes against first constitution
    June. Election of Second Constituent Assembly
    October. Second constitution accepted by referendum
1947 January. Election of Vincent Auriol as President
    March. Anglo-French Treaty of Dunkirk
    April. Formation of Gaullist Rassemblement
    Revolt in Madagascar
    May. Ramadier dismisses Communist ministers
    June. Marshall speech on aid
    November–December. Communist-led strikes
    Albert Camus's *La Peste*
1948 January. Formation of Third Force
    March. Treaty of Mutual Assistance
    October–November. Strikes
1949 April. Signature of North Atlantic Treaty
1950 May. Schuman proposes coal and steel plan
    October. Pleven plan for European army
1951 April. Coal and steel agreement between France, Germany,
    Italy, and Benelux
    May. Electoral reform bill
    June. General election
1952 March. Government of Pinay
1953 Formation of Poujadist league
    December. Election of René Coty as President
1954 May. Fall of Dien Bien Phu
    June. Government of Mendès-France
    July. French Assembly approves Indo-China settlement and
    rejects European Defence Community
    November. Algerian revolt

1955 June. Agreement with Néo-Destour in Tunisia
1956 January. General election
Front Républicain government under Guy Mollet
March. Independence of Morocco and Tunisia recognized
June. Law extending self-government in colonies
November. Suez affair
December. Return of Saar to German sovereignty
1957 March. Rome Treaties for Common Market ratified by
Assembly
May. Resignation of Mollet government
August. Partial devaluation of franc
1958 16 April. Fall of Gaillard government
13 May. Revolt of Europeans and Army in Algeria
14 May. Government of Pflimlin
1 June. Government of General de Gaulle accepted by
Assembly
3 June. French parliament adjourns till October
28 September. Constitution of Fifth Republic accepted by
referendum
21 December. General de Gaulle elected President
27 December. Devaluation of franc
1959 8 January. General de Gaulle proclaimed President of Fifth
Republic; Michel Debré, Premier
1960 January. Introduction of 'new' franc
February. First French nuclear bomb exploded
1961 January. Referendum on future of Algeria
April. Army revolt in Algeria collapses
1962 March. Franco-Algerian agreement
April. Resignation of Debré
July. Independence of Algeria proclaimed
October. Referendum approves future presidential election
by universal suffrage

FURTHER READING

Some of the works mentioned in the reading list to volume 2 must be repeated here, among them the general histories – Lavisse: *Histoire de France contemporaine* (1920-2), vol. 8; Ch. Seignobos: *L'Évolution de la Troisième République* (1875-1914); Renouvin, Préclin et Hardy: *La Paix armée et la Grande Guerre, 1871-1939* (Clio, 2nd ed. 1947); J. P. T. Bury: *France, 1814-1940* (2nd ed. 1951); Lefebvre, Pouthas et Baumont: *Histoire de la France pour tous les Français* (1950); M. Reinhard (ed.): *Histoire de France, ii, de 1715 à 1946* (1954). To these may be added Gordon Wright: *France in modern times, 1760 to the present* (1962), a thoughtful and informed survey, with very full bibliographical discussions which should be consulted; D. W. Brogan: *The Development of Modern France* (1940), encyclopedic in its scope; and David Thomson's *Democracy in France* (3rd ed. 1958), the best single analysis of French politics since 1871. The texts of successive French constitutions are given in Duguit, Monnier et Bonnard, *Les Constitutions et les principales lois politiques de la France depuis 1789* (various editions: the earlier ones contain an introduction which is the best short survey of French constitutional history since 1789).

General interpretations of the course of French politics are R. Rémond: *La Droite en France de 1815 à nos jours* (1954), and F. Goguel: *La Politique des partis sous la IIIe République* (1946), both interesting and suggestive, but both also tending to reduce French political history to an unduly artificial pattern. D. W. S. Lidderdale's *The Parliament of France* (1951) is essential for understanding the weakness of parliamentary institutions in France.

An interesting contemporary English interpretation of the first quarter-century of the Third Republic is J. E. C. Bodley's *France* (revised ed. 1902). The opening years of the Third Republic are those that have been best served by historians. The constitutional debates are described in detail by M. Deslandres: *Histoire constitutionelle de la France*, iii, *L'Avènement de la IIIe République, la constitution de 1875* (1937). *The Beginning of the Third Republic in France* (1940), by F. H. Brabant, is a witty account with sympathetic sketches of the Legitimist, Orleanist, and republican personalities of the time. Daniel Halévy provides an individual interpretation in *La Fin des notables* (1930) and *La République des ducs* (1937). The contribution that can be made to historical interpretation by a scholarly piece of electoral analysis is shown by J. Goualt's *Comment la France est devenue républicaine* (1954). The classic work in the field of political analysis is A. Siegfried's *Tableau politique de la France de l'Ouest sous la III*^{e} *République* (1913). Among recent books on the Dreyfus Affair are G. Chapman's *The Dreyfus Case* (1955) and Dr Johnson's *France and the Dreyfus Affair* (1966). A clear analysis of the political institutions of the Third Republic is J. Barthélemy's *Le Gouvernement de la France* (ed. of 1934). W. L. Middleton's *The French Political System* (1932) is a lively description, and A. Siegfried gives a pungent verdict on French parties in *Tableau des partis en France* (1930). Right-wing critiques of the republican parties are R. de Jouvenel's *La République des camarades* (1934) and A. Thibaudet's *La République des professeurs* (1927).

It is not easy to find party or social histories in France which are not over-committed. A thorough and detailed, but excessively orthodox history of the Socialist Party is *Histoire du socialisme en France (1871–1961)* (1962), by D. Ligou. E. Dolléans's *Histoire du mouvement ouvrier, 1830 à nos jours* (1947–53) is useful but also rather uncritical. A rather ambivalent history is G. Walker's *Histoire du parti communiste français* (1948). A good, reasonably short account of *The Action Française* (1962) is by E. R. Tannenbaum. *Republican Ideas and the Liberal Tradition in France 1870–1914* (1951) by J. A. Scott is interesting but tries to link the politics of the Third Republic rather too closely to political traditions inherited from the French Revolution. The political ideas of the French parties are best studied in the writings of the time, for example, *Éléments d'une doctrine radicale* (1925) by Alain, Léon Blum's *L'Histoire jugera* (1945), a selection of articles and speeches, and *Une politique de grandeur française* (1945) by Maurice Thorez. To the last of these it would be wise to add some of the material that the Party would prefer to suppress, such as *Les Cahiers du bolchevisme pendant la campagne 1939–40* (1951) collected by A. Rossi. A lively and penetrating survey of the period when French party divisions reached almost to the point of civil war was made by the English left-wing journalist, A. Werth, in *The Twilight of France, 1933–40* (1942). There are hardly any outstanding biographies for this period, though the English reader will find J. Hampden Jackson's *Clemenceau and the Third Republic* (1946) an interesting sketch of the most striking individual in its political history.

The economic history of France has been neglected. Val Lorwin

Further Reading

has written on *The French Labor Movement* (1954). *Bilan de l'économie française, 1919-46* (1947) by C. Bettelheim is a useful survey of the period, with a fair amount of statistical information. On religion the best account is A. Dansette's *Histoire religieuse de la France contemporaine* (1948-51); and on the colonies, up to the dates of their publication, H. Blet's *Histoire de la colonisation française* (1946) and H. Deschamps's *Méthodes et doctrines coloniales de la France du XVI*e *siècle à nos jours* (1953). On foreign policy general histories of international relations are apt to give a more balanced picture than histories of the policy of a single country. In addition to the appropriate volumes of P. Renouvin's *Histoire des relations internationales: Le XIX*e *siècle, ii, de 1871 à 1914* (1955); *Le crise du XX*e *siècle, i, de 1914 à 1929; ii, de 1929 à 1945* (1958) give clear, short summaries of international affairs from a French point of view; and there is also J.-B. Duroselle's *Histoire diplomatique de 1919 à nos jours* (1957). Two difficult phases in French foreign policy are studied by J. C. King in *Foch versus Clemenceau* (1960) and Adrienne Hytier in *Two Years of French Foreign Policy: Vichy 1940-1942* (1958). The crucial problem of relations between Great Britain and France during the inter-war years is considered by A. Wolfers in *Britain and France between the Two Wars* (1940) and W. M. Jordan in *Great Britain, France and the German Problem, 1918-39* (1943).

The last phase of the Third Republic was described by a great historian, Marc Bloch, in *L'Étrange défaite* (1949), translated as *Strange Defeat*. The most revealing of many memoirs on the Vichy régime is by Pétain's first secretary, Henri du Moulin de Labarthète, *Le Temps des illusions: souvenirs juillet 1940-avril 1942* (1946). An account of Vichy France based on contemporary sources is given in my contribution to *Hitler's Europe* (1954), pp. 338-434, edited by A. and V. M. Toynbee. There is a short sketch of the Resistance in H. Michel's *Histoire de la résistance* (1950), though much more material on this struggle is gradually being brought out. General de Gaulle's *Mémoires de guerre* (1954-9) is a classic. R. Aron, who has written a history of Vichy, has also collected much first-hand material in *Histoire de la libération de la France* (1959), translated as *De Gaulle before Paris* (1962) and *De Gaulle triumphant* (1964). Gordon Wright describes the complicated political manoeuvres before the setting up of the Fourth Republic in *The Reshaping of French Democracy* (1948); and the Fourth Republic itself is ably analysed by Dorothy Pickles in *French Politics: the First Year of the Fourth Republic* (1953) and Philip Williams in *Politics in Post-war*

France (2nd ed., 1958). Mrs Pickles has continued her conscientious and perceptive study of French politics in *The Fifth French Republic* (1960). The most thorough account, so far, of the important series of Plans is *Economic Planning in France* (1963) by J. and A.-M. Hackett.

To pick out a limited number of works of fiction which throw light on the history of recent times is even more difficult than to make a selection for earlier periods. The development of nationalist feeling is illustrated by the novels of Maurice Barrès, such as *Les Déracinés*. Anatole France's *L'Île des pingouins* is a satiric history of the earlier years of the Third Republic, and Georges Duhamel's *Chronique des Pasquier* (1933–45) a sober account of the fortunes of a bourgeois family. Marcel Proust in the many volumes of *À la recherche du temps perdu* not only looks back to the apparently stable society of the years before the First World War but also prophetically forward to an age of decay and disaster. Direct responses to the tragedy of war, such as Henri Barbusse's *Le Feu*, show the intensity of feeling it aroused, but now seem to go less deep than Proust's more indirect approach to an age of national decay. Disillusionment and despair are reflected in Céline's *Voyage au bout de la nuit* (1932) and Camus' *La Peste* (1947). The plays of Sartre, written mostly after the Second World War, continue to reflect the state of depression of the inter-war years; Simone de Beauvoir's semi-autobiographical *Les Mandarins*, on a lower artistic level, gives an impression of the self-questioning futility of politicians and intellectuals after the Second World War. The new France is so far little reflected in literature; one would hardly expect, or perhaps even desire, to find a technological revolution in the poetry or fiction of a nation.

INDEX

Index

Blanquists, 34, 44, 45, 69
Bloc National, 70, 123, 125, 127
Bloy, Léon, 81
Blum, Léon, 53, 129, 165–6, 168, 171, 184
Bolo, 116
Bonapartism, 11, 13, 17, 20, 47, 83, 182, 211
Boncourt, Paul, 140
Bonnet, Georges, 170, 173, 175, 177
Bordeaux, 9, 111, 178
Bordeaux, Archbishop of, 132
Boulanger, General, Boulangism, 33–6, 38, 44, 46–7, 83
Boule-de-suif, 76
Bourgeois, Léon, 37, 42, 67, 120
Bourguiba, 224
Bourses de Travail, 45
Braque, Georges, 74, 227
Breton, André, 228
Briand, Aristide, 53, 63–5, 69, 98, 111, 113, 116–17, 123, 125, 134, 136–7, 160–61, 215
Broglie, Albert de, 9, 14, 17, 19–21, 25
Brunot, Ferdinand, 53
Brussels Pact, 216
Budget, French, *see* finances

Cachin, Marcel, 129
Cagoulards, 149
Caillaux, Joseph, 57, 67, 98–102, 115–17, 127, 134, 155, 164
Caillaux, Mme, 101
Cambodia, 93, 223
Cambon, Jules, 96
Cambon, Paul, 96–7
Camelots du roi, 87, 143, 149
Cameroons, French, 98, 195
Camus, Albert, 230, 232
Candide, 144
Carmen, 75
Carnet B, 108
Carnot, Sadi, President, 33, 37, 46
Cartel des Gauches, 127–8, 130, 133–5
Casablanca, 192
Casimir-Périer, President, 37, 46
Cassagnac, Paul de, 90
Castelnau, General de, 132
Catholics, Integral, 78
Catholics, Social, 39
Catroux, General, 181
Céline, Louis-Ferdinand, 229
Cézanne, Paul, 74
Chamberlain, Austen, 160
Chamberlain, Neville, 170–71, 173
Chamber of Deputies of Third Republic, 18–19, 22; of 1914, 102; of 1919, 121
Chambord, comte de, 12–13, 15, 32, 38
Chambrun, marquis de, 182
Chanak, 125

Château-Thierry, 118
Chautemps, Camille, 140–41, 169, 173, 197
Chevau-légers, 17, 19
Chiappe, Jean, 142, 144, 188
Church in France, Roman Catholic, 15–17, 25, 38–40, 63–6, 183–4, 231
Le Cimetière marin, 227
Cinema, French, 79, 229–30
Citroën, André, 157
Clair, René, 229
Claudel, Paul, 85, 227
Clemenceau, Georges, 10, 31–3, 36–8, 50, 53, 66–7, 117–21, 123, 177
clericalism, 15–16, 25–6, 40
Clichy, 154
coal and steel agreement of 1951, 217
Cochin-China, 93
Cocteau, Jean, 229
Colette, 227, 229
Collaboration, 144, 187–8, 194, 199
Colonial convention, Franco-British, 94
Colonies, colonial policy, 28–9, 92–4, 133, 188–9, 222–4, 234–8, 241–3
Combes, Émile, 60–63, 65, 97
Comité des Forges, 122, 157
Comité Secret de l'Action Révolutionnaire (C.S.A.R.), 149
Common Market, 234, 245
Communards, amnesty of, 23–4
Commune of Paris, 9, 23, 37, 77
Communist Party, Communism, Communists, 122, 127, 129–30, 133, 135–6, 140, 145–7, 151–4, 171–2, 174, 177, 190–91, 196–7, 200–207, 209, 211–14, 216, 221, 225, 231, 233, 239–41, 246
Compiègne, 179
Comte, Auguste, 76
Concordat, Napoleonic, 63–4
Confédération Générale du Travail (C.G.T.), 69, 130, 154, 170–71, 212–13, 247
Confédération Générale du Travail Unitaire (C.G.T.U.), 130
Congress of Berlin, 91
conscription, three years law, 101–2
Constituent Assembly of 1945, 203–4
Constitutional Laws of Third Republic, 18–19
Constitution of Fifth Republic, 238–9
Constitution of Fourth Republic, 206–7
Coppée, François, 55
cordon sanitaire, 124
Corot, Jean-Baptiste, 74
Correspondance de Rome, 78
Corsica, liberation of, 196; Corsica, in 1958, 236
Coty, François, 143
Coty, René, President, 205, 225, 238
Council of the Republic, 206

266

Index

Index

Index

Index